Discovering the American Past

SIXTH EDITION

Discovering the American Past

A Look at the Evidence

VOLUME II: SINCE 1865

William Bruce Wheeler

University of Tennessee

Susan D. Becker

University of Tennessee, Emerita

Houghton Mifflin Company   Boston   New York

Publisher: Charles Hartford
Senior Sponsoring Editor: Sally Constable
Development Editor: Lisa Kalner Williams
Senior Project Editor: Christina Horn
Editorial Assistant: Kristen Truncellito
Senior Art and Design Coordinator: Jill Haber
Senior Photo Editor: Jennifer Meyer Dare
Composition Buyer: Chuck Dutton
Associate Strategic Buyer: Brian Pieragostini
Senior Marketing Manager: Sandra McGuire
Market Specialist: Molly Parke

Cover image: Blackberry and Day-timer.

Cover photograph: © Kathleen Finlay/Masterfile.

The song lyrics on page 264 are reprinted courtesy of International Business Machines Corporation. Copyright © 1935 International Business Machines Corporation.

Printed in the U.S.A.

Library of Congress Control Number: 2005935024

Instructor's exam copy:
ISBN 13: 978-0-618-73255-5
ISBN 10: 0-618-73255-1

For orders, use student text ISBNs:
ISBN 13: 978-0-618-52260-6
ISBN 10: 0-618-52260-3

1 2 3 4 5 6 7 8 9-CRS-10 09 08 07 06

Contents

CHAPTER **3**

How They Lived: Middle-Class Life, 1870–1917

CHAPTER **4**

Progressives and the Family: The Redefinition of Childhood, 1880–1920

CHAPTER **5**

Homogenizing a Pluralistic Nation: Propaganda During World War I

CHAPTER **6**

The "New" Woman: Social Science Experts and the Redefinition of Women's Roles in the 1920s

CHAPTER **10**

A Generation in War and Turmoil: The Agony of Vietnam

CHAPTER **11**

A Nation of Immigrants: The California Experience

Preface

During the July 4 weekend of 2005, motion picture studios, investors, and producers were frantic. For almost two years attendance at movie theaters had been in a noticeable decline. By mid-2005 the slump was the worst in almost twenty years. At the same time, television executives were in a panic. In spite of the enormous number of choices via network, cable, and satellite dish offerings, television viewership too was down.

In the midst of these disturbing statistics (disturbing at least for motion picture and television executives), more Americans than ever before were *reading*—reading everything from Harry Potter novels to books about America's past. Anticipating the three hundredth anniversary of the birth of Benjamin Franklin in 2006, readers gobbled up first-rate biographies penned by Edmund Morgan, Walter Isaacson, and Gordon Wood. David McCullough and the late Shelby Foote became celebrities for their historical studies. In fact, McCullough's latest book, *1776* (Simon & Schuster, 2005), was the cover story in the May 23, 2005, issue of *Newsweek;* the newsmagazine claimed that McCullough's books "have become the most widely ready nonfiction of the age."[1] And McCullough's work is not alone: Edmund Morgan's *Benjamin Franklin* (Yale University Press, 2002), a more traditionally scholarly work, sold over 170,000 copies as of September 2005.[2]

In all, those cynical men and women who a few years ago accused Americans of no longer being readers joyously retracted their warnings of reading's demise. The American public was reading again, and history books were being purchased and consumed by more people than ever.

How can we account for this welcome phenomenon? It is possible that, in the midst of a tangled and confusing era fraught with both domestic and foreign challenges and dangers, Americans were seeking in their collective past the origins of their own contemporary greatness—and difficulties. As educator Diane Ravitch put it in a 2001 address to the New Jersey Council for History Education, "we study history because it provides us with knowledge, vocabulary, idioms, and language in which to make connections between the

---

1. *Newsweek*, May 23, 2005. The newsmagazine also published a short excerpt of *1776*, thus making it immediately available even before the book's publication to its readers.
2. Figures given to authors by Yale University Press, September 2005.

past, the present and the future."[3] Putting Ravitch's theory into practice, many readers have returned to the dark and uncertain days of America's own struggle for independence and survival or to its agonizing Civil War, to snatch the kernels of their past vision and strength that they surely need to navigate the treacherous road ahead. Others have returned to their own past to see how Americans dealt with civil rights, imperialism, government propaganda, diversity, gender issues, and so forth. In short, American readers were coming to see history as not only entertaining but also important in their efforts to understand themselves—where they had come from, where they were at present, and where they might be going.

As with previous editions, we began this book with an urgent desire to tap into the interest students have in the past and a firm belief that the study of American history can contribute to an understanding of the contemporary world. *Discovering the American Past* does this in two important ways: (1) putting the present in perspective by giving us an appreciation of the trends, forces, and people who served to shape present-day American life; and (2) teaching us the skills we need to examine and analyze our present environment and culture. Our goals, therefore, are to increase students' interest in historical issues and to help them develop and sharpen the critical skills they will need to live in today's world.

In order to truly appreciate both the writings about the past as well as the people, events, and epochs of the past itself, these students of history have to go to the evidence—the "raw material" of history that historians like McCullough, Morgan, Isaacson, Wood, and others use to attempt to reconstruct the past. *Discovering the American Past* is intended to help those interested in history to find, assess, arrange, and use such historical evidence. We aim to provide an engaging mixture of types of primary sources, ranging from the more traditional sources such as letters, newspapers, public documents, speeches, and oral reminiscences to the less traditional sources such as photographs, architecture, statistics, art, films, and cartoons. We also establish a healthy balance among political, social, diplomatic, intellectual, economic, and cultural history. As much as possible, we have tried "to let the evidence speak for itself" and have avoided (we hope) leading students toward one particular interpretation or another. In this book, then, we have created a kind of historical sampler that we believe will help students learn the methods and skills all educated people must be able to use, as well as help them learn the historical content. Over the years, we have found this approach to be effective

3. See Diane Ravitch, "Obstacles to Teaching History Today," excerpts from a speech delivered to the New Jersey Council for History Education on March 15, 2001, and published in *History Matters!* 13 (June 2001), pp. 1, 6–7.

in many different classroom situations, including seminars, small classes, and large lecture classes.

Format of the Book

Each chapter is divided into six parts: The Problem, Background, The Method, The Evidence, Questions to Consider, and Epilogue. Each of these parts builds upon the others, creating a uniquely integrated chapter structure that helps guide the reader through the analytical process. "The Problem" section begins with a brief discussion of the central issues of the chapter and then states the questions students will explore. A "Background" section follows, designed to help students understand the historical context of the problem. The section called "The Method" gives students suggestions for studying and analyzing the evidence. "The Evidence" section is the heart of the chapter, providing a variety of primary source material on the particular historical event or issue described in the chapter's "Problem" section. "Questions to Consider," the section that follows, focuses students' attention on specific evidence and on linkages among different evidence material. The "Epilogue" section gives the aftermath or the historical outcome of the evidence—what happened to the people involved, who won an election, how a debate ended, and so on.

Changes in the Sixth Edition

Each chapter in this edition has had to pass three important screening groups: (1) the authors (and some of our graduate students) who used the chapters to teach our students, (2) student evaluators who used *Discovering the American Past* in class, and (3) instructors who either used the book or read and assessed the new and revised chapters. With advice from our screeners, we have made the following alterations that we believe will make *Discovering the American Past* even more useful and contemporary: For example, Volume I contains three entirely new chapters: Chapter 9, "The Diplomacy, Politics, and Intrigue of 'Manifest Destiny': The Annexation of Texas"; Chapter 10, "'No More Pint o' Salt for Me': The Port Royal Experiment, 1861–1865"; and Chapter 11, "The Reconstruction Era: Farmers and Workers in the West and North, 1866–1877." Chapter 3 now focuses entirely on the Chesapeake Bay colonies and on the evolution of the slave-based plantation system. Chapters 1 and 6 both have incorporated more Native American voices. Chapter 4 includes more evidence from the 1770 trial of Captain Thomas Preston. Chapters 2, 5, 7, and 8 have been revised to reflect the most recent scholarship.

Volume II offers two completely new chapters—Chapter 4, "Progressives and the Family: The Redefinition of Childhood, 1880–1920," and Chapter 8, "Going to War with Japan: A Problem in Diplomacy and Causation"—in addition to "The Reconstruction Era: Farmers and Workers in the West and North, 1866–1877." Chapter 2 has added an additional focus on African American manhood. Chapter 3 offers a more precise selection of material artifacts. Chapter 5 has sharpened its treatment of government-initiated propaganda. Chapter 10 connects Vietnam with more recent U.S. military operations in Bosnia, Somalia, Afghanistan, and Iraq. Finally, significant new material has been provided in Chapters 6, 7, 9, and 11, the last one addressing the issue of post-9/11 immigration.

Instructor's Resource Manual

Because we value the teaching of American history and yet fully understand how difficult it is to do well, we have written our own Instructor's Resource Manual to accompany *Discovering the American Past*. In this manual, we explain our specific content and skills objectives for each chapter. In addition, we include an expanded discussion of the method and evidence sections. We also answer some of students' frequently asked questions about the material in each problem. Our suggestions for teaching and evaluating student learning draw not only upon our own experiences but also upon the experiences of those of you who have shared your classroom ideas with us. Finally, we wrote updated bibliographic essays for each problem.

Acknowledgments

We would like to thank all the students and instructors who have helped us in developing and refining our ideas for this edition. We are also appreciative of Ms. Mary Ann Bright, who assisted in the preparation of the manuscript. At Houghton Mifflin, we are especially grateful for the hard work and encouragement of Lisa Kalner Williams and Christina Horn, professional in every sense of the word. Finally we are indebted to colleagues at both our own and at other institutions who reviewed the manuscript and made significant contributions to this edition: Stephen V. Ash, University of Tennessee; Thomas J. Brown, University of South Carolina; John Davies, University of Delaware; Matthew Dennis, University of Oregon; Todd M. Kerstetter, Texas Christian University; Michael L. Krenn, Appalachian State University; Lorraine M. Lees, Old Dominion University; Margaret A. Lowe, Bridgewater State College; Pamela Riney-Kehrberg, Iowa State University; and Matthew C. Whitaker, Arizona State University.

Over the years, former students have written to us to express their appreciation for the knowledge and skills they learned from this book. It is we, however, who have learned at least as much from them: that most students do not want to be just silent note-takers but rather *active participants* in their own educations and their own world. We dedicate this edition to them, as well as to students of the present and future who will learn that lesson.

W. B. W.
S. D. B.

1

The Reconstruction Era: Farmers and Workers in the West and North, 1866–1877

The Problem

The Civil War tore the nation apart, sometimes even splitting individual families, and pitted Union soldiers against Confederate soldiers for four long years. In the period between the firing on Fort Sumter in 1861 and Lee's surrender at Appomattox Court House in 1865, over 630,000 people were killed and many thousands more were wounded. Deaths during the Civil War, both in numbers and in proportion to total population, far exceeded deaths during any other war in our nation's history.

Those who survived were faced with uncertainties about their roles in a rapidly changing world. Daniel Sawtelle was the Republican son of a Democratic New England farmer. After enlisting in the 8th Maine Infantry at age 23, he served in Florida and South Carolina, later reenlisting as a sharpshooter and a member of the occupation army in Virginia. Ill and exhausted when he finally returned home in 1866, he wrote in his memoirs: "Only think of a big boy, man grown, almost twenty-eight, wanting mother more than anything else on earth. Sick and worn with my long journey, I was too glad to cry and too sick to laugh."[1] Restless after a few months at home, he decided that there were more opportunities for farmers out West and moved first to Wisconsin, then Minnesota, then South Dakota, and finally Oregon.

Elisha Hunt Rhodes was the son of a Rhode Island sea captain who had drowned on a voyage. At the age of 16, Rhodes was supporting his family by working as a clerk. Nineteen years old when he enlisted as a private in the 2nd Rhode Island Volunteers, he was discharged as a colonel in 1865. Writing in his diary on the day he said good-bye to his regiment, he reflected:

It was sad, yet joyful, for the war is over and we are at home. No more suf-

1. Peter H. Buckingham, ed., *All's for the Best: The Civil War Reminiscences and Letters of Daniel W. Sawtelle* (Knoxville: University of Tennessee Press, 2001), p. 200.

✦ CHAPTER 1

The Reconstruction
Era: Farmers and
Workers in the West
and North,
1866–1877

fering, no more scenes of carnage and death. Thank God it is over and that the Union is restored. And so at last I am a simple citizen.[2]

Rhodes returned to his home state, married, and later traveled throughout the South and West as a representative for woolen and cotton mills. Active in veterans' affairs, he often took his grandsons to visit Civil War battlefields. "I don't think that Grandpa owned a house," wrote one of Rhodes's grandsons years later. "He and Grandma used to board on Benefit Street and out at Fruit Hill, and sometimes they stayed with Aunt Alice. . . ."[3]

These two Union soldiers' experiences were similar to those of thousands of young men during the Reconstruction era immediately following the Civil War. Popular literature of the times exhorted young men to strive to be successful. Some, like Sawtelle, went West to try their luck at farming on the plains. Others, like Rhodes, went to the newly expanding cities, lured by the opportunities offered by business and industry. What characteristics were thought to be essential for "success?" What difficulties did farmers and workers face in the decade following the War? What actions did they take to try to overcome these problems?

✦

Background

Historians generally treat Reconstruction as the story of the South, defeated by the Union and occupied by as many as 200,000 federal troops immediately after the Civil War. Economically devastated, with their crops, homes, transportation, and monetary system destroyed, the former Confederate states also faced a political crisis with the disenfranchisement of their former leaders. Overshadowing the economic and political problems, however, were questions related to the newly freed slaves. No one knew what the place of the free African Americans would be in Southern society nor the nature of the future relationships between blacks and whites.

During Reconstruction, white Southerners began to restrict the rights of African Americans through coercive labor contracts, labor "gangs" that resembled work patterns under slavery, black codes limiting mobility, and vagrancy laws. Vigilante violence occurred and organizations such as the Ku Klux Klan were formed to intimidate African Americans, while sharecropping, tenant farming, and the crop lien system increased among blacks and poor whites, trapping them in a permanent cycle of indebtedness.

In the North, President Ulysses Grant's administration, as well as state and city governments, were marked by scandals, corruption, and bribery. The presidential election of 1876 was between two very similar men, both former reform governors: Republican

2. Robert Hunt Rhodes, ed., *All for the Union* (Lincoln: Andrew Mowbray Inc., 1985), p. 248.
3. Ibid., p. 249.

Rutherford Hayes of Ohio and Democrat Samuel Tilden of New York. Both sides claimed fraud, and a special electoral commission, voting along strict party lines, gave the election to Hayes. As part of the subsequent political compromise in 1877, the activities of federal troops in the South were curtailed and the rights of freed blacks in the former Confederate states were left without any federal protection.

There is no question that the story of the South, along with the political situation in the North, is central to our understanding of the Reconstruction era, 1866–1877. However, in many ways Reconstruction was truly a *national* phenomenon, involving the incorporation of far-reaching economic and social changes that had begun long before the Civil War but were accelerated by the War. Three of the most significant trends of the postwar era were industrialization, urbanization, and the westward expansion of farming into the Great Plains. By focusing only on the struggles of black and white Southerners and the political battles and corruption in the North during the Reconstruction era, we sometimes overlook the important experiences of the millions of other Americans who went West hoping to become prosperous farmers or who left their rural and small town homes to go to nearby cities in search of new economic opportunities in manufacturing, business, and the professions.

The westward movement, of course, had been a constant element of the nineteenth century. With the rapid expansion of railroads and favorable legislation from both the U.S. Congress and state legislatures, railroad companies acquired enormous power to set their own rates and schedules. Railroads also possessed large land grants along their routes, which they sold at a profit to land companies and farmers.

Although the Homestead Act of 1862 had granted 160-acre farms to settlers who would live on the land and improve it, this farm size was too small to be profitable for farmers on the plains. Most settlers had to buy more land and often borrowed money to purchase their farmsteads. Extremes of temperature and precipitation; the lack of trees to provide wood for houses, fences, and fuel; the need for oxen or horses to plow the ground and reap the crop; and the unsuitability of eastern seeds and crops for plains agriculture—all made the work of establishing successful, productive farms in states such as Kansas and Nebraska very difficult. Family farms depended on the work of women and children, who had to perform heavy physical labor cleaning, cooking, and washing, as well as helping with outdoor chores. Often geographically isolated, farm women depended upon distant women neighbors for help in childbirth, sickness, and other emergencies. In spite of these challenges, the census reveals the striking fact that in 1870 there were 2.7 million farms on the plains and prairies, and ten years later there were 4 million farms.

Struggling western farmers resented the roles played by eastern bankers and capitalists, the middlemen who operated grain-storage elevators, and the railroad owners whose monopoly on regional transportation systems enabled them to set arbitrary rate and time schedules. As early as 1867, a social

◆ CHAPTER 1

The Reconstruction
Era: Farmers and
Workers in the West
and North,
1866–1877

and educational organization for farmers had been founded, the National Grange of the Patrons of Husbandry. As a result of the depression of 1873 and the increasing competition from overseas farmers, agricultural prices began to fall. By the mid-1870s, with over 1.5 million members, the Grange had become an important political and economic force in midwestern states such as Wisconsin, Minnesota, Illinois, and Iowa. In the late 1870s, after some political successes on the state level, the Grange gradually reverted to its original functions as an educational and social organization for farm families.

As successive waves of miners, cattle and sheep ranchers, and farm families moved West, they came into increasing conflict with the Native American inhabitants. In response to Eastern demands for fairer treatment of Indians, President Grant had announced a "peace policy" that called for the establishment of reservations where Native Americans could live and be instructed in Christianity and agriculture. Little was done to implement any sort of government aid, however, and Indian affairs fell victim to the same corruption that characterized the rest of the Grant administration. The same railroads that made it easier for settlers to emigrate to the West also encouraged commercial and "sport" hunting of buffalo. During the 1870s, such hunting resulted in the slaughter of over *5 million* buffalo. The big herds, upon which the Indians depended, had been exterminated by the end of the decade. Native Americans raided wagon trains travelling across the plains and defeated Custer and his troops at Little Big Horn, but eventually they succumbed to the Army's determined efforts to contain Indians on reservations and punish those who resisted.

Like the westward movement, the emigration of Americans from rural areas and villages into towns and cities had begun earlier, continued during the war, and increased dramatically in the last quarter of the nineteenth century. The real population gains in the late 1860s and 1870s were to be found in medium-sized cities and large towns. The number of towns with populations between 10,000 and 25,000 doubled between 1860 and 1870, and increased by another 26 percent by 1880. The number of cities with populations between 50,000 and 100,000 doubled between 1860 and 1870, and increased by 27 percent more by 1880.

Along with the increase in urbanization came the expansion of business and industry. Many of the emerging, wealthy business elite, such as John D. Rockefeller, had avoided military service and laid the foundation of their later industrial fortunes during the Civil War. Below the business elite were the new, salaried managers, whose well-being depended on the degree to which they contributed to the profitability of the business through adopting new technologies and increasing workers' productivity. Generally speaking, both the government and the courts were favorable to business interests during the Reconstruction era. Social Darwinism, as popularized in the United States through self-help literature, seemed to give legitimacy to ideas about the "survival of the fittest."

The power and influence of big business did not go unchallenged, however.

From the founding of the short-lived National Labor Union in 1866 to that of the broad, all-encompassing Noble Order of the Knights of Labor in 1869, workers and reformers tried to gain more equality for labor. The prolonged depression that began in 1873 affected workers as well as farmers. Historians estimate that in the years between 1873 and 1877, only two out of ten people in the labor force had full-time, steady employment. Another two out of ten were unemployed, and about four out of ten worked only six or seven months of each year. Violent demonstrations and strikes occurred throughout the 1870s, for example when mounted police charged into a crowd of unemployed workers in New York City in 1874, beating them with billy clubs.

Labor activism in the mining industry, which the mine operators blamed on the secret labor society the Molly Maguires, also ended in violence, characterized by the use of spies, private police, and Italian strikebreakers. By the summer of 1877, labor unrest was widespread. Pennsylvania railroad workers, who worked shifts as long as 15 to 18 hours and whose wages had already been cut by more than one-third, were informed that there would be another wage cut. Spontaneous strikes occurred in cities throughout Pennsylvania and spread to West Virginia, Illinois, and Ohio. Many of these strikes included workers not connected with the railroads, and ended in riots during which federal troops fired on crowds of people. In total, the railroad strikes of 1877 destroyed more than $10 million worth of railroad property.

In this problem, you will be examining some self-help literature to see the characteristics that were considered essential for young men who wished to "succeed" in the post–Civil War era. You will also look at some experiences of farmers and workers in the West and North. What challenges and difficulties did they face? How did they try to solve these problems through organizations such as the Grange and the Knights of Labor?

The Method

For many years, historians who studied major events such as the American Revolution, urbanization, or industrialization focused mainly on the events themselves. This meant that the majority of people who lived during the times being studied became somewhat secondary to the understanding of the times. In other words, they were *acted upon*, rather than being *actors* in historical events or periods of important changes. To the degree that any people were important historical figures, it was because they were generals or presidents or business leaders who were in positions of power and influence.

During the 1960s and 1970s, some European historians continued to see history this way, especially those who studied large geographical areas such as the Mediterranean region over very long periods of time. Historians who believe that certain theories can ex-

♦ CHAPTER 1

The Reconstruction
Era: Farmers and
Workers in the West
and North,
1866–1877

plain historical change and events also tend to conclude that people are acted upon by major forces over which they have no control. In the United States, however, historians' new interest in ordinary people's lives and experiences led them in a different direction. Although no one would deny that people are influenced by major geographical, economic, social, and political forces, historians began to study the ways in which people chose from among alternatives and took action.

In this problem, you will be looking at farmers and workers who lived in a period of economic and social change, and who were affected by these changes. Yet they were not merely *acted upon,* but rather they had choices and took action to solve what they perceived as their problems. In examining the evidence, it is very important for you to place farmers and workers firmly into their historical setting and then to determine why and how they acted to change their situations.

♦

The Evidence

EXCERPTS FROM INSPIRATIONAL LITERATURE

Source 1 from Horatio Alger, Jr., *Ragged Dick and Mark, the Match Boy* (New York: Collier/Macmillan, 1962), pp. 43–44, 75, 110–111.

1. *Ragged Dick* (1867).

[*When we are first introduced to Ragged Dick, he is a boy about twelve years old, dirty, and wearing torn and tattered clothing. He sleeps on the street in doorways, carts, or old boxes. He also has some bad habits: he smokes cigarettes, gambles, goes to the theater, and occasionally eats in taverns. He is a "bootblack" who shines shoes for a living.*]

I have mentioned Dick's faults and defects, because I want it understood, to begin with, that I don't consider him a model boy. But there were some good points about him nevertheless. He was above doing anything mean or dishonorable. He would not steal, or cheat, or impose upon younger boys, but was frank and straight-forward, manly and self-reliant. His nature was a noble one, and had saved him from all mean faults. I hope my young readers will like him as I do, without being blind to his faults. Perhaps, although he was only a bootblack, they may find something in him to imitate. . . .

[*When Ragged Dick encounters a young boy, Frank, who is visiting his uncle on his way to boarding school, Dick offers to show Frank around New York City. None of Dick's friends recognize him, as he is wearing clothes that Frank gives him. Frank tells Dick that he could make a better life for himself.*]

"A good many distinguished men have once been poor boys. There's hope for you, Dick, if you'll try."

"Nobody ever talked to me so before," said Dick. "They just called me Ragged Dick, and told me I'd grow up to be a vagabone (boys who are better educated need not be surprised at Dick's blunders) and come to the gallows."

"Telling you so won't make it turn out so, Dick. If you'll try to be somebody, and grow up into a respectable member of society, you will. You may not become rich,—it isn't everybody that becomes rich, you know,—but you can obtain a good position, and be respected."

"I'll try," said Dick, earnestly. "I needn't have been Ragged Dick so long if I hadn't spent my money in goin' to the theatre, and treatin' boys to oyster-stews, and bettin' money on cards, and such like." . . .

[By the end of the day, Ragged Dick and Frank have become friends, and they promise to write to each other.]

"Uncle, Dick's ready to go," said Frank.

"Good-by, my lad," said Mr. Whitney. "I hope to hear good accounts of you sometime. Don't forget what I have told you. Remember that your future position depends mainly upon yourself, and that it will be high or low as you choose to make it."

He held out his hand, in which was a five-dollar bill. Dick shrunk back.

"I don't like to take it," he said. "I haven't earned it."

"Perhaps not," said Mr. Whitney; "but I give it to you because I remember my own friendless youth. I hope it may be of service to you. Sometime when you are a prosperous man, you can repay it in the form of aid to some poor boy, who is struggling upward as you are now."

"I will, sir," said Dick, manfully.

He no longer refused the money, but took it gratefully, and, bidding Frank and his uncle good-by, went out into the street.

[Ragged Dick changes his ways and gives up his bad habits after Frank leaves. He rents a room, saves his money, and studies on his own. After diving off a ferry to save the life of a young boy, Dick is rewarded by the boy's father, who gives him a job as a clerk in his bank. Ragged Dick now calls himself Richard Hunter, Esquire.]

◆ CHAPTER 1

The Reconstruction
Era: Farmers and
Workers in the West
and North,
1866–1877

Source 2 from Russell Conwell, *Acres of Diamonds* (Westwood, N.J.: Fleming H. Revell Company, 1960), pp. 24–27.

2. "Acres of Diamonds" Lecture (1870).

[Conwell begins his lecture by telling the story of an ancient Persian, Ali Hafed, a wealthy farmer who owned a large, prosperous farm. One day, a visitor tells Ali Hafed about diamonds and the immense wealth that they bring to their owners. Hafed becomes restless and discontented, sells his farm, leaves his family, and goes in search of diamonds. In all his travels, he never finds any diamonds, and he dies poor and unhappy. In the meantime, the man who bought Ali Hafed's farm finds a fabulous lode of diamonds in his own garden. Opportunity for success, Conwell insisted in his lecture, can be found in your own "backyard."]

I say that you ought to get rich, and it is your duty to get rich. How many of my pious brethren say to me, "Do you, a Christian minister, spend your time going up and down the country advising young people to get rich, to get money?" "Yes, of course I do." They say, "Isn't that awful! Why don't you preach the gospel instead of preaching about man's making money?" "Because to make money honestly is to preach the gospel." That is the reason. The men who get rich may be the most honest men you find in the community.

"Oh," but says some young man here tonight, "I have been told all my life that if a person has money he is very dishonest and dishonorable and mean and contemptible." My friend, that is the reason why you have none, because you have that idea of people. The foundation of your faith is altogether false. Let me say here clearly, and say it briefly, though subject to discussion which I have not time for here, ninety-eight out of one hundred of the rich men of America are honest. That is why they are rich. That is why they are trusted with money. That is why they carry on great enterprises and find plenty of people to work with them. It is because they are honest men.

Says another young man, "I hear sometimes of men that get millions of dollars dishonestly." Yes, of course you do, and so do I. But they are so rare a thing in fact that the newspapers talk about them all the time as a matter of news until you get the idea that all the other rich men got rich dishonestly.

My friend, you take and drive me—if you furnish the auto—out into the suburbs of Philadelphia, and introduce me to the people who own their homes around this great city, those beautiful homes with gardens and flowers, those magnificent homes so lovely in their art, and I will introduce you to the very best people in character as well as in enterprise in our city, and you know I will. A man is not really a true man until he owns his own home, and they that own their homes are made more honorable and honest and pure, and true and economical and careful, by owning the home. . . .

Money is power, and you ought to be reasonably ambitious to have it. You ought because you can do more good with it than you could without it. . . . The man who gets the largest salary can do the most good with the power that is furnished to him. Of course he can if his spirit be right to use it for what it is given to him.

I say, then, you ought to have money. If you can honestly attain unto riches in Philadelphia, it is your Christian and godly duty to do so. It is an awful mistake of these pious people to think you must be awfully poor in order to be pious.

Some men say, "Don't you sympathize with the poor people?" Of course I do, or else I would not have been lecturing these years. I won't give in but what I sympathize with the poor, but the number of poor who are to be sympathized with is very small. To sympathize with a man whom God has punished for his sins, thus to help him when God would still continue a just punishment, is to do wrong, no doubt about it, and we do that more than we help those who are deserving. While we should sympathize with God's poor— that is, those who cannot help themselves—let us remember there is not a poor person in the United States who was not made poor by his own shortcomings, or by the shortcomings of someone else. It is all wrong to be poor, anyhow.

Source 3 from Samuel Smiles, *Character* (New York: Harper & Bros, 1877 [?]), pp. 13, 48–49, 165–166.

3. *Character* (1871).

Character is one of the greatest motive powers in the world. In its noblest embodiments, it exemplifies human nature in its highest forms, for it exhibits man at his best. . . .

Although genius always commands admiration, character most secures respect. The former is more the time, afterwards springing up in acts and thoughts and habits. Thus the mother lives again in her children. They unconsciously mould themselves after her manner, her speech, her conduct, and her method of life. Her habits become theirs; and her character is visibly repeated in them.

This maternal love is the visible providence of our race. . . . It begins with the education of the human being at the outstart of life, and is prolonged by virtue of the powerful influence which every good mother exercises over her children through life. When launched into the world, each to take part in its

◆ CHAPTER 1

The Reconstruction
Era: Farmers and
Workers in the West
and North,
1866–1877

labors, anxieties, and trials, they still turn to their mother for consolation, if not for counsel, in their time of trouble and difficulty. The pure and good thoughts she has implanted in their minds when children continue to grow up into good acts long after she is dead. . . .

Man is the brain, but woman is the heart of humanity; he its judgment, she its feeling; he its strength, she its grace, ornament, and solace. Even the understanding of the best woman seems to work mainly through her affections. And thus, though man may direct the intellect, woman cultivates the feelings, which mainly determine the character. While he fills the memory, she occupies the heart. She makes us love what he can only make us believe, and it is chiefly through her that we are enabled to arrive at virtue. . . .

Work is one of the best educators of practical character. It evokes and disciplines obedience, self-control, attention, application, and perseverance; giving a man deftness and skill in his special calling, and aptitude and dexterity in dealing with the affairs of ordinary life.

It is idleness that is the curse of man—not labor. . . . it is this power which constitutes the real distinction between a physical and a moral life, and that forms the primary basis of individual character.

WESTERN FARMERS

Source 4 photos from Long Collection, Kansas Collection; Wisconsin Historical Society.

4. Sod House Pictures.

A. An early, simple sod house in Kansas.

B. A nineteenth-century sod house on the prairie.

Sources 5 and 6 from Cass G. Barns, *The Sod House* (Lincoln: University of Nebraska Press, 1970), pp. 90, 217.

5. Grasshoppers (1875).

This year we had another very dry season resulting in light crops on which the grasshoppers came down by multiplied millions. Great destitution and suffering followed. . . . The grasshoppers came in such swarms that they looked in the distance like fast-gathering rain clouds flying through the air. In some places on the fields of grain they were so numerous that the grain was completely hid from sight. If they had kept still, a man with a scoop shovel could have filled a common wagon bed with them in a few minutes. For a number of years it seemed to be our lot to meet with the grasshoppers, which would take meat, bread and other things from our table.

6. Bugs (1876).

In moving into all kinds of houses we find all kinds of insects that prey upon human blood. One house we found as nearly alive with bugs as a house could be, and not walk off. Soon after going to bed the first night, the bugs sallied out upon us by the hundreds, as if we were sent there on purpose to feed them. . . . After killing the first squad that came out of ambush, we began to count as fast as we destroyed them, and by actual count we killed more than two hundred besides the many we had deprived of life before beginning to count.

Source 7 from Howard Ruede, *Sod-House Days: Letters from a Kansas Homesteader, 1877–78* (New York: Columbia University Press, 1937), pp. 28–29, 50, 52–53.

7. A Homesteader's Experience in Kansas (1877).

[*Howard Ruede traveled from Pennsylvania to Kansas by train, a trip that took three days and three nights. Writing home to his family, Ruede explained how sod houses were built and described the dugout that he and his friends were building. Many of his letters and diary entries were also about food.*]

The sod wall is about 2 feet thick at the ground, and slopes off on the outside to about 14 inches at the top. The roof is composed of a ridge pole and rafters

◆ CHAPTER 1

The Reconstruction
Era: Farmers and
Workers in the West
and North,
1866–1877

of rough split logs, on which is laid corn stalks, and on top of those are two layers of sod. The roof has a very slight pitch, for if it had more, the sod would wash off when there is a heavy rain. . . .

Occasionally a new comer has a "bee," and the neighbors for miles around gather at his claim and put up his house in a day. Of course there is no charge for labor in such cases. The women come too, and while the men lay up the sod walls, they prepare dinner for the crowd, and have a very sociable hour at noon. A house put up in this way is very likely to settle and get out of shape, but it is seldom deserted for that reason.

At first these sod houses are unplastered, and this is thought perfectly all right, but such a house is somewhat cold in the winter, as the crevices between the sods admit some cold air; so some of the houses are plastered with a kind of "native lime," made of sand and a very sticky native clay. . . . I will have to be contented with a very modest affair for a while, but perhaps I can improve it later. . . .

AT THE DUGOUT, KILL CREEK, KANSAS

Turned out about 6 and made fire. Forgot to put the beans to soak last evening, so it took a little longer to boil. Wind n.w., and the fire smokes a good deal, but that kills the meat flies, so I can stand it. While the breakfast was cooking I went out and cut wood so it will be drying out. Rather cloudy this morning. Levin took his ink with him, so I'll have to get a bottle when I go to town again. About 9 o'clock went to chopping again. Guess I'll have to quit, because it makes me short-breathed. Quit about 11, and got as far as Hoot's, on the way back. He was at work on a breaking plow and I stopped to help him a bit. It was raining right smart, and we had showers all day. We tinkered away at the plow till noon, and then I would have left, but they asked me to stop, so I went in and had a square meal. The meat he told me to guess at. I guessed veal, but it was coon. Learned a little about setting the rolling cutter on a breaking plow by watching him and Snyder. When I left for the ranch I bought a loaf of bread from Mrs. Snyder, and I felt as good as if I had drawn a prize in the lottery. Tried a new dodge with the cornmeal. Mixed it with a little water and salt, and baked it over the fire, and it went down a heap better than mush. My supper will be a slice of ham boiled with beans, and a slice of bread. How is that for high toned? The wind is n.e. and the room is full of smoke. . . .

AT THE DUGOUT, KILL CREEK, KANSAS

Turned out about 6, and after breakfast went over to Snyder's. John was shelling corn, and I turned in and helped him. He soon left, to go and herd the cattle, but I kept on till near noon; and I stayed to dinner to pay for my work. . . . As I have no oil, I go to bed with the sun, and try to get up with it, though as yet I have not done so. . . . The start we have made goes very slow, but I think we will get ahead so that next spring we can go to farming and not have to work round. I have a hard time with the meat flies and have taken thousands of eggs off of the ham. I have no dark or smoky place to keep it in, and they get inside of the paper in which it is wrapped. Hardly know what to do with it. It weighs 20 lb. and was twice as big as I wanted, but I could not get a smaller one. The provisions I bought on the 16th cost $2.80. I'll see how long they last. Pickled or smoked hog meat costs 10¢ per lb., corn meal $1.25 per cwt. Hope I'll get papers or a letter with this evening's mail.

Source 8 from John Stands-in-Timber and Margot Liberty, *Cheyenne Memories*, 2nd ed. (New Haven: Yale University Press, 1998), pp. 276–278.

8. Native Americans and Western Farming (1877).

Farming and Gardening

The government started the Indians raising gardens as soon as they surrendered. Some had gardens of corn and other crops at Fort Keogh. They had forgotten how, though they all used to garden in the old days before they hunted buffalo. Now they were learning about new crops as well, things they had never seen before. The Dull Knife people got to Oklahoma in 1877 about the time the watermelons ripened, and when the Southern Cheyennes gave them some they cut them up and boiled them like squash. They did not know you could eat them raw. But later when they planted their own they put sugar with the seeds. They said it would make them sweeter when they grew.

When they reached Tongue River every man was supposed to have a garden of his own. A government farmer went around to teach them. And many of them worked hard, even carrying buckets of water from the river by hand. . . .

Another time when they practiced plowing down there, one man plowed up a bull snake and the next man plowed up a rattlesnake, and after that they were all afraid to go.

In Montana they began to help each other. The government issued plows to quite a few men, and in Birney the Fox Military Society used to plow together as soon as the frost was out. They would all gather at the farthest place up the river and work together until that was done, and then move to the next. They had seven or eight plows and it went faster that way. Besides, it was more fun.

[15]

✦ CHAPTER 1

The Reconstruction
Era: Farmers and
Workers in the West
and North,
1866–1877

One year they decided to finish every garden in ten days, and any member who did not show up would be punished. Everything was fine for several days, until they got to Black Eagle's place. And Looks Behind never came. The rest of them finished plowing for Black Eagle and Medicine Top and Broken Jaw. Then they all got on their horses, and us kids followed them to the Medicine Bull place on Tie Creek and there was Looks Behind, fixing his fence.

They all yelled and fired their guns, and galloped by and hit him with their quirts. There were twenty or thirty of them. Looks Behind had a shovel and at first he was going to fight, but he took it. Afterwards he could hardly talk. They made him get on his horse and go back and start plowing right away.

Source 9 from John L. Commons, et al., *A Documentary History of American Industrial Society,* Vol. X, (Cleveland: Arthur H. Clark Company, 1911). pp. 76–79, 132–136.

9. The Grange.

A. Circular announcing the formation of the Grange (1868).

National Grange, Washington, D.C., September, 1868.

In response to numerous inquiries in regard to the organization and objects of our Order, this circular is issued. . . . It is founded upon the axioms that the products of the soil comprise the basis of all wealth; that individual happiness depends upon general prosperity, and that the wealth of a country depends upon the general intelligence and mental culture of the producing classes. . . .

Women are admitted into our Order, as well as young persons of both sexes over the age of sixteen and eighteen respectively. In its proceedings a love for rural life will be encouraged, the desire for excitement and amusement, so prevalent in youth, will be gratified, instead of being repressed; not, however, in frivolities, as useless for the future as they are for the present, but by directing attention to the wonder-workings of nature, and leading the mind to enjoy and appreciate that never-ending delight which follows useful studies, relating to the animal, vegetable, and mineral kingdoms. . . .

Its objects, as already indicated, are to advance education, to elevate and dignify the occupation of the farmer, and to protect its members against the numerous combinations by which their interests are injuriously affected.

There is no association that secures so many advantages to its members as this.

The Order of the Patrons of Husbandry will accomplish a thorough and systematic organization among farmers and horticulturists throughout the

United States, and will secure among them intimate social relations and acquaintance with each other, for the advancement and elevation of its pursuits, with an appreciation and protection of their true interests. By such means may be accomplished that which exists throughout the country in all other avocations, and among all other classes—combined co-operative association for individual improvement and common benefit. . . .

Among other advantages which may be derived from the Order, can be mentioned, systematic arrangements for procuring and disseminating, in the most expeditious manner, information relative to crops, demand and supply, prices, markets, and transportation throughout the country, and for the establishment of depots for the sale of special or general products in the cities; also for the purchase and exchange of stock, seeds, and desired varieties of plants and trees, and for the purpose of procuring help at home or from abroad, and situations for persons seeking employment; also for ascertaining and testing the merits of newly invented farming implements, and those not in general use, and for detecting and exposing those that are unworthy, and for protecting by all available means, the farming interests from fraud and deception of every kind.

In conclusion, we desire that agricultural societies shall keep step with the music of the age, and keep pace with improvements in the reaping machine and steam engine. In this Order we expect to accomplish these results.

B. Excerpts from the 13th National Meeting of the Grange (1879).

Thirteen years' experience and association in the Grange has satisfied the American farmers, whom we represent, that their grievances will never be removed until farmers are elected as representatives to the law-making bodies of our states, and to the national legislatures, in such numbers as will constitute those bodies with a fair share of our people. . . . To this end we recommend farmers to make such alliance, whenever representatives to the state legislatures or to the national legislature are to be chosen, as will enable them by their votes to elect from their own number an even handed, fair share of representatives. . . . The assumption of this constitutional right is but the assertion of our manhood, and we cannot longer be dominated by party associations which deny us our equality, or support a partizan press that ignores the association of American farmers.

American farming is growing less profitable and less encouraging. In a country possessing so many facilities of cheap production this discouraging aspect of agriculture must be and is the result of other than natural causes. The annual additions of wealth under the enlightened system of agriculture

◆ CHAPTER 1

The Reconstruction
Era: Farmers and
Workers in the West
and North,
1866–1877

are enormous, but from the unequal divisions of the profits of labor and the unjust discriminations made against it, the enlistments of property show that the farmers of the United States are not prospering. . . .

The farmers of America have on all occasions shown themselves to be a patient and enduring people, and further submission to wrong and injustice will be a sacrifice of manhood and exhibition of cowardice. Stirred with a just sense of right and supported by the integrity of our purpose, the National Grange of the Patrons of Husbandry, in the name and interests of the farmers of the United States, sternly demand—

1st. That the Department of Agriculture shall be made an Executive Department, and the Commissioner a Cabinet officer.

2d. That the Agricultural Department shall be sustained and supported by annual appropriations commensurate with the importance of the great and permanent industry it represents.

3d. That commercial treaties shall be made with all foreign countries, giving to American products equal and unrestricted intercourse with the markets of the world.

4th. That governments be administered in a cheaper and simpler manner, consonant with the conditions of the people.

5th. That a more rigid economy in the expenditures of public moneys be reestablished.

6th. That the laws shall be plain and simple, to the end that justice shall be speedy, crime punished, and good government maintained.

7th. That the creation or allowing of monopolies to exist is in violation of the spirit and genius of free republican government.

8th. That the tariffs of freight and fare over railroads and all transportation companies shall be regulated, and all unjust discriminations inhibited by law.

9th. That taxation shall be equal and uniform, and all values made to contribute their just proportion to the support of the government.

10th. That the revenue laws of the United States shall be so adjusted as to bear equally upon all classes of property, to the end that agriculture shall be relieved of the disproportion of burdens it bears.

11th. That the patent laws of the United States be so revised that innocent purchasers of patent rights shall be protected, and fraudulent venders alone held responsible for infringements of rights and violations of law.

12th. That a system of elementary agricultural education shall be adopted in the common schools of the country.

13th. That we are entitled to and should have a fair representation in the legislative halls of the country, chosen from the ranks of the farmers. . . .

With manly dignity we boldly declare our rights and interests, and with unwavering devotion will maintain and defend them on all occasions, and this warning is defiantly thrown to the world.

NORTHERN WORKERS

Source 10 from James C. Sylvis, *The Life, Speeches, Labors & Essays of William H. Sylvis* (New York: Augustus M. Kelley, 1968), pp. 296, 316–318.

10. National Labor Union, Letter to the *Evening Advocate* from William Sylvis (1868).

WHAT WE WANT.

We now want:

1. A new department at Washington, to be called THE DEPARTMENT OF LABOR, the head of said department to be called the Secretary of Labor, and to be chosen directly from the ranks of workingmen. To this department should be referred all questions of wages and the hours of labor in the navy-yards and all other government workshops, the registry and regulation of trades-unions and co-operative associations, the disposition of public lands, and all other questions directly connected with and affecting labor.

2. The unconditional repeal of all laws bearing upon the disposition of the public domain.

3. The adoption of a plain, unvarnished law for the giving away of the public lands to actual settlers in parcels of not less than forty nor more than one hundred acres, no man being allowed to hold in his own name, the name of his wife, nor any other name, more than one tract.

4. Every man taking up land to be required to proceed to live upon, improve, and cultivate it within one year, or forfeit his claim.

5. Appropriations to be made from the United States Treasury to assist workingmen who desire to locate upon the public domain, but who are destitute of the means to do so.

6. No grants of public land to be made to railroad companies or to other corporations, nor to individuals, except actual settlers, under any circumstances, nor for any purpose.

7. All lands granted to railroad companies or other corporations, or individuals, remaining unoccupied and uncultivated at the end of five years from the date of said grant, to revert back to the government, and be sold at government price ($1.25 per acre), the proceeds to go to the person or persons to whom the grant was made. This provision should apply to *all* grants that have been made.

✦ CHAPTER 1

The Reconstruction
Era: Farmers and
Workers in the West
and North,
1866–1877

8. All uncultivated lands held by grant of Congress, by any person or persons, shall pay a tax of *ten cents per acre* into the treasury of the United States until said lands are cultivated, or have reverted to the government.

9. All uncultivated lands now held by grant of Congress, by any person or persons, shall be immediately placed in the market at one dollar and twenty-five cents per acre.

Anticipating the opposition that will be made to the proposition to give the public lands away, and pay the expenses of the poor workingmen who desire to move upon and cultivate these lands, upon the ground that they cost the government something, I will answer, that whatever these lands did cost for surveys, etc., came out of the public treasury; and all the money that is or ever was in said treasury was put there by *the labor of the country*. The lands belong to the people, were paid for by the people, and the people have a right to enjoy them without paying for them a second time. And, all things considered, the proposition to assist the very poor in getting to these lands is a very modest one. We only ask that a very little of the taxes paid by labor be returned to those who paid it, while hundreds of millions are being appropriated for other purposes.

Source 11 from Terence V. Powderly, *Thirty Years of Labor, 1859–1889* (New York: Augustus M. Kelley, 1967), pp. 64–65.

11. Excerpts from the Preamble of the Knights of Labor (1870).

"The recent alarming development and aggression of aggregated wealth, which, unless checked, will inevitably lead to the pauperization and hopeless degradation of the toiling masses, render it imperative, if we desire to enjoy the blessings of the government bequeathed to us by the founders of the Republic, that a check should be placed upon its power and unjust accumulation, and a system adopted which will secure to the laborer the fruits of his toil; and as this much-desired object can only be accomplished by the thorough unification of labor, and the united efforts of those who obey the divine injunction, 'In the sweat of thy face shalt thou eat bread,' we have formed the INDUSTRIAL BROTHERHOOD, with a view of securing the organization and direction, by co-operative effort, of the power of the industrial classes; and we submit to the people of the United States the objects sought to be accomplished by our organization, calling upon all who believe in securing 'the greatest good to the greatest number' to aid and assist us:

"I. To bring within the folds of organization every department of productive industry, making knowledge a standpoint for action, and industrial, moral and social worth—not wealth—the true standard of individual and national greatness.

"II. To secure to the toilers a proper share of the wealth that they create; more of the leisure that rightly belongs to them; more societary advantages; more of the benefits, privileges and emoluments of the world; in a word, all those rights and privileges necessary to make them capable of enjoying, appreciating, defending and perpetuating the blessings of republican institutions.

"III. To arrive at the true condition of the producing masses in their educational, moral and financial condition, we demand from the several States and from the national government the establishment of bureaus of labor statistics.

"IV. The establishment of co-operative institutions, productive and distributive.

"V. The reserving of the public lands, the heritage of the people, for the actual settler—not another acre for railroads or speculators.

"VI. The abrogation of all laws that do not bear equally upon capital and labor, the removal of unjust technicalities, delays and discriminations in the administration of justice, and the adoption of measures providing for the health and safety of those engaged in mining, manufacturing or building pursuits.

"VII. The enactment of a law to compel chartered corporations to pay their employes at least once in every month in full for labor performed during the preceding month in the lawful money of the country.

"VIII. The enactment of a law giving mechanics and other laborers a first lien on their work.

"IX. The abolishment of the contract system on national, State and municipal work.

"X. To inaugurate a system of public markets, to facilitate the exchange of the productions of farmers and mechanics, tending to do away with middlemen and speculators.

"XI. To inaugurate systems of cheap transportation to facilitate the exchange of commodities.

"XII. The substitution of arbitration for strikes, whenever and wherever employers and employes are willing to meet on equitable grounds.

"XIII. The prohibition of the importation of all servile races, the discontinuance of all subsidies granted to national vessels bringing them to our shores, and the abrogation of the Burlingame Treaty.

"XIV. To advance the standard of American mechanics by the enactment and enforcement of equitable apprentice laws.

◆ CHAPTER 1

The Reconstruction
Era: Farmers and
Workers in the West
and North,
1866–1877

"XV. To abolish the system of contracting the labor of convicts in our prisons and reformatory institutions.

"XVI. To secure for both sexes equal pay for equal work.

"XVII. The reduction of the hours of labor to eight per day, so that laborers may have more time for social enjoyment and intellectual improvement, and be enabled to reap the advantages conferred by labor-saving machinery, which their brains have created.

"XVIII. To prevail upon the government to establish a just standard of distribution between capital and labor by providing a purely national circulating medium based upon the faith and resources of the nation, issued directly to the people, without the intervention of any system of banking corporations, which money shall be a legal tender in the payment of all debts, public or private, and interchangeable at the option of the holder for government bonds, bearing a rate of interest not to exceed three and sixty-five hundredths per cent., subject to future legislation of Congress."

Source 12 from John Garraty, ed., *The Transformation of American Society, 1870–1890* (Columbia: University of South Carolina Press, 1969), pp. 88–96.

12. Massachusetts Bureau of Statistics of Labor Report (1878).

From a Carpet-Mill Operative.—I am satisfied with sixty hours a week: it is plenty time for any man, although there are some employed in the same place over that time, and get nothing extra for it. . . .

From a Shoemaker.—I think there ought to be an eight-hour law all over the country. There is not enough work to last the year round, and work over eight hours a day, or forty-eight hours a week. There can be only about so much work to do any way: and, when that is done, business has got to stop, or keep dragging the year round, so that a man has to work for almost any price offered. . . .

From a Carpenter.—I think that eight hours a day is enough for a man to work at his trade. Then I think there would be more work; and he would have time to make his house and garden look more tidy, if he has one, or to study and improve the mind. I think that a man would do more work at home when he is at work than he would when unemployed; for he is down-hearted, and does not feel like working at home. I find too, that, the lower wages are, the more work they expect a man to do. . . .

From a Carpenter.—In regard to the number of hours a day's work should consist of, I think ten hours is a fair day's work, and do not think an eight-hour law would be any help to the laboring class. There are some who would make good use of their spare time; and there are others who would not. This same class would want pay for ten hours, and would strike if they could not get it. I for one never could see where the laboring class gains any lasting good by a strike. I think a man should make the best terms possible with his boss; and, if he cannot get as much as he wants, he should try other places. He cannot expect to have every thing as he did in good times. If he gets enough to eat, and plain clothes to wear, he should be content for the present. Better times will come soon. . . .

From a Harness-Maker.—In answer to the question, "Do you consider yourself overworked?" I answered, "Yes"; and it is my honest and firm conviction that I am, by at least two hours a day. With the great increase in machinery within the last fifteen or twenty years, I think, in justice, there ought to be some reduction in the hours of labor. Unless the hours of labor are shortened in proportion to the increase of machinery, I consider machinery an injury rather than a benefit to humanity. I tell you that ten hours a day, hard, steady work, is more than any man can stand for any length of time without injuring his health, and therefore shortening his life. For my own part, although my work is not very laborious, when I stop work in the evening, I feel completely played out. I would like to study some; but I am too fatigued. In fact it is as much as I can do to look over the evening paper; and I am almost certain that this is the condition of a majority of workingmen. . . .

From a Shoe-Finisher.—Some piece hands work more than ten hours. Under these circumstances, I consider that, in boot and shoe towns, the laboring classes are overworked, having no time for social enjoyment or self-culture, or for acquiring information. If they get the time, they are unfit for it after ten hours' hard labor. . . .

From a Machinist.—In reply to your question concerning overwork, I wish to say, that, in employment requiring close application of mind or body, to be successful, the diligent and conscientious workman often, I might say always, finds his energy exhausted long before his ten hours are up. . . . I do not think I should be able to follow up work in this way until the age of sixty-five. Hope to find some way to avoid some of the long hours and some of the heavy work before then. I do not mean to complain; but it does seem as if the burdens and the pleasures of this world were very unequally divided. . . .

From a Boot and Shoe Cutter.—Tax machinery. Bring it in common with hand labor, so a man can have twelve months' work in a year, instead of six or eight months. Protect hand labor, same as we protect trade from Europe, by tax or tariff.

From a Machinist.—Machinery and the swarms of cheap foreign labor are

◆ CHAPTER 1

The Reconstruction
Era: Farmers and
Workers in the West
and North,
1866–1877

fast rendering trades useless, and compelling the better class of mechanics to change their occupation, or go to farming. . . .

From a Clerk in a Country Store.—I do believe that, if a person enjoys good health, and is willing to work, he may earn an honest living, and perhaps lay aside a few dollars for future wants. A large portion of our poor people have poor ways: they will sit around the corner groceries and saloons, chew and smoke tobacco, swear and curse those who seem to be prospering, complain of the hard times and their hard luck. . . .

From a Machinist.—The great need now of the laboring man is honesty and contentment. I mean, being willing to do an honest day's work, and contented with the wages his labor will bring in the market. The idea that a man can get rich, without hard work of some kind, must be given up. Thirty-three years of hard work, and yet far from being rich, is my condition.

From a Shoe-Cutter.—There is no way I think I could be paid more fairly than I now am. I do not consider that my employers profit unfairly by my labor. My labor is in the market for sale. My employers buy it just as they buy a side of leather, and expect, and I think are willing to pay, a fair market price for it. . . . All trades-unions and combinations I also consider as injurious to the mass of working-people. A few profit by these associations, and the many pay the bills. If working-people would drop the use of beer, tobacco, and every thing else that is not of real benefit, and let such men as_____and a host of others earn their own living, they would have far more money for the general expenses of a family than they now have. I live in a village of about two thousand inhabitants; and I do not know of a family in destitute circumstances which has let alone vicious expenditures, and been industrious. It is the idle, unthrifty, beer-drinking, don't-care sort of people, who are out at the elbows, and waiting for some sort of legislation to help them. The sooner working-people get rid of the idea that somebody or something is going to help them, the better it will be for them. In this country, as a general thing, every man has an equal chance to rise. In our village there are a number of successful business men, and all began in the world without any thing but their hands and a will to succeed. The best way for working-people to get help is to help themselves. . . .

From a Steam and Gas Fitter.—The war created a class of money aristocrats. . . . Fifteen years ago a man could start a successful business with from one hundred to three hundred dollars; while it now requires one to three or more thousand, thereby making a poor man's chances poorer every year. In fifteen years this country will be worse off than the old countries of Europe and Asia. The rich will be very rich, the poor very poor, and the government will be controlled by the moneyed class. . . .

From a Custom Shoemaker.—The best thing the government (national) can do for workingmen is to let them alone. The wise and the prudent need no help; for the unwise and imprudent nothing effectual can be done. Forethought and economy, carefully practised in early life as well as age, would banish poverty; and nothing else ever will.

From a Comb-Maker.—I do not know of any legislation that will help the workingman, and not affect the successful employer. He has the capital; and, if he cannot employ it so as to make it pay more than in other investments, he would not be likely to employ many workingmen at very high prices.

Source 13 from Samuel Gompers, *Seventy Years of Life and Labour: An Autobiography,* Vol. I, (New York: Augustus M. Kelley, 1967), pp. 155–157.

13. Samuel Gompers's "Strike Baby" (1878).

The Cigar Manufacturers' Association had declared that under no circumstances would any leaders of the strike be employed for at least six months. As a consequence, for nearly four months I was out of employment. I had parted with everything of any value in the house, and my wife and I were every day expecting a newcomer in addition to the five children we already had.

My family helped in every way possible. Part of the time they were hungry and without the necessaries of life. Never once did my wife falter. Blacklisted, I desperately sought employment, going home at night where my brave wife prepared soup out of water, salt, pepper, and flour. . . .

Once I was ready to commit murder. All the children were ill, probably because of winter cold and under-nourishment; they were subject to illness and fever. I walked around looking for work and could not find it, and as I left my wife in the morning again to look for work there were indications that the newcomer was about due, but by previous experience I thought that that condition would last a couple of days. But when I came home, my sister-in-law, who was living with us and sharing whatever little we had, told me that the child was born. There had been nobody to help the mother or the child. I stood by, dazed, and then rushed to the man who had acted as our physician. He was the physician paid by the Hand-in-Hand Society. But he was not in and like a madman I rushed back, but the situation was the same as it was before.

It dawned on me that there was a physician on the next block and I went to him and told him of the condition and that I wanted him to come down and attend to my wife. He asked me if I had money. When I told him I did not, he re-

◆ CHAPTER 1

The Reconstruction
Era: Farmers and
Workers in the West
and North,
1866–1877

plied that he was not our regular physician. I said I knew that but my wife was in such a serious condition and the child there and I wanted him to come to attend her right away. He said, "Well, I do not feel like it and I won't do it."

I walked up to him, looked him square in the eye and said, "Yes you will, you will come and see my wife now." He said, "Well, I will not." I put my hand on his coat collar and said, "You will come now with me or you will never make another move." He said he wanted me to pay him and I said: "I have got no money. I have been out of work, but I will promise to pay you everything I can gather tonight, but you will come with me without another minute's hesitation or I will not be responsible for what I will do to you. Come along." He put on his hat and coat and he went with me. While he was attending the mother and child, I went around among the members of my family and gathered up two dollars and gave it to him. He prescribed some medicine and I did not have the money to get the prescription filled and finally prevailed upon the druggist with whom I was acquainted through living in the neighborhood to trust me for it and we pulled her through. The baby was my Al. He was our strike baby, born in the forenoon of February 28, 1878.

◆

Questions to Consider

In this problem, you are examining western farmers' and northern workers' experiences in the immediate post–Civil War era. As you saw in the Method section, your focus is on the ways in which people were *actors* in their own lives rather than merely *acted upon* by forces beyond their control. However, it is very important to situate these farmers and workers firmly in their own historical time period first, before examining the choices they made. The first three pieces of evidence (Sources 1 through 3) should help you understand how people thought about "success" and what characteristics they believed were necessary to achieve it.

Horatio Alger was a Harvard graduate who became a Unitarian minister under pressure from his father, even though his real love was literature and writing. Prevented from enlisting in the Civil War by a series of physical mishaps, he began writing short stories, novels, and, later in his career, biographies of self-made men. *Ragged Dick* (Source 1), an enormously popular bestseller, was followed by more than 130 other books, mostly fiction about poor newsboys, shoeshine boys, messengers, and street musicians who overcame all obstacles to become successful. Russell Conwell was a Civil War veteran and lawyer who became a Baptist minister in 1879 and later founded Temple University in Philadelphia. He was famous for his inspirational lecture, "Acres of Diamonds" (Source 2), which he claimed to have delivered—with variations—over 6,000 times. Samuel Smiles, one of eleven children, grew up in Scotland and was a self-made man who became a doctor and a writer. Source 3 is an excerpt from his book, *Character*, the sequel to his very popular book, *Self-Help* (1860). These two advice books, along with Smiles's *Thrift* (1875) and *Duty* (1880), sold over a million copies in the United States.

What do these three authors believe constitutes "success" for young men? What qualities would a successful young man possess? Smiles also writes about women's roles, although Alger and Conwell do not. In what ways does "success" for women differ from "success" for men?

The second group of evidence (Sources 4 through 9) examines western farmers' lives and activities. Source 4 consists of two pictures of the sod houses in which farmers lived. How would you describe these houses and their surroundings to a student who could not see the pictures? Sources 5 and 6 reveal the conditions faced by a young Methodist minister and his family in Kansas. What happened to them? Howard Ruede (Source 7) was a twenty-three year old Pennsylvanian who emigrated to Kansas to file a homestead claim in 1877. His father, two younger brothers, mother, and sister eventually joined him. Like many settlers, Ruede first built a dugout (a partially underground shelter), and he worked for the town printer or on other people's farms. Sometimes he earned wages; sometimes he worked in return for food or the use of farm equipment. What were some of the hardships he faced?

During the same period, the federal government insisted that Native Americans who were living on reservations take up plains farming. John Stands-in-Timber, a Cheyenne, discusses these efforts (Source 8). How and why did the Indians' farming experiences differ from those of the white settlers? As farming expanded westward and became more dependent on the transportation of farm products to distant markets, farmers sought relief from some of their problems. What were the general purposes of the Patrons of Husbandry, commonly known as the Grange (Source 9)? What grievances did the farmers voice at the 13th meeting of the Grange?

Workers' attempts to organize had begun well before the Civil War and continued during the war itself. What economic changes did William Sylvis, head of the National Labor Union, ask for in his letter (Source 10)? In the 1870s, the Knights of Labor, a broad-based labor union that included both skilled and unskilled workers, superseded the National Labor Union. Which of the Knights' demands, outlined in Source 11, were similar to those of the National Labor Union? Which were different?

Source 12 is a sample of some workers' responses to a Massachusetts labor survey taken in 1878. What were their major complaints? Do any of these workers' statements reflect the ideas found in the self-help literature written by Alger, Conwell, and Smiles? Influenced by the Great Railroad Strike of 1877, many other workers also struck for better wages in 1877–1878. In New York City, Cigarmakers' Union president Samuel Gompers tried

◆ CHAPTER 1

The Reconstruction
Era: Farmers and
Workers in the West
and North,
1866–1877

to help striking cigar makers who worked in tenement houses. What working-class family dilemmas does his story about the "strike baby" (Source 13) illustrate?

Finally, return to the central questions of this chapter. How would you sum up the popular attitudes of the 1870s toward success? What was the impact of these ideas? What problems did the farmers and workers face? What actions did they take to try to solve these problems?

◆

Epilogue

In the summer of 1877, California newspaperman Henry George began writing a book entitled *Progress and Poverty*. In it, he argued that the extremes of wealth and poverty in the United States were caused by rich Americans' monopolistic control of the land and the rents they charged. George advocated a "single tax" on the increasing value of land, which would enable the government to abolish all other forms of taxation. As a result, George believed, the gap between the rich and the poor would narrow. The evils that resulted from the unequal and unfair distribution of wealth, George wrote, "are not incidents of progress, but tendencies which must bring progress to a halt; that they will not cure themselves, but, on the contrary, must, unless their cause is removed, grow greater and greater. . . ."[4] When *Progress and Poverty* was published in 1879, it sold more than two million copies in the United States and was also widely read and admired abroad.

During the decade of the 1880s, farm prices continued to fall. Wheat, which had sold for $1.20 a bushel in 1881, was 70 cents a bushel in 1889; during the same years, the price of cotton fell from 11 cents a pound to less than a penny a pound. Farmers' Alliances gained membership rapidly in the South and West, including a Colored Alliance that had nearly a quarter of a million African American members. After demonstrating their power in the elections of 1890, farmers formed the Populist party. Their candidates ran on a platform of far-reaching political and economic reforms, and the party enjoyed considerable success on the state level. In fact, many of the Populist party reforms were implemented in the first quarter of the twentieth century.

Under the Dawes Act of 1887, Native Americans were granted 160-acre farms on their reservations, and the "extra" land was sold to white settlers. The opening in 1889 of Oklahoma, a territory reserved for Indians since the 1820s, reduced the Indian landholdings to just one-third of their previous total. Finally, fearing a Sioux uprising during the Ghost Dance movement of 1891, the army, using machine guns, killed 146 Native Americans at Wounded

4. Henry George, *Progress and Poverty* (New York: Modern Library, 1929 [1879]), p. 544.

Knee Creek on a reservation in South Dakota.

Workers also suffered serious setbacks in the 1880s and 1890s, as police, private security forces, and federal troops were regularly called out to quell labor disturbances. In the Haymarket Affair of 1886, a bomb exploded during an outdoor labor meeting in Chicago, resulting in the arrests of eight people and the execution of four of them. The 1892 Homestead Strike against Carnegie Steel Works outside Pittsburgh involved a gun battle between the strikers and private security guards; federal troops were called in to break the 1894 Pullman strike near Chicago. The Knights of Labor declined after a series of unsuccessful strikes in the 1880s and was replaced by the more conservative American Federation of Labor. Organized in 1888, the AF of L included only unions of skilled, white workers and confined its demands to the "bread-and-butter" issues of wages and hours. The use of child labor peaked during the late nineteenth century, thousands of workers were killed or injured each year on the job, and another depression in 1894 had severe, long-lasting effects on working-class families.

CHAPTER

2

The Road to
True Freedom:
African American
Alternatives in
the New South

◆

The Problem

By 1895, when the venerable Frederick Douglass died, African Americans in the South had been free for thirty years. Yet in many ways, their situation had barely improved from that of servitude, and in some ways, it had actually deteriorated. Economically, very few had been able to acquire land of their own, and the vast majority continued to work for white landowners under various forms of labor arrangements and sometimes under outright peonage.[1] Political and civil rights supposedly had been guaranteed under the Fourteenth and Fifteenth amendments to the Constitution (ratified in 1868 and 1870, respectively), but those

rights often were violated, federal courts offered little protection, and, beginning in the early 1890s, southern states began a successful campaign to disfranchise black voters and to institute legal segregation through legislation that collectively became known as Jim Crow laws.[2] In some ways more threatening, violence against African Americans was increasing and in most cases going unpunished. Between 1889 and 1900, 1,357 lynchings of African Americans were recorded in the United States, the vast majority in the states of the former Confederacy. In 1898, in New Bern, North Carolina, one white orator proposed "choking the Cape Fear River with the bodies of Negroes."

1. Whatever names were given to these labor arrangements (tenancy, sharecropping, and so on), in most of the arrangements a white landowner or merchant furnished farm workers with foodstuffs and fertilizer on credit, taking a percentage of the crops grown in return. For a fascinating description of how the system worked, see Theodore Rosengarten, *All God's Dangers: The Life of Nate Shaw* (New York: Alfred A. Knopf, 1974).

2. The term *Jim Crow,* generally used to refer to issues relating to African Americans, originated in the late 1820s with white minstrel singer Thomas "Daddy" Rice, who performed the song "Jump Jim Crow" in blackface makeup. By the 1840s, the term was used to refer to racially segregated facilities in the North.

In truth, by the 1890s it had become evident for all who cared to see that Lincoln's emancipation of southern slaves had been considerably less than complete.

Economic semiservitude, disfranchisement, assaults on black women, and widespread lynchings combined to undercut the African American male's sense of his own manhood. Alternately portrayed by whites as childlike creatures or as brutish sexual predators, black males tried desperately though not always successfully to assert their manhood. At the beginning of the Spanish-American War in 1898, many African American men rushed to enlist in the armed services, and one unit actually rescued Theodore Roosevelt's Rough Riders from a difficult situation in their soon-to-be-famous "charge up San Juan Hill."

Many whites, however, refused to allow African American men to express their masculinity. Indeed, more than a few white men actually believed that *they themselves* displayed their own masculinity by keeping blacks in their "place." During the racially charged North Carolina state elections in 1898, one newspaper published a poem that specifically expressed that sentiment:

Rise, ye sons of Carolina!
Proud Caucasians, one and all;
Be not deaf to Love's appealing—
Hear your wives and daughters call,
See their blanched and anxious faces,
Note their frail, but lovely forms
Rise, defend their spotless virtue
With your strong and manly arms.[3]

3. *Wilmington (NC) Messenger,* November 8, 1898, quoted in Glenda Elizabeth Gilmore, *Gender and Jim Crow: Women and the Politics*

Thus in the eyes of many African Americans, their collective star appeared not to be rising but rather descending. A number of spokespersons offered significantly different strategies for improving the situation of African Americans in the South. For this chapter's Evidence section, we have chosen five such spokespersons, all of them well known to blacks in the New South. Ida B. Wells (1862–1931) was a journalist, lecturer, and crusader who was well known in both the United States and Europe. Booker T. Washington (1856–1915) was a celebrated educator, author, and political figure who many believed should have inherited the mantle of Frederick Douglass as the principal spokesperson for African Americans. Henry McNeal Turner (1834–1915) was a bishop of the African Methodist Episcopal Church and a controversial speaker and writer. W. E. B. Du Bois (pronounced *Du Boys',* 1868–1963) was an academician and editor and one of the founders of the National Association for the Advancement of Colored People (NAACP). Finally, Frances Ellen Watkins Harper (1825–1911) was a popular poet and writer who gave numerous speeches in support of both African American and women's rights. Each of these spokespersons offered a contrasting alternative for African Americans in the New South.

In this chapter, you will be analyzing the situation that African Americans in the New South faced in the years after

of White Supremacy in North Carolina, 1896–1920 (Chapel Hill: University of North Carolina Press, 1996), p. 91. Gilmore's study is highly recommended for anyone who wishes to delve more deeply into this topic.

✦ CHAPTER 2

The Road to True
Freedom:
African American
Alternatives in
the New South

Reconstruction and identifying the principal alternatives open to them. What different strategies did Wells, Washington, Turner, Du Bois, and Harper offer African Americans? Were there other options they did not address? Based on your examination of the different alternatives advocated by these five African American spokespersons, what do you think were the strengths and weaknesses of each approach? Finally, keep in mind that the five spokepersons advocated taking different paths to the *same* ultimate goal: full equality for African Americans.

Background

The gradual end of Reconstruction by the federal government left the South in the hands of political and economic leaders who chose to call themselves "redeemers." Many of these men came from the same landowner and planter-lawyer groups that had led the South prior to the Civil War, thus giving the post-Reconstruction South a high degree of continuity with earlier eras. Also important, however, was a comparatively new group of southerners, men who called for a "New South" that would be highlighted by increased industrialization, urbanization, and diversified agriculture.

In many ways, the New South movement was an undisguised attempt to imitate the industrialization that was sweeping through the North just prior to, during, and after the Civil War. Indeed, the North's industrial prowess had been one reason for its ultimate military victory. As Reconstruction gradually came to an end in the southern states, many southern bankers, business leaders, and editors became convinced that the South should not return to its previous, narrow economic base of plantations and one-crop agriculture but instead should follow the North's lead toward modernization through industry. Prior to the Civil War, many of these people had been calling for economic diversification, but they had been overwhelmed by the plantation aristocracy that controlled southern state politics and had used that control to further its own interests. By the end of Reconstruction, however, the planter elite had lost a good deal of its power, thus creating a power vacuum into which advocates of a New South could move.

Nearly every city, town, and hamlet of the former Confederacy had its New South boosters. Getting together in industrial societies or chambers of commerce, the boosters called for the erection of mills and factories. Why, they asked, should southerners export their valuable raw materials elsewhere, only to see them return from northern and European factories as costly finished products? Why couldn't southerners set up their own manufacturing establishments and become prosperous within a self-contained economy? And if the southerners were short of capital, why not encourage rich northern investors to put up money in return for promises of great profits? In fact, the

South had all the ingredients required of an industrial system: raw materials, a rebuilt transportation system, labor, potential consumers, and the possibility of obtaining capital. As they fed each other's dreams, the New South advocates pictured a resurgent South, a prosperous South, a triumphant South, a South of steam and power rather than plantations and magnolias.

Undoubtedly, the leading spokesman of the New South movement was Henry Grady, editor of the *Atlanta Constitution* and one of the most influential figures in the southern states. Born in Athens, Georgia, in 1850, Grady was orphaned in his early teens when his father was killed in the Civil War. Graduating from his hometown college, the University of Georgia, Grady began a long and not particularly profitable career as a journalist. In 1879, aided by northern industrialist Cyrus Field, he purchased a quarter interest in the *Atlanta Constitution* and became that newspaper's editor. From that position, he became the chief advocate of the New South movement.

Whether speaking to southern or northern audiences, Grady had no peer. Addressing a group of potential investors in New South industries in New York in 1886, he delighted his audience by saying that he was glad the Confederacy had lost the Civil War, for that defeat had broken the power of the plantation aristocracy and provided the opportunity for the South to move into the modern industrial age. Northerners, Grady continued, were welcome: "We have sown towns and cities in the place of theories, and put business above politics . . . and have . . . wiped out the place where Mason and Dixon's line used to be."[4]

To those southerners who envisioned a New South, the central goal was a harmonious, interdependent society in which each person and thing had a clearly defined place. Most New South boosters stressed industry and the growth of cities because the South had few factories and mills and almost no cities of substantial size. But agriculture also would have its place, although it would not be the same as the cash-crop agriculture of the pre–Civil War years. Instead, New South spokespersons advocated a diversified agriculture that would still produce cash crops for export but would also make the South more self-sufficient by producing food crops and raw materials for the anticipated factories. Small towns would be used for collection and distribution, a rebuilt railroad network would transport goods, and northern capital would finance the entire process. Hence, each part of the economy and, indeed, each person would have a clearly defined place and role in the New South, a place and role that would ensure everyone a piece of the New South's prosperity.

But even as Grady and his counterparts were fashioning their dreams of a New South and selling those dreams to both northerners and southerners, a less beneficial, less prosperous side of the New South was taking shape. In spite of the New South advocates' successes in establishing factories and mills (for example, Knoxville, Tennes-

4. Grady's speech is in Richard N. Current and John A. Garraty, eds., *Words That Made American History* (Boston: Little, Brown, 1962), Vol. II, pp. 23–31.

◆ CHAPTER 2

The Road to True
Freedom:
African American
Alternatives in
the New South

see, witnessed the founding of more than ninety such enterprises in the 1880s alone), the post-Reconstruction South remained primarily agricultural. Furthermore, many of the farms were worked by sharecroppers or tenant farmers who eked out a bare subsistence while the profits went to the landowners or to the banks. This situation was especially prevalent in the lower South, where by 1910 a great proportion of farms were worked by tenants: South Carolina (63.0 percent), Georgia (65.6 percent), Alabama (60.2 percent), Mississippi (66.1 percent), and Louisiana (55.3 percent).[5] Even as factory smokestacks were rising on portions of the southern horizon, a high percentage of southerners remained in agriculture and in poverty.

Undeniably, African Americans suffered the most. More than four million African American men, women, and children had been freed by the Civil War. During Reconstruction, some advances were made, especially in the areas of public education and voter registration. Yet even these gains were either impermanent or incomplete. By 1880 in Georgia, only 33.7 percent of the black school-age population was enrolled in school, and by 1890 (twenty-five years after emancipation), almost half of all blacks aged ten to fourteen in the Deep South were still illiterate.[6] As for voting rights, the vast majority of African Americans chose not to exer-

cise them, fearing intimidation and violence.

Many blacks and whites at the time recognized that African Americans would never be able to improve their situation economically, socially, or politically without owning land. Yet even many Radical Republicans were reluctant to give land to the former slaves. Such a move would mean seizing land from the white planters, a proposal that clashed with the notion of the sanctity of private property. As a result, most African Americans were forced to take menial, low-paying jobs in southern cities or to work as farmers on land they did not own. By 1880, only 1.6 percent of the landowners in Georgia were black, and most of them owned the most marginal and least productive land.

As poor urban laborers or tenant farmers, African Americans were dependent on their employers, landowners, or bankers and prey to rigid vagrancy laws, the convict lease system, peonage, and outright racial discrimination. Moreover, the end of Reconstruction in the southern states was followed by a reimposition of rigid racial segregation, at first through a return to traditional practices and later (in the 1890s) by state laws governing nearly every aspect of southern life. For example, voting by African Americans was discouraged, initially by intimidation and then by more formal means such as poll taxes and literacy tests. African Americans who protested or strayed from their "place" were dealt with harshly. Between 1880 and 1918, more than twenty-four hundred African Americans were lynched by southern white mobs, each action being a

5. Bureau of the Census, *Farm Tenancy in the United States* (Washington: Government Printing Office, 1924), pp. 207–208.
6. Roger L. Ransom and Richard Sutch, *One Kind of Freedom: The Economic Consequences of Emancipation* (Cambridge: Cambridge University Press, 1977), pp. 28, 30.

grim reminder to African Americans of what could happen to those who challenged the status quo. For their part, the few southern whites who spoke against such outrages were themselves subjects of intimidation and even violence. Indeed, although most African American men and women undoubtedly would have disagreed, African Americans' relative position in some ways had deteriorated since the end of the Civil War.

To be sure, a black middle class did exist and was growing in the South, principally in cities such as New Orleans, Richmond, Durham, and elsewhere. Most were men and women who served the African American community (editors, teachers, clergy, undertakers, retailers, restauranteurs, real estate owners, and so forth), people who owned their own homes, saw to it that their sons and daughters received good educations, and maintained a standard of living superior to the majority of whites and blacks in the South.[7] Although some of them spoke out in the interests of fellow African Americans, still more preferred to live out of the spotlight and challenged the region's status quo quietly—when they did so at all.

Many New South advocates openly worried about how potential northern investors and politicians might react to the disturbing erosion of African Americans' position or to the calls of some middle-class blacks for racial justice. Although the dream of the New South rested on the concept of a harmonious, interdependent society in which each component (industry or agriculture, for example) and each person (white or black) had a clearly defined place, it appeared that African Americans were being kept in their "place" largely by intimidation and force. Who would want to invest in a region where the status quo of mutual deference and "place" often was maintained by force? To calm northern fears, Grady and his cohorts assured northerners that African Americans' position was improving and that southern society was one of mutual respect between the races. "We have found," Grady stated, "that in the summing up the free Negro counts more than he did as a slave."[8] Most northerners believed Grady because they wanted to, because they had no taste for another bitter Reconstruction, and in many cases because they shared white southerners' prejudice against African Americans. Grady was able to reassure them because they wanted to be reassured.

Thus for southern African Americans, the New South movement had done little to better their collective lot. Indeed, in some ways their position had deteriorated. Tied economically either to land they did not own or to the lowest-paying jobs in towns and cities, subjects of an increasingly rigid code of racial segregation and loss of political rights, and victims of an upswing in racially directed violence, African Americans in the New South had every reason to question the oratory of Henry

7. On home ownership, in North Carolina in 1870 only 5.6 percent of African Americans owned their own homes. By 1910 that figure had risen to 26 percent. Gilmore, *Gender and Jim Crow,* p. 15.

8. *The New South: Writings and Speeches of Henry Grady* (Savannah: The Beehive Press, 1971), p. 8.

◆ CHAPTER 2

The Road to True
Freedom:
African American
Alternatives in
the New South

Grady and other New South boosters. Jobs in the New South's mills and factories generally were reserved for whites, so the opportunities that European immigrants in the North had to work their way gradually up the economic ladder were closed to southern blacks.

How did African Americans respond to this deteriorating situation? In the 1890s, numerous African American farmers joined the Colored Alliance, part of the Farmers' Alliance Movement that swept the South and Midwest in the 1880s and 1890s. This movement attempted to reverse the farmers' eroding position through the establishment of farmers' cooperatives (to sell their crops together for higher prices and to purchase manufactured goods wholesale) and by entering politics to elect candidates sympathetic to farmers (who would draft legislation favorable to farmers). Many feared, however, that this increased militancy of farmers—white and black—would produce a political backlash that would leave them even worse off. Such a back-

lash occurred in the South in the 1890s with the defeat of the Populist revolt.

Wells, Washington, Turner, Du Bois, and Harper offered southern African Americans five other ways to confront the economic, social, and political difficulties they faced. And, as African American men and women soon discovered, there were other options as well.

Your task in this chapter is to analyze the evidence in order to answer the following central questions:

1. What were the different alternatives offered by Wells, Washington, Turner, Du Bois and Harper?
2. Were there other options those five spokespersons did not mention?
3. What were the strengths and weaknesses of each alternative? Note: Remember that you are evaluating the five alternatives *not* from a present-day perspective but in the context and time in which they were advocated (1892–1906).
4. How would you support your assessment of the strengths and weaknesses of each alternative?

The Method

In this chapter, the evidence is from speeches delivered by five well-known African Americans or from their writings that were also given as speeches. Although all five spokespersons were known to southern African Americans, they were not equally well known. It is almost impossible to tell which of the five was the best known (or least known) in her or his time, although fragmentary evidence suggests that

Washington and Harper were the most well-known figures among African Americans in various socioeconomic groups.

The piece by Ida B. Wells (Source 1) is excerpted from a pamphlet published simultaneously in the United States and England in 1892, but it is almost certain that parts of it were delivered as a speech by Wells in that same year. The selections by Booker T. Washington (Source 2), Henry NcNeal Turner (Source 3), W. E. B. Du Bois (Sources 4 and 5), and Frances E. W. Harper (Source 6) are transcriptions, or printed versions, of speeches delivered in September 1895, December 1895, 1903, 1906, and November 1892, respectively.

Ida Bell Wells was born a slave in Holly Springs, Mississippi, in 1862. After emancipation, her father and mother, as a carpenter and a cook, respectively, earned enough money to send her to a freedmen's school. In 1876, her parents died in a yellow fever epidemic. Only fourteen years old, Wells lied about her age and got a job teaching in a rural school for blacks, eventually moving to Memphis, Tennessee, to teach in the city's schools for African Americans. In 1884, she was forcibly removed from a railroad passenger car for refusing to move to the car reserved for "colored" passengers; she sued the railroad company.[9] About this time, Wells began writing articles for many black-owned newspapers, mostly on the subject of unequal educational opportunities for whites and blacks in Memphis. As a result, the Memphis school board discharged her, and she became a full-time journalist and lecturer. By 1892, she had become co-owner of the *Memphis Free Speech* newspaper. In 1895, she married black lawyer-editor Ferdinand Lee Barnett and from that time went by the name Ida Wells-Barnett, a somewhat radical practice in 1895.

Like Wells, Booker T. Washington was born a slave, in Franklin County,

Virginia. Largely self-taught before entering Hampton Institute, a school for African Americans, at age seventeen, he worked his way through school, mostly as a janitor. At age twenty-five, he was chosen to organize a normal school for blacks at Tuskegee, Alabama. Washington spent thirty-four years as the guiding force at Tuskegee Institute, shaping the school into his vision of what African Americans must do to better their lot. In great demand as a speaker to white and black audiences alike, Washington received an honorary degree from Harvard College in 1891. Four years later, he was chosen as the principal speaker at the opening of the Negro section of the Cotton States and International Exposition in Atlanta.

Henry McNeal Turner was born a free black near Abbeville, South Carolina. Mostly self-taught, he joined the Methodist Episcopal Church, South, in 1848 and was licensed to preach in 1853. In 1858, he abandoned that denomination to become a minister in the African Methodist Episcopal (AME) Church, and by 1862 he was the pastor of the large Israel Church in Washington, D.C. In 1863, he became a chaplain in the Union army, assigned to the 1st U.S. Colored Regiment. After the war, he became an official of the Freedmen's Bureau in Georgia and afterward held a succession of political appointments. One of the founders of the Republican party in Georgia, Turner was made bishop of the AME Church in Georgia in 1880. In that position, he met and became a friend of Ida B. Wells, who also was a member of the AME Church.

William Edward Burghardt Du Bois was born in Great Barrington, Massa-

9. The Tennessee Supreme Court ruled in favor of the Chesapeake and Ohio Railroad and against Wells in 1887.

◆ CHAPTER 2

The Road to True
Freedom:
African American
Alternatives in
the New South

chusetts, one of approximately fifty blacks in a town of five thousand people. He was educated with the white children in the town's public school and in 1885 was enrolled at Fisk University, a college for African Americans in Nashville, Tennessee. It was there, according to his autobiography, that he first encountered overt racial prejudice. Graduated from Fisk in 1888, he entered Harvard as a junior. He received his bachelor's degree in 1890 and his Ph.D. in 1895. His book *The Philadelphia Negro* was published in 1899. In this book, Du Bois asserted that the problems African Americans faced were the results of their history (slavery and racism) and environment, not of some imagined genetic inferiority.

Frances Ellen Watkins Harper was born in Maryland in 1825, the only child of free parents. Orphaned at an early age, she was raised by an aunt, who enrolled her in a school for free blacks run by an uncle, who headed the Academy for Negro Youth and was a celebrated African American abolitionist (he was friends with both William Lloyd Garrison and Benjamin Lundy). Ending her formal education at the age of thirteen, Harper worked as a seamstress and needlework teacher. But she yearned to write and, in 1845, published her first book of poetry. It was later followed by ten more volumes of poetry (all commercially successful), a short story—the first to be published by a black woman—in 1859, and an immensely popular novel in 1892. She was a founder and vice president of the

National Association of Colored Women. In 1860, she married Fenton Harper, who died in 1864. The couple had one child, a daughter, who was in continuous poor health and died in 1909.

This is not the first time that you have had to analyze speeches. Our society is almost literally bombarded by speeches delivered by politicians, business figures, educators, and others, most of whom are trying to convince us to adopt a set of ideas or actions. As we listen to such speeches, we invariably weigh the options presented to us, often using other available evidence (in this case, the Background section of this chapter) to help us make our decisions. One purpose of this exercise is to help you think more critically and use evidence more thoroughly when assessing different options.

It is logical to begin by analyzing each of the speeches in turn. As you read each selection, make a rough chart like the one on the next page to help you remember the main points.

Once you have carefully defined the alternatives presented by Wells, Washington, Turner, Du Bois, and Harper, return to the Background section of this chapter. As you reread that section, determine the strengths and weaknesses of each alternative offered for African Americans living in the New South in the late nineteenth and early twentieth centuries. What evidence would you use to determine each alternative's strengths and weaknesses?

African American Alternatives		How Does Speaker Develop Her/His Arguments?	Strengths and Weaknesses (Fill in later)
Speaker	Suggested Alternatives		
Wells			
Washington			
Turner			
Du Bois			
Harper			

◆

The Evidence

Source 1 from Ida B. Wells, *United States Atrocities* (London: Lux Newspaper and Publishing Co., 1892), pp. 13–18. In the United States, the pamphlet was titled *Southern Horrors*. See Jacqueline Jones Royster, ed., *Southern Horrors and Other Writings: The Anti-Lynching Campaign of Ida B. Wells, 1892–1900* (Boston: Bedford Books, 1997), pp. 49–72.

1. Ida B. Wells's *United States Atrocities,* 1892 (excerpt).

Mr. Henry W. Grady, in his well-remembered speeches in New England and New York, pictured the Afro-American as incapable of self-government. Through him and other leading men the cry of the South to the country has been "Hands off! Leave us to solve our problem." To the Afro-American the South says, "The white man must and will rule." There is little difference between the Ante-bellum South and the New South. Her white citizens are wedded to any method however revolting, any measure however extreme, for the subjugation of the young manhood of the dark race. They have cheated him out of his ballot, deprived him of civil rights or redress in the Civil Courts thereof, robbed him of the fruits of his labour, and are still murdering, burning and lynching him.

The result is a growing disregard of human life. Lynch Law has spread its insidious influence till men in New York State, Pennsylvania and on the free Western plains feel they can take the law in their own hands with impunity,

[39]

◆ CHAPTER 2

The Road to True
Freedom:
African American
Alternatives in
the New South

especially where an Afro-American is concerned. The South is brutalised to a degree not realised by its own inhabitants, and the very foundation of government, law, and order are imperilled.

Public sentiment has had a slight "reaction," though not sufficient to stop the crusade of lawlessness and lynching. The spirit of Christianity of the great M. E. Church was sufficiently aroused by the frequent and revolting crimes against a powerless people, to pass strong condemnatory resolutions at its General Conference in Omaha last May. The spirit of justice of the grand old party[10] asserted itself sufficiently to secure a denunciation of the wrongs, and a feeble declaration of the belief in human rights in the Republican platform at Minneapolis, June 7th. A few of the great "dailies" and "weeklies" have swung into line declaring that Lynch Law must go. The President of the United States issued a proclamation that it be not tolerated in the territories over which he has jurisdiction. . . .

These efforts brought forth apologies and a short halt, but the lynching mania has raged again through the past twelve months with unabated fury. The strong arm of the law must be brought to bear upon lynchers in severe punishment, but this cannot and will not be done unless a healthy public sentiment demands and sustains such action. The men and women in the South who disapprove of lynching and remain silent on the perpetration of such outrages are *particeps criminis*—accomplices, accessories before and after the fact, equally guilty with the actual law-breakers, who would not persist if they did not know that neither the law nor militia would be deployed against them.

In the creation of this healthier public sentiment, the Afro-American can do for himself what no one else can do for him. The world looks on with wonder that we have conceded so much, and remain law-abiding under such great outrage and provocation.

To Northern capital and Afro-American labour the South owes its rehabilitation. If labour is withdrawn capital will not remain. The Afro-American is thus the backbone of the South. A thorough knowledge and judicious exercise of this power in lynching localities could many times effect a bloodless revolution. The white man's dollar is his god, and to stop this will be to stop outrages in many localities.

The Afro-Americans of Memphis denounced the lynching of three of their best citizens, and urged and waited for the authorities to act in the matter, and bring the lynchers to justice. No attempt was made to do so, and the black men left the city by thousands, bringing about great stagnation in every branch of business. Those who remained so injured the business of the street car company by staying off the cars, that the superintendent, manager, and

10. *Grand old party* refers to the Republican party, the GOP.

treasurer called personally on the editors of the *Free Speech,* and asked them to urge our people to give them their patronage again. Other business men became alarmed over the situation, and the *Free Speech* was suppressed that the coloured people might be more easily controlled. A meeting of white citizens in June, three months after the lynching, passed resolutions for the first time condemning it. *But they did not punish the lynchers.* Every one of them was known by name because they had been selected to do the dirty work by some of the very citizens who passed these resolutions! Memphis is fast losing her black population, who proclaim as they go that there is no protection for the life and property of any Afro-American citizen in Memphis who will not be a slave. . . .

[*Wells then urged African Americans in Kentucky to boycott railroads in the state, since the legislature had passed a law segregating passenger cars. She claimed that such a boycott would mean a loss to the railroads of $1 million per year.*]

The appeal to the white man's pocket has ever been more effectual than all the appeals ever made to his conscience. Nothing, absolutely nothing, is to be gained by a further sacrifice of manhood and self-respect. By the right exercise of his power as the industrial factor of the South, the Afro-American can demand and secure his rights, the punishment of lynchers, and a fair trial for members of his race accused of outrage.

Of the many inhuman outrages of this present year, the only case where the proposed lynching did *not* occur, was where the men armed themselves in Jacksonville, Florida, and Paducah, Kentucky, and prevented it. The only times an Afro-American who was assaulted got away has been when he had a gun, and used it in self-defence. The lesson this teaches, and which every Afro-American should ponder well, is that a Winchester rifle should have a place of honour in every black home, and it should be used for that protection which the law refuses to give. When the white man, who is always the aggressor, knows he runs a great risk of biting the dust every time his Afro-American victim does, he will have greater respect for Afro-American life. The more the Afro-American yields and cringes and begs, the more he has to do so, the more he is insulted, outraged, and lynched.

econ + guns

◆ CHAPTER 2

The Road to True
Freedom:
African American
Alternatives in
the New South

Source 2 from Louis R. Harlan, ed., *The Booker T. Washington Papers* (Urbana: University of Illinois Press, 1974), Vol. III, pp. 583–587.

2. Booker T. Washington's Atlanta Exposition Address (standard printed version), September 1895.

[Atlanta, Ga., Sept. 18, 1895]

Mr. President and Gentlemen of the Board of Directors and Citizens:

One-third of the population of the South is of the Negro race. No enterprise seeking the material, civil, or moral welfare of this section can disregard this element of our population and reach the highest success. I but convey to you, Mr. President and Directors, the sentiment of the masses of my race when I say that in no way have the value and manhood of the American Negro been more fittingly and generously recognized than by the managers of this magnificent Exposition at every stage of its progress. It is a recognition that will do more to cement the friendship of the two races than any occurrence since the dawn of our freedom.

Not only this, but the opportunity here afforded will awaken among us a new era of industrial progress. Ignorant and inexperienced, it is not strange that in the first years of our new life we began at the top instead of at the bottom; that a seat in Congress or the state legislature was more sought than real estate or industrial skill; that the political convention or stump speaking had more attractions than starting a dairy farm or truck garden.

A ship lost at sea for many days suddenly sighted a friendly vessel. From the mast of the unfortunate vessel was seen a signal, "Water, water; we die of thirst!" The answer from the friendly vessel at once came back, "Cast down your bucket where you are." A second time the signal, "Water, water; send us water!" ran up from the distressed vessel, and was answered, "Cast down your bucket where you are." And a third and fourth signal for water was answered, "Cast down your bucket where you are." The captain of the distressed vessel, at last heeding the injunction, cast down his bucket, and it came up full of fresh, sparkling water from the mouth of the Amazon River. To those of my race who depend on bettering their condition in a foreign land or who underestimate the importance of cultivating friendly relations with the Southern white man, who is their next-door neighbour, I would say: "Cast down your bucket where you are"—cast it down in making friends in every manly way of the people of all races by whom we are surrounded.

Cast it down in agriculture, mechanics, in commerce, in domestic service, and in the professions. And in this connection it is well to bear in mind that whatever other sins the South may be called to bear, when it comes to business, pure and simple, it is in the South that the Negro is given a man's chance in the commercial world, and in nothing is this Exposition more eloquent than in emphasizing this chance. Our greatest danger is that in the great leap from slavery to freedom we may overlook the fact that the masses of us are to live by the productions of our hands, and fail to keep in mind that we shall prosper in proportion as we learn to dignify and glorify common labour, and put brains and skill into the common occupations of life; shall prosper in proportion as we learn to draw the line between the superficial and the substantial, the ornamental gewgaws of life and the useful. No race can prosper till it learns that there is as much dignity in tilling a field as in writing a poem. It is at the bottom of life we must begin, and not at the top. Nor should we permit our grievances to overshadow our opportunities.

To those of the white race who look to the incoming of those of foreign birth and strange tongue and habits for the prosperity of the South, were I permitted I would repeat what I say to my own race, "Cast down your bucket where you are." Cast it down among the eight millions of Negroes whose habits you know, whose fidelity and love you have tested in days when to have proved treacherous meant the ruin of your firesides. Cast down your bucket among these people who have, without strikes and labour wars, tilled your fields, cleared your forests, builded your railroads and cities, and brought forth treasures from the bowels of the earth, and helped make possible this magnificent representation of the progress of the South. Casting down your bucket among my people, helping and encouraging them as you are doing on these grounds, and to education of head, hand, and heart, you will find that they will buy your surplus land, make blossom the waste places in your fields, and run your factories. While doing this, you can be sure in the future, as in the past, that you and your families will be surrounded by the most patient, faithful, law-abiding, and unresentful people that the world has seen. As we have proved our loyalty to you in the past, in nursing your children, watching by the sick-bed of your mothers and fathers, and often following them with tear-dimmed eyes to their graves, so in the future, in our humble way, we shall stand by you with a devotion that no foreigner can approach, ready to lay down our lives, if need be, in defense of yours, interlacing our industrial, commercial, civil, and religious life with yours in a way that shall make the interests of both races one. In all things that are purely social we can be as separate as the fingers, yet one as the hand in all things essential to mutual progress.

There is no defense or security for any of us except in the highest intelligence and development of all. If anywhere there are efforts tending to curtail the fullest growth of the Negro, let these efforts be turned into stimulating, encouraging, and making him the most useful and intelligent citizen. Effort

◆ CHAPTER 2

The Road to True
Freedom:
African American
Alternatives in
the New South

or means so invested will pay a thousand per cent interest. These efforts will be twice blessed—"blessing him that gives and him that takes."

There is no escape through law of man or God from the inevitable:—

"The laws of changeless justice bind
　Oppressor with oppressed;
And close as sin and suffering joined
　We march to fate abreast."

Nearly sixteen millions of hands will aid you in pulling the load upward, or they will pull against you the load downward. We shall constitute one-third and more of the ignorance and crime of the South, or one-third [of] its intelligence and progress; we shall contribute one-third to the business and industrial prosperity of the South, or we shall prove a veritable body of death, stagnating, depressing, retarding every effort to advance the body politic.

Gentlemen of the Exposition, as we present to you our humble effort at an exhibition of our progress, you must not expect overmuch. Starting thirty years ago with ownership here and there in a few quilts and pumpkins and chickens (gathered from miscellaneous sources), remember the path that has led from these to the inventions and production of agricultural implements, buggies, steam-engines, newspapers, books, statuary, carving, paintings, the management of drug stores and banks, has not been trodden without contact with thorns and thistles. While we take pride in what we exhibit as a result of our independent efforts, we do not for a moment forget that our part in this exhibition would fall far short of your expectations but for the constant help that has come to our educational life, not only from the Southern states, but especially from Northern philanthropists, who have made their gifts a constant stream of blessing and encouragement.

The wisest among my race understand that the agitation of questions of social equality is the extremest folly, and that progress in the enjoyment of all the privileges that will come to us must be the result of severe and constant struggle rather than of artificial forcing. No race that has anything to contribute to the markets of the world is long in any degree ostracized. It is important and right that all privileges of the law be ours, but it is vastly more important that we be prepared for the exercise of these privileges. The opportunity to earn a dollar in a factory just now is worth infinitely more than the opportunity to spend a dollar in an opera-house.

In conclusion, may I repeat that nothing in thirty years has given us more hope and encouragement, and drawn us so near to you of the white race, as this opportunity offered by the Exposition; and here bending, as it were, over the altar that represents the results of the struggles of your race and mine, both starting practically empty-handed three decades ago, I pledge that in your effort to work out the great and intricate problem which God has laid at the doors of the South, you shall have at all times the patient, sympathetic help of my race; only let this be constantly in mind, that, while from representations in these buildings of the product of field, of forest, of mine, of factory, letters, and art, much good will come, yet far above and beyond material benefits will be that higher good, that, let us pray God, will come, in a blotting out of sectional differences and racial animosities and suspicions in a determination to administer absolute justice, in a willing obedience among all classes to the mandates of law. This, coupled with our material prosperity, will bring into our beloved South a new heaven and a new earth.

Source 3 from Edwin S. Redkey, ed., *Respect Black: The Writings and Speeches of Henry McNeal Turner* (New York: Arno Press, 1971), pp. 167–171. Reprinted by permission.

3. Henry McNeal Turner's "The American Negro and His Fatherland," December 1895 (excerpt).

It would be a waste of time to expend much labor, the few moments I have to devote to this subject, upon the present status of the Negroid race in the United States. It is too well-known already. However, I believe that the Negro was brought to this country in the providence of God to a heaven-permitted if not a divine-sanctioned manual laboring school, that he might have direct contact with the mightiest race that ever trod the face of the globe.

The heathen Africans, to my certain knowledge, I care not what others may say, eagerly yearn for that civilization which they believe will elevate them and make them potential for good. The African was not sent and brought to this country by chance, or by the avarice of the white man, single and alone. The white slave-purchaser went to the shores of that continent and bought our ancestors from their African masters. The bulk who were brought to this country were the children of parents who had been in slavery a thousand years. Yet hereditary slavery is not universal among the African slaveholders. So that the argument often advanced, that the white man went to Africa and stole us, is not true. They bought us out of a slavery that still exists over a large portion of that continent. For there are millions and millions of slaves in Africa today. Thus the superior African sent us, and the white man brought us, and we remained in slavery as long as it was necessary to learn that a God, who is a spirit, made the world and controls it, and that that Supreme Being could be sought and found by the exercise of faith in His only begotten Son. Slavery then went down, and the colored man was thrown upon his own re-

✦ CHAPTER 2

The Road to True
Freedom:
African American
Alternatives in
the New South

sponsibility, and here he is today, in the providence of God, cultivating self-reliance and imbibing a knowledge of civil law in contradistinction to the dictum of one man, which was the law of the black man until slavery was overthrown. I believe that the Negroid race has been free long enough now to begin to think for himself and plan for better conditions [than] he can lay claim to in this country or ever will. *There is no manhood future in the United States for the Negro.* He may eke out an existence for generations to come, but he can never be a *man*—full, symmetrical and undwarfed. . . .

[*Here Turner asserted that a "great chasm" continued to exist between the races, that whites would have no social contact with blacks, and (without using Booker T. Washington's name) that any black who claimed that African Americans did not want social equality immediately "is either an ignoramus, or is an advocate of the perpetual servility and degradation of his race. . . ."*]

. . . And as such, I believe that two or three millions of us should return to the land of our ancestors, and establish our own nation, civilization, laws, customs, style of manufacture, and not only give the world, like other race varieties, the benefit of our individuality, but build up social conditions peculiarly our own, and cease to be grumblers, chronic complainers and a menace to the white man's country, or the country he claims and is bound to dominate.

The civil status of the Negro is simply what the white man grants of his own free will and accord. The black man can demand nothing. He is deposed from the jury and tried, convicted and sentenced by men who do not claim to be his peers. On the railroads, where the colored race is found in the largest numbers, he is the victim of proscription, and he must ride in the Jim Crow car or walk. The Supreme Court of the United States decided, October 15th, 1883, that the colored man had no civil rights under the general government,[11] and the several States, from then until now, have been enacting laws which limit, curtail and deprive him of his civil rights, immunities and privileges, until he is now being disfranchised, and where it will end no one can divine. . . .

The discriminating laws, all will concede, are degrading to those against which they operate, and the degrader will be degraded also. "For all acts are reactionary, and will return in curses upon those who curse," said Stephen A. Douglass [*sic*], the great competitor of President Lincoln. Neither does it re-

11. On October 15, 1883, the Supreme Court handed down one decision that applied to five separate cases that had been argued before the Court, all of them having to do with racial segregation by private businesses (inns, hotels, theaters, and a railroad). Writing for the majority, Justice Joseph P. Bradley ruled that the Thirteenth, Fourteenth, and Fifteenth amendments did not give the federal government the power to outlaw discriminatory practices by private organizations, but only by states. See 109 U.S. 3, 3 S. Ct., 18, 27, L. Ed. 835 (1883).

quire a philosopher to inform you that degradation begets degradation. Any people oppressed, proscribed, belied, slandered, burned, flayed and lynched will not only become cowardly and servile, but will transmit that same servility to their posterity, and continue to do so *ad infinitum,* and as such will never make a bold and courageous people. The condition of the Negro in the United States is so repugnant to the instincts of respected manhood that thousands, yea hundreds of thousands, of miscegenated will pass for white, and snub the people with whom they are identified at every opportunity, thus destroying themselves, or at least *unracing* themselves. They do not want to be black because of its ignoble condition, and they cannot be white, thus they become monstrosities. Thousands of young men who are even educated by white teachers never have any respect for people of their own color and spend their days as devotees of white gods. Hundreds, if not thousands, of the terms employed by the white race in the English language are also degrading to the black man. Everything that is satanic, corrupt, base and infamous is denominated *black,* and all that constitutes virtue, purity, innocence, religion, and that which is divine and heavenly, is represented as *white.* Our Sabbath-school children, by the time they reach proper consciousness, are taught to sing to the laudation of white and to the contempt of black. Can any one with an ounce of common sense expect that these children, when they reach maturity, will ever have any respect for their black or colored faces, or the faces of their associates? But, without multiplying words, the terms used in our religious experience, and the hymns we sing in many instances, are degrading, and will be as long as the black man is surrounded by the idea that *white* represents God and black represents the devil. The Negro should, therefore, build up a nation of his own, and create a language in keeping with his color, as the whites have done. Nor will he ever respect himself until he does it. . . .

What the black man needs is a country and surroundings in harmony with his color and with respect for his manhood. Upon this point I would delight to dwell longer if I had time. Thousands of white people in this country are ever and anon advising the colored people to keep out of politics, but they do not advise themselves. If the Negro is a man in keeping with other men, why should he be less concerned about politics than any one else? Strange, too, that a number of would-be colored leaders are ignorant and debased enough to proclaim the same foolish jargon. For the Negro to stay out of politics is to level himself with a horse or a cow, which is no politician, and the Negro who does it proclaims his inability to take part in political affairs. If the Negro is to be a man, full and complete, he must take part in everything that belongs to manhood. If he omits a single duty, responsibility or privilege, to that extent he is limited and incomplete.

◆ CHAPTER 2

The Road to True
Freedom:
African American
Alternatives in
the New South

Time, however, forbids my continuing the discussion of this subject, roughly and hastily as these thoughts have been thrown together. Not being able to present a dozen or two more phases, which I would cheerfully and gladly do if opportunity permitted, I conclude by saying the argument that it would be impossible to transport the colored people of the United States back to Africa is an advertisement of folly. Two hundred millions of dollars would rid this country of the last member of the Negroid race, if such a thing was desirable, and two hundred and fifty millions would give every man, woman and child excellent fare, and the general government could furnish that amount and never miss it, and that would only be the pitiful sum of a million dollars a year for the time we labored for nothing, and for which somebody or some power is responsible. The emigrant agents at New York, Boston, Philadelphia, St. John, N.B., and Halifax, N.S., with whom I have talked, establish beyond contradiction, that over a million, and from that to twelve hundred thousand persons, come to this country every year, and yet there is no public stir about it. But in the case of African emigration, two or three millions only of self-reliant men and women would be necessary to establish the conditions we are advocating in Africa.

Source 4 from Nathan Huggins, comp., *W. E. B. Du Bois Writings* (New York: Library of America, 1986), pp. 842, 846–848, 860–861.

4. W. E. B. Du Bois's "The Talented Tenth," 1903 (excerpt).

The Negro race, like all races, is going to be saved by its exceptional men. The problem of education, then, among Negroes must first of all deal with the Talented Tenth; it is the problem of developing the Best of this race that they may guide the Mass away from the contamination and death of the Worst, in their own and other races. Now the training of men is a difficult and intricate task. Its technique is a matter for educational experts, but its object is for the vision of seers. If we make money the object of man-training, we shall develop money-makers but not necessarily men; if we make technical skill the object of education, we may possess artisans but not, in nature, men. Men we shall have only as we make manhood the object of the work of the schools—intelligence, broad sympathy, knowledge of the world that was and is, and of the relation [of] men to it—this is the curriculum of that Higher Education which must underlie true life. On this foundation we may build bread-winning skill of hand and quickness of brain, with never a fear lest the child and man mistake the means of living for the object of life. . . .

[Here Du Bois argued against those who asserted that African American "leadership should have begun at the plow and not in the Senate" by stating that for 250 years blacks had been at the plow and were still "half-free serfs" without political rights. He then went on to say that many people focused their attention on "death, disease, and crime" among blacks, ignoring those who had achieved education, professions, homes, and the like.]

Can the masses of the Negro people be in any possible way more quickly raised than by the effort and example of this aristocracy of talent and character? Was there ever a nation on God's fair earth civilized from the bottom upward? Never; it is, ever was and ever will be from the top downward that culture filters. The Talented Tenth rises and pulls all that are worth the saving up to their vantage ground. This is the history of human progress; and the two historic mistakes which have hindered that progress were the thinking first that no more could ever rise save the few already risen; or second, that it would better the unrisen to pull the risen down.

How then shall the leaders of a struggling people be trained and the hands of the risen few strengthened? There can be but one answer: The best and most capable of their youth must be schooled in the colleges and universities of the land. We will not quarrel as to just what the university of the Negro should teach or how it should teach it—I willingly admit that each soul and each race-soul needs its own peculiar curriculum. But this is true: A university is a human invention for the transmission of knowledge and culture from generation to generation, through the training of quick minds and pure hearts, and for this work no other human invention will suffice, not even trade and industrial schools.

All men cannot go to college but some men must; every isolated group or nation must have its yeast, must have for the talented few centers of training where men are not so mystified and befuddled by the hard and necessary toil of earning a living, as to have no aims higher than their bellies, and no God greater than Gold. This is true training, and thus in the beginning were the favored sons of the freedmen trained.

Thus, again, in the manning of trade schools and manual training schools we are thrown back upon the higher training as its source and chief support. There was a time when any aged and wornout carpenter could teach in a trade school. But not so to-day. Indeed the demand for college-bred men by a school like Tuskegee, ought to make Mr. Booker T. Washington the firmest friend of higher training. Here he has as helpers the son of a Negro senator, trained in Greek and the humanities, and graduated at Harvard; the son of a Negro congressman and lawyer, trained in Latin and mathematics, and graduated at Oberlin; he has as his wife, a woman who read Virgil and Homer in the same class room with me; he has as college chaplain, a classical graduate

◆ CHAPTER 2

The Road to True
Freedom:
African American
Alternatives in
the New South

of Atlanta University; as teacher of science, a graduate of Fisk; as teacher of history, a graduate of Smith,—indeed some thirty of his chief teachers are college graduates, and instead of studying French grammars in the midst of weeds, or buying pianos for dirty cabins, they are at Mr. Washington's right hand helping him in a noble work. And yet one of the effects of Mr. Washington's propaganda has been to throw doubt upon the expediency of such training for Negroes, as these persons have had.

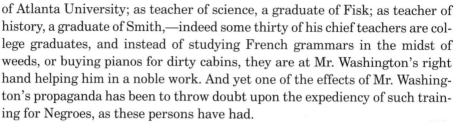

Men of America, the problem is plain before you. Here is a race transplanted through the criminal foolishness of your fathers. Whether you like it or not the millions are here, and here they will remain. If you do not lift them up, they will pull you down. Education and work are the levers to uplift a people. Work alone will not do it unless inspired by the right ideals and guided by intelligence. Education must not simply teach work—it must teach Life. The Talented Tenth of the Negro race must be made leaders of thought and missionaries of culture among their people. No others can do this work and Negro colleges must train men for it. The Negro race, like all other races, is going to be saved by its exceptional men.

Source 5 from Herbert Atheker, ed., *Pamphlets and Leaflets by W. E. B. Du Bois* (White Plains, N.Y.: Kraus-Thomson Organization Ltd., 1986), pp. 63–65.

5. Du Bois's Niagara Address, 1906 (excerpt).[12]

In detail our demands are clear and unequivocal. First, we would vote; with the right to vote goes everything: Freedom, manhood, the honor of your wives, the chastity of your daughters, the right to work, and the chance to rise, and let no man listen to those who deny this.

We want full manhood suffrage, and we want it now, henceforth and forever.

Second. We want discrimination in public accommodation to cease. Separation in railway and street cars, based simply on race and color, is un-American, undemocratic, and silly. We protest against all such discrimination.

Third. We claim the right of freemen to walk, talk, and be with them that wish to be with us. No man has a right to choose another man's friends, and to attempt to do so is an impudent interference with the most fundamental human privilege.

12. The Niagara Movement was organized by Du Bois in 1905. It called for agitation against all forms of segregation. This is a selection from Du Bois's address to the group in 1906.

Fourth. We want the laws enforced against rich as well as poor; against Capitalist as well as Laborer; against white as well as black. We are not more lawless than the white race, we are more often arrested, convicted and mobbed. We want justice even for criminals and outlaws. We want the Constitution of the country enforced. We want Congress to take charge of Congressional elections. We want the Fourteenth Amendment carried out to the letter and every State disfranchised in Congress which attempts to disfranchise its rightful voters. We want the Fifteenth Amendment enforced and no State allowed to base its franchise simply on color.

The failure of the Republican Party in Congress at the session just closed to redeem its pledge of 1904 with reference to suffrage conditions [in] the South seems a plain, deliberate, and premeditated breach of promise, and stamps that party as guilty of obtaining votes under false pretense.

Fifth. We want our children educated. The school system in the country districts of the South is a disgrace and in few towns and cities are the Negro schools what they ought to be. We want the national government to step in and wipe out illiteracy in the South. Either the United States will destroy ignorance or ignorance will destroy the United States.

And when we call for education we mean real education. We believe in work. We ourselves are workers, but work is not necessarily education. Education is the development of power and ideal. We want our children trained as intelligent human beings should be, and we will fight for all time against any proposal to educate black boys and girls simply as servants and underlings, or simply for the use of other people. They have a right to know, to think, to aspire.

These are some of the chief things which we want. How shall we get them? By voting where we may vote, by persistent, unceasing agitation, by hammering at the truth, by sacrifice and work.

We do not believe in violence, neither in the despised violence of the raid nor the lauded violence of the soldier, nor the barbarous violence of the mob, but we do believe in John Brown, in that incarnate spirit of justice, that hatred of a lie, that willingness to sacrifice money, reputation, and life itself on the altar of right. And here on the scene of John Brown's martyrdom we reconsecrate ourselves, our honor, our property to the final emancipation of the race which John Brown died to make free.

Our enemies, triumphant for the present, are fighting the stars in their courses. Justice and humanity must prevail. We live to tell these dark brothers of ours—scattered in counsel, wavering and weak—that no bribe of money or notoriety, no promise of wealth or fame, is worth the surrender of a people's manhood or the loss of a man's self-respect. We refuse to surrender the

◆ CHAPTER 2

The Road to True
Freedom:
African American
Alternatives in
the New South

leadership of this race to cowards and trucklers. We are men; we will be treated as men. On this rock we have planted our banners. We will never give up, though the trump of doom find us still fighting.

And we shall win. The past promised it, the present foretells it. Thank God for John Brown! Thank God for Garrison and Douglass! Sumner and Phillips, Nat Turner and Robert Gould Shaw,[13] and all the hallowed dead who died for freedom! Thank God for all those today, few though their voices be, who have not forgotten the divine brotherhood of all men, white and black, rich and poor, fortunate and unfortunate.

We appeal to the young men and women of this nation, to those whose nostrils are not yet befouled by greed and snobbery and racial narrowness: Stand up for the right, prove yourselves worthy of your heritage and whether born north or south dare to treat men as men. Cannot the nation that has absorbed ten million foreigners into its political life without catastrophe absorb ten million Negro Americans into that same political life at less cost than their unjust and illegal exclusion will involve?

Courage, brothers! The battle for humanity is not lost or losing. All across the skies sit signs of promise. The Slav is rising in his might, the yellow millions are tasting liberty, the black Africans are writhing toward the light, and everywhere the laborer, with ballot in his hand, is voting open the gates of Opportunity and Peace. The morning breaks over blood-stained hills. We must not falter, we may not shrink. Above are the everlasting stars.

Source 6 from Frances Smith Foster, ed., *A Brighter Coming Day: A Frances Ellen Watkins Harper Reader* (New York: Feminist Press, 1990), pp. 285–292.

6. Frances E. W. Harper's "Enlightened Motherhood," an Address to the Brooklyn Literary Society, November 15, 1892 (excerpt).

It is nearly thirty years since an emancipated people stood on the threshold of a new era, facing an uncertain future—a legally unmarried race, to be taught the sacredness of the marriage relation; an ignorant people, to be taught to read the book of the Christian law and to learn to comprehend more fully the claims of the gospel of the Christ of Calvary. A homeless race, to be gathered into homes of peaceful security and to be instructed how to plant around their firesides the strongest batteries against the sins that degrade and the

13. Robert Gould Shaw was a Massachusetts white man who during the Civil War commanded African American troops. While leading those soldiers into battle, Shaw was killed on July 18, 1863. He was portrayed in the 1989 film *Glory.*

race vices that demoralize. A race unversed in the science of government and unskilled in the just administration of law, to be translated from the old oligarchy of slavery into the new commonwealth of freedom, and to whose men came the right to exchange the fetters on their wrists for the ballots in their right hands—a ballot which, if not vitiated by fraud or restrained by intimidation, counts just as much as that of the most talented and influential man in the land.

While politicians may stumble on the barren mountain of fretful controversy, and men, lacking faith in God and the invisible forces which make for righteousness, may shrink from the unsolved problems of the hour, into the hands of Christian women comes the opportunity of serving the ever blessed Christ, by ministering to His little ones and striving to make their homes the brightest spots on earth and the fairest types of heaven. The school may instruct and the church may teach, but the home is an institution older than the church and antedates school, and that is the place where children should be trained for useful citizenship on earth and a hope of holy companionship in heaven. . . .

The home may be a humble spot, where there are no velvet carpets to hush your tread, no magnificence to surround your way, nor costly creations of painter's art or sculptor's skill to please your conceptions or gratify your tastes; but what are the costliest gifts of fortune when placed in the balance with the confiding love of dear children or the true devotion of a noble and manly husband whose heart can safely trust in his wife? You may place upon the brow of a true wife and mother the greenest laurels; you may crowd her hands with civic honors; but, after all, to her there will be no place like home, and the crown of her motherhood will be more precious than the diadem of a queen. . . .

Marriage between two youthful and loving hearts means the laying [of] the foundation stones of a new home, and the woman who helps erect that home should be careful not to build it above the reeling brain of a drunkard or the weakened fibre of a debauchee. If it be folly for a merchant to send an argosy, laden with the richest treasures, at midnight on a moonless sea, without a rudder, compass, or guide, is it not madness for a woman to trust her future happiness, and the welfare of the dear children who may yet nestle in her arms and make music and sunshine around her fireside, in the unsteady hands of a characterless man, too lacking in self-respect and self-control to hold the helm and rudder of his own life; who drifts where he ought to steer, and only lasts when he ought to live?

The moment the crown of motherhood falls on the brow of a young wife, God gives her a new interest in the welfare of the home and the good of soci-

✦ CHAPTER 2

The Road to True
Freedom:
African American
Alternatives in
the New South

ety. If hitherto she had been content to trip through life a lighthearted girl, or to tread amid the halls of wealth and fashion the gayest of the gay, life holds for her now a high and noble service. She must be more than the child of pleasure or the devotee of fashion. Her work is grandly constructive. A helpless and ignorant babe lies smiling in her arms. God has trusted her with a child, and it is her privilege to help that child develop the most precious thing a man or woman can possess on earth, and that is a good character. Moth may devour our finest garments, fire may consume and floods destroy our fairest homes, rust may gather on our silver and tarnish our gold, but there is an asbestos that no fire can destroy, a treasure which shall be richer for its service and better for its use, and that is a good character. . . .

Are there not women, respectable women, who feel that it would wring their hearts with untold anguish, and bring their gray hairs in sorrow to the grave, if their daughters should trail the robes of their womanhood in the dust, yet who would say of their sons, if they were trampling their manhood down and fettering their souls with cords of vice, "O, well, boys will be boys, and young men will sow their wild oats."

I hold that no woman loves social purity as it deserves to be loved and valued, if she cares for the purity of her daughters and not her sons; who would gather her dainty robes from contact with the fallen woman and yet greet with smiling lips and clasp with warm and welcoming hands the author of her wrong and ruin. How many mothers to-day shrink from a double standard for society which can ostracise the woman and condone the offense of the man? How many mothers say within their hearts, "I intend to teach my boy to be as pure in his life, as chaste in his conversation, as the young girl who sits at my side encircled in the warm clasp of loving arms?" How many mothers strive to have their boys shun the gilded saloon as they would the den of a deadly serpent? Not the mother who thoughtlessly sends her child to the saloon for a beverage to make merry with her friends. How many mothers teach their boys to shrink in horror from the fascinations of women, not as God made them, but as sin has degraded them? . . .

I would ask, in conclusion, is there a branch of the human race in the Western Hemisphere which has greater need of the inspiring and uplifting influences that can flow out of the lives and examples of the truly enlightened than ourselves? Mothers who can teach their sons not to love pleasure or fear death; mothers who can teach their children to embrace every opportunity, employ every power, and use every means to build up a future to contrast with the old sad past. Men may boast of the aristocracy of blood; they may glory in the aristocracy of talent, and be proud of the aristocracy of wealth, but there is an aristocracy which must ever outrank them all, and that is the aristocracy of character.

The work of the mothers of our race is grandly constructive. It is for us to build above the wreck and ruin of the past more stately temples of thought and action. Some races have been overthrown, dashed in pieces, and destroyed; but to-day the world is needing, fainting, for something better than the results of arrogance, aggressiveness, and indomitable power. We need mothers who are capable of being character builders, patient, loving, strong, and true, whose homes will be an uplifting power in the race. This is one of the greatest needs of the hour. No race can afford to neglect the enlightenment of its mothers. If you would have a clergy without virtue or morality, a manhood without honor, and a womanhood frivolous, mocking, and ignorant, neglect the education of your daughters. But if, on the other hand, you would have strong men, virtuous women, and good homes, then enlighten your women, so that they may be able to bless their homes by the purity of their lives, the tenderness of their hearts, and the strength of their intellects. From schools and colleges your children may come well versed in ancient lore and modern learning, but it is for us to learn and teach, within the shadow of our own homes, the highest and best of all sciences, the science of a true life. When the last lay of the minstrel shall die upon his ashy lips, and the sweetest numbers of the poet cease to charm his death-dulled ear; when the eye of the astronomer shall be too dim to mark the path of worlds that roll in light and power on high; and when all our earthly knowledge has performed for us its mission, and we are ready to lay aside our environments as garments we have outworn and outgrown: if we have learned the science of a true life, we may rest assured that this acquirement will go with us through the valley and shadow of death, only to grow lighter and brighter through the eternities.

Questions to Consider

The Background section of this chapter strongly suggests that the prospects for African Americans in the post-Reconstruction South were bleak. Although blacks certainly preferred sharecropping or tenancy to working in gangs as in the days of slavery, neither sharecropping nor tenancy offered African Americans much chance to own their own land. Furthermore, the industrial opportunities available to European immigrants, which allowed many of them gradually to climb the economic ladder, for the most part were closed to southern blacks, in part because the South was never able to match the North in the creation of industrial jobs and in part because what jobs the New South industrialization did create often were closed to blacks. As we have seen, educational opportunities for African Americans in the South were severely limited—so much so that by 1890, more than 75 percent of the adult

◆ CHAPTER 2

The Road to True
Freedom:
African American
Alternatives in
the New South

black population in the Deep South still was illiterate (as opposed to 17.1 percent of the adult white population). In addition, rigid segregation laws and racial violence had increased dramatically. Indeed, the prospects for southern blacks were far from promising.

Begin by analyzing Ida B. Wells's response (Source 1) to the deteriorating condition of African Americans in the South. In her view, how did blacks in Memphis and Kentucky provide a model for others? What was that model? In addition to that model, Wells tells us how blacks in Jacksonville, Florida, and Paducah, Kentucky, were able to prevent lynchings in those towns. What alternative did those blacks present? Was Wells advocating it? Finally, what role did Wells see the African American press playing in preventing lynchings?

The alternative offered by Booker T. Washington (Source 2) differs markedly from those offered by Wells. In his view, what *process* should African Americans follow to enjoy their full rights? How did he support his argument? What did Washington conceive the role of southern whites in African Americans' progress to be? Before you dismiss Washington's alternative, remember that his *goals* were roughly similar to those of Wells. Also use some inference to imagine how Washington's audiences would have reacted to his speech. How would southern whites have greeted his speech? southern blacks? What about northern whites? northern blacks? To whom was Washington speaking?

Now move on to Henry McNeal Turner's alternative (Source 3). At first Bishop Turner seems to be insulting

blacks. What was he really trying to say? Why did he think that God ordained blacks to be brought to America in chains? In Turner's view, once blacks were freed, what was their best alternative? Why? Turner's view of whites is at serious odds with that of Washington. How do the two views differ on this point? How did Turner use his view of whites to support his alternative for blacks?

Taken together, the two speeches by W. E. B. Du Bois (Sources 4 and 5) present a consistent view, even though their subject matter and emphasis are different. What was the "talented tenth"? In Du Bois's view, what crucial role must that group play? How is that view at odds with Washington's view? In his Niagara Address of 1906, Du Bois states what the goals of the "talented tenth" should be. What are those objectives? How does his suggested *process* differ from that of Washington? Furthermore, how does Du Bois's view differ from Washington's with respect to timing? tactics? tone? Remember, however, that the long-term goals of both men were similar.

Perhaps you have been struck by the fact that both Turner and Du Bois pinned their hopes for progress on African American *men*. Turner refers frequently to "manhood" and Du Bois to "exceptional men." Why do you think this was so? Why do you think the concept of African American manhood was important to these two thinkers?

For Frances E. W. Harper (Source 6), the hopes of African Americans lay not with black men but with black *women*. Why did she believe this was so? As opposed to education, work, or the political arena, in Harper's view what was the importance of the African American home? Would Harper have agreed or disagreed with Wells? Washington? Turner? Du Bois? How might African American men such as Washington, Turner, and Du Bois have reacted to her arguments?

After you have examined each of the alternatives, move on to your assessment of the strengths and weaknesses of each argument. As noted earlier, you will need to review the Background section of this chapter in order to establish the historical context in which the five arguments were made. Then, keeping in mind that context, try to imagine the reactions that these alternatives might have elicited in the following situations:

1. What would have happened if southern African Americans had adopted Wells's alternatives? Where might the process outlined by Wells have led? Were there any risks for African Americans? If so, what were they?

2. What would have happened if southern African Americans had adopted Washington's alternative? How long would it have taken them to realize Washington's goals? Were there any risks involved? If so, what were they?

3. What would have happened if southern African Americans had adopted Turner's alternative? Were there any risks involved? How realistic was Turner's option?

4. What would have happened if southern African Americans had adopted Du Bois's alternative? How long would Du Bois's process have taken? Were there any risks involved?

5. Was white assistance necessary according to Wells? to Washington? to Turner? to Du Bois? How did each spokesperson perceive the roles of the federal government and the federal courts? How did the government and courts stand on this issue at the time? [*Clue:* What was the Supreme Court decision in *Plessy v. Ferguson* (1896)?]

6. How might blacks and whites have reacted to Harper's arguments? black women? black men? As with the ideas of Washington, how long would it have taken African Americans who embraced Harper's ideas to reach the goals of social, economic, and political equality?

To be sure, it is very nearly impossible for us to put ourselves completely in the shoes of these men and women. Although racism still is a strong force in American life today, the intellectual and cultural environment was dramatically different in the time these five spokespersons were offering their ideas to African Americans. Even so, by placing each spokesperson in a historical context, we should be able to evaluate the strengths and weaknesses of his or her argument.

◆ CHAPTER 2

The Road to True
Freedom:
African American
Alternatives in
the New South

◆

Epilogue

For the advocates of a New South, the realization of their dream seemed to be just over the horizon, always just beyond their grasp. Many of the factories did make a good deal of money. But profits often flowed out of the South to northern investors. And factory owners often maintained profits by paying workers pitifully low wages, which led to the rise of a poor white urban class that lived in slums and faced enormous problems of malnutrition, poor health, family instability, and crime. To most of those who had left their meager farms to find opportunities in the burgeoning southern cities, life there appeared even worse than it had been in the rural areas. Many whites returned to their rural homesteads disappointed and dispirited by urban life.

For an increasing number of southern African Americans, the solution seemed to be to abandon the South entirely. Beginning around the time of World War I (1917–1918), a growing number of African Americans migrated to the industrial cities of the Northeast, Midwest, and West Coast (see Source 7). But there, too, they met racial hostility and racially inspired riots.

But in the North, African Americans could vote and thereby influence public policy. By the late 1940s, it had become clear that northern urban African American voters, by their very number, could force American politicians to deal with racial discrimination. By the 1950s, it was evident that the South would have to change its racial policies, if not willingly then by force. It took federal courts, federal marshals, and occasionally federal troops, but the crust of discrimination in the South began to be broken in the 1960s. Attitudes changed slowly, but the white southern politician draped in the Confederate flag and calling for resistance to change became a figure of the past. Although much work still needed to be done, changes in the South had been profound, laying the groundwork for more changes ahead. Indeed, by the 1960s, the industrialization and prosperity (largely through in-migration) of the Sunbelt seemed to show that Grady's dream of a New South might become a reality.

And yet, for all the hopeful indications (black voting and officeholding in the South, for instance), in many ways the picture was a somber one. By the 1970s, several concerned observers, both black and white, feared that the poorest 30 percent of all black families, instead of climbing slowly up the economic ladder, were in the process of forming a permanent underclass, complete with a social pathology that included broken families, crime, drugs, violence, and grinding poverty. Equally disturbing in the 1980s was a new wave of racial intolerance among whites, a phenomenon that even invaded many American colleges and universities. In short, although much progress had been made since the turn of the nineteenth century, in many ways, as in the New South, the dream of equality and tolerance remained just over the horizon.

By this time, of course, Wells, Washington, Turner, Du Bois, and Harper

Source 7 from U.S. Bureau of the Census, *Historical Statistics of the United States, Colonial Times to 1970* (Washington, D.C.: U.S. Government Printing Office, 1975), Vol. I, p. 95.

7. Estimated Net Intercensal Migration* of Negro Population by Region, 1870–1920 (in thousands).

Region	1870–1880	1880–1890	1890–1900	1900–1910	1910–1920
New England[1]	4.5	6.6	14.2	8.0	12.0
Middle Atlantic[2]	19.2	39.1	90.7	87.2	170.1
East North Central[3]	20.8	16.4	39.4	45.6	200.4
West North Central[4]	15.7	7.9	23.5	10.2	43.7
South Atlantic[5]	−47.9	−72.5	−181.6	−111.9	−158.0
East South Central[6]	−56.2	−60.1	−43.3	−109.6	−246.3
West South Central[7]	45.1	62.9	56.9	51.0	−46.2

*A net intercensal migration represents the amount of migration that took place between U.S. censuses, which are taken every ten years. The net figure is computed by comparing in-migration to with out-migration from a particular state. A minus figure means that out-migration from a state was greater than in-migration to it.

1. Maine, New Hampshire, Vermont, Massachusetts, Rhode Island, and Connecticut.
2. New York, New Jersey, and Pennsylvania.
3. Ohio, Indiana, Illinois, Michigan, and Wisconsin.
4. Minnesota, Iowa, Missouri, North Dakota, South Dakota, Nebraska, and Kansas.
5. Delaware, Maryland, District of Columbia, Virginia, West Virginia, North Carolina, South Carolina, Georgia, and Florida.
6. Kentucky, Tennessee, Alabama, and Mississippi.
7. Arkansas, Louisiana, Oklahoma, and Texas.

were dead. Wells continued to write militant articles for the African American press, became deeply involved in the women's suffrage movement, and carried on a successful crusade to prevent the racial segregation of the Chicago city schools. She died in Chicago in 1931. For his part, Washington publicly clung to his notion of self-help while secretly supporting more aggressive efforts to gain political rights for African Americans. He died in Tuskegee, Alabama, in 1915.

Turner's dream of thousands of blacks moving to Africa never material-ized. In response, he grew more strident and was especially critical of African Americans who opposed his ideas. In 1898, Turner raised a storm of protest when his essay "God Is a Negro" was published. The essay began, "We have as much right . . . to believe that God is a Negro, as you buckra, or white, people have to believe that God is a fine looking, symmetrical and ornamented white man."[14] He died while on

14. Edwin S. Redkey, ed., *Respect Black: The Writings and Speeches of Henry McNeal Turner* (New York: Arno Press, 1971), pp. 176–177.

◆ CHAPTER 2

The Road to True
Freedom:
African American
Alternatives in
the New South

a speaking trip to Canada in 1915. As for Du Bois, he eventually turned away from his championship of a "talented tenth" in favor of more mass protests. As a harbinger of many African Americans of the 1960s and 1970s, he embraced pan-Africanism, combining it with his long-held Marxist ideas. He died in Africa in 1963.

Harper was one of the most popular poets of her time. After her husband's death, she became increasingly vocal on feminist issues, was a friend and ally of Susan B. Anthony, and, in 1866, delivered a moving address before the National Women's Rights Convention. She died in Philadelphia, Pennsylvania, from heart disease in 1911. Her home has been preserved as a national historic landmark.

Wells and Harper were not the only African American women who attempted to offer solutions to the black dilemma. Another such person was Julia Haywood Cooper (1858–1964), who was born a slave in North Carolina, earned her BA and MA degrees from Oberlin College, and for many years was a teacher and principal at the District of Columbia's only black high school (later named Dunbar High School). Her book, *A Voice from the South* (1892) advocated equal educational opportunities for black women. In 1925, at the age of 64, she earned a Ph.D. from the Sorbonne in Paris.[15]

In their time, Wells, Washington, Turner, Du Bois, and Harper were important and respected figures. Although often publicly at odds with one another, they shared the same dream of African Americans living with pride and dignity in a world that recognized them as complete men and women. In an era in which few people championed the causes of African Americans in the New South, these five spokespersons stood out as courageous individuals.

15. *A Voice from the South, by a Black Woman of the South* (New York: Oxford University Press, photocopy of the 1892 edition, 1988).

3

How They Lived: Middle-Class Life, 1870–1917

◆

The Problem

In the 1870s, Heinrich Schliemann, a middle-aged German archaeologist, astonished the world with his claim that he had discovered the site of ancient Troy. As all educated people of the time knew, Troy was the golden city of heroes that the blind poet Homer (seventh century B.C.E.) made famous in his *Iliad* and *Odyssey*. Although archaeologists continued to argue bitterly about whether it was really Troy or some other ancient city that Schliemann was excavating, the general public was fascinated with the vases, gold and silver cups, necklaces, and earrings that were unearthed.

Not only the relics and "treasure" interested Americans, however. As the magazine *Nation* pointed out in 1875, these discoveries offered an opportunity to know about Troy as it had actually existed and to understand something about the daily lives of the inhabitants. Nineteenth-century Americans were intensely curious about the art, religion, burial customs, dress, and even the foods of the ancient Greeks. "Real Trojans," noted a magazine editor in 1881, "were very fond of oysters." (He based his conclusion on the large amounts of oyster shells uncovered at the archaeological digs.)

Material culture study is the use of artifacts to understand people's lives. In this chapter, you will be looking at some artifacts of the late nineteenth and early twentieth centuries—advertisements and house plans—to try to reconstruct the lives of middle-class white Americans during a period when the country was changing rapidly. What were Americans' hopes and fears during this era? What were their values?

◆

Background

The age from approximately 1870 to 1900 was characterized by enormous and profound changes in American life. Unquestionably, the most important changes were the nation's rapid industrialization and urbanization. Aided and accelerated by the rapid growth of railroads, emerging industries could extend their tentacles throughout the nation, collecting raw materials and fuel for the factories and distributing finished products to the growing American population. By 1900, that industrial process had come to be dominated by a few energetic and shrewd men, captains of industry to their friends and robber barons to their enemies. Almost every conceivable industry, from steel and oil to sugar refining and meat packing, was controlled by one or two gigantic corporations that essentially had the power to set prices on the raw materials bought and the finished products sold. In turn, the successes of those corporations created a new class of fabulously rich industrialists, and names like Swift, Armour, Westinghouse, Pillsbury, Pullman, Rockefeller, Carnegie, and Duke literally became almost household words, as much for the notoriety of the industrialists as for the industries and products they created.

As America became more industrialized, it also became more urban. In the past, the sizes of cities had been limited by the availability of nearby food, fuel, and employment opportunities. But the network of railroads and the rise of large factories had removed those limitations, and American cities grew phenomenally. Between 1860 and 1910, urban population increased sevenfold, and by 1920 more than half of all Americans lived in cities.[1] These urban complexes not only dominated the regions in which they were located but eventually set much of the tone for the entire nation as well.

Both processes—industrialization and urbanization—profoundly altered nearly every facet of American life. Family size began to decrease; the woman who might have had five or six children in 1860 was replaced by the "new" woman of 1900 who had only three or four children. The fruits of industrialization, distributed by new marketing techniques, could be enjoyed by a large portion of the American population. Electric lights, telephones, and eventually home appliances virtually revolutionized the lives of the middle and upper classes, as did Ford's later mass production of the Model T automobile.

The nature of the work also was changed because factories required a higher degree of regimentation than did farm work or the "putting-out" system. Many industries found it more profitable to employ women and children than adult males, thus altering the home lives of many of the nation's working-class citizens. Moreover, the lure of employment brought millions of immigrants to the United States, most of whom huddled together in cities, found low-paying jobs, and dreamed of the future. And as the cities grew grimy with factory soot and became increasingly populated by laborers, immigrants, and what one observer referred to as the "dangerous classes," upper- and middle-class Americans began to abandon the urban cores and retreat to fashionable suburbs on the peripheries, to return to the cities either in their automobiles or on streetcars only for work or recreation. In fact, the com-

---

1. The census defined *city* as a place with a population over twenty-five hundred people. Thus, many of the cities referred to in this chapter are what we would call towns, or even small towns.

forts of middle-class life were made possible, in part, by the exploitation of industrial workers.

Industrialization and urbanization not only changed how most Americans lived but how they *thought* as well. Faith in progress and technology was almost boundless, and there was widespread acceptance of the uneven distribution of wealth among Americans. Prior to the turn of the century, many upper- and middle-class Americans believed that life was a struggle in which the fittest survived. This concept, which applied Charles Darwin's discoveries about biological evolution to society, was called social Darwinism. The poor, especially the immigrant poor, were seen as biologically and morally inferior. It followed, then, that efforts to help the less fortunate through charity or government intervention were somehow tampering with both God's will and Darwinian evolution. In such a climate of opinion, the wealthy leaders of gigantic corporations became national heroes, superior in prestige to both preachers and presidents.

The response of the working classes varied; although many workers rejected the concepts of social Darwinism and Victorian morality, others aspired to middle-class status. In spite of long hours, low pay, and hazardous conditions, the men and women of the working classes engaged in a series of important labor protests and strikes during this period. A rich working-class culture developed in the saloons, vaudeville theaters, dance halls, and streets of medium-size and larger cities. Many workers sought alternatives in some form of socialism; many others, however, strove to achieve the standard of living of the rapidly expanding middle class. Across the country, young boys read the rags-to-riches tales of Horatio Alger, and girls learned to be "proper ladies" so that they would not embarrass their future husbands as they rose in society together.

Social critics and reformers of the time were appalled by the excesses of the "fabulously rich" and the misery of the "wretchedly poor." And yet a persistent belief in the opportunity to better one's position (or one's children's position) led many people to embrace an optimistic attitude and to focus on the acquisition of material possessions. New consumer goods were pouring from factories, and the housing industry was booming. Middle-class families emulated the housing and furnishing styles of the wealthy, and skilled blue-collar workers and their families aspired to own modest suburban homes on the streetcar line.

After 1900, widespread concern about the relationship of wages to the cost of maintaining a comfortable standard of living led to numerous studies of working-class families in various parts of the country. Could workers realistically hope to own homes and achieve decent standards of living as a result of their labor? In 1909, economist Robert Coit Chapin estimated that a family of five needed an annual income of about $900 to live in a decent home or apartment in New York City. A follow-up study of Philadelphia in 1917 estimated that same standard of living at approximately $1,600. Yet the average annual pay of adult male wage workers during these years ranged from only $600 to $1,700. Several other factors affected family income, however. Average wages are misleading, because skilled workers earned significantly more than unskilled or semiskilled workers. Even within the same industry and occupation, midwestern workers earned more than northeastern workers, and southern workers earned the lowest wages of all. Adult women workers, 80 percent of whom lived with families as wives or unmarried daughters, added their wages (approximately $300 to $600 a year) to the family income, as did working children. Many families, especially those of recent immigrants, also took in boarders and lodgers, who paid rent.

Finally, the cost of land and building materials was much more expensive in large cities than in smaller cities and towns. In his investigation of New York, Chapin found that 28 percent of working-class families in nine upstate cities owned their own homes, compared with only 1 percent in New York City. Another study in 1915 also sharply illustrated regional differences in homeownership. Twenty percent of Paterson, New Jersey, silk workers were homeowners, but only 10 percent of Birmingham, Alabama, steelworkers owned homes. Nineteen percent of Milwaukee's working-class families owned their own homes, compared to 4.4 percent of Boston's working-class families. Nor were all these homes in the central city. Working-class suburbs expanded along streetcar lines or were developed near industries on the fringes of a city, such as the suburb of Oakwood just outside Knoxville, Tennessee.[2] In this

community near textile mills and a major railroad repair shop, house lots measuring 50 by 140 feet sold for less than $100; most homes were built for under $1,000. Nearly half of the one thousand families who moved to Oakwood between 1902 and 1917 came from the older industrial sections of Knoxville.

Completely reliable income and cost statistics for early twentieth-century America do not exist, but it seems reasonable to estimate that at least one-fourth of working-class families owned or were paying for homes and that many more aspired to homeownership. But fully half of all working-class families, usually concentrated in large cities, lived in or near poverty and could not hope to own their own homes. Those with middle-class, white-collar occupations were more fortunate. Lawyers, doctors, businessmen, ministers, bank tellers, newspaper editors, and even schoolteachers could—through careful budgeting and saving—realistically expect to buy or build a house.

Although technological advances and new distribution methods put many modern conveniences and new products within the reach of all but the poorest Americans, the economic growth of the period was neither constant nor steady. The repercussions from two major depressions—one in 1873 and one in 1893—made "getting ahead" difficult, if not impossible, for many lower-middle-class and blue-collar families. Furthermore, at times everything seemed to be changing so rapidly that many people felt insecure. Yet within middle-class families, this sense of insecurity and even fear often

2. Knoxville's population in 1900 was 32,637; the city had experienced a 237 percent growth in population from 1880 to 1900.

coexisted with optimism and a faith in progress.

One way to understand the lives of middle-class Americans during the post–Civil War era is to look at the *things* with which they surrounded themselves: their clothes, the goods and services they bought, and even their houses. Why did such fashions and designs appeal to Americans of the late nineteenth and early twentieth centuries? What kind of an impression were these people trying to make on other people? How did they really feel about themselves? Sometimes historians, like archaeologists, use artifacts such as clothes, furniture, houses, and so forth to reconstruct the lives of Americans in earlier times. Indeed, each year many thousands of tourists visit historic homes such as Jefferson's Monticello, retrace the fighting at Gettysburg, or stroll through entire restored communities such as Colonial Williamsburg. But historians of the post–Civil War period also may use advertisements (instead of the products or services themselves) and house plans (instead of the actual houses) to understand how middle-class Americans lived and what their values and concerns were.

Every day, Americans are surrounded, even bombarded, by advertising that tries to convince them to buy some product, use some service, or compare brand X with brand Y. Television, radio, billboards, magazines, and newspapers spread the message to potential consumers of a variety of necessary—and unnecessary—products. Underlying this barrage of advertisements is an appeal to a wide range of emotions: ambition, elitism, guilt, and anxiety. A whole new "science" has arisen, called market research, that analyzes consumers' reactions and predicts future buying patterns.

Yet advertising is a relatively new phenomenon, one that began to develop after the Civil War and did not assume its modern form until the 1920s. P. T. Barnum, the promoter and impresario of mid-nineteenth-century entertainment, pointed the way with publicity gimmicks for his museum and circuses and, later, for the relatively unknown Swedish singer Jenny Lind. (Barnum created such a demand for Lind's concert tickets that they sold for as much as two hundred dollars each.) But at the time of the Civil War, most merchants still announced special sales of their goods in simple newspaper notices, and brand names were virtually unknown.

Businesses, both large and small, expanded enormously after the Civil War. Taking advantage of the country's greatly improved transportation and communication systems, daring business leaders established innovative ways to distribute products, such as the mail-order firm and the department store. Sears Roebuck & Company was founded in 1893, and its "wish book," or catalogue, rapidly became popular reading for millions of people, especially those who lived in rural areas. Almost one thousand pages long, these catalogues offered a dazzling variety of consumer goods and were filled with testimonial letters from satisfied customers. Lewis Thomas from Jefferson County, Alabama, wrote in 1897,

I received my saddle and I must say that I am so pleased and satisfied with my saddle, words cannot express my thanks for the benefit that I received from the pleasure and satisfaction given me. I know that I have a saddle that will by ordinary care last a lifetime, and all my neighbors are pleased as well, and I am satisfied so well that you shall have more of my orders in the near future.

And from Granite, Colorado, Mrs. Laura Garrison wrote, "Received my suit all right, was much pleased with it, will recommend your house to my friends."

For those who lived in cities, the department store was yet another way to distribute consumer goods. The massive, impressively decorated buildings erected by department store owners were often described as consumer "cathedrals" or "palaces." In fact, no less a personage than President William Howard Taft dedicated the new Wanamaker's department store in Philadelphia in 1911. "We are here," Taft told the crowd, "to celebrate the completion of one of the most important instrumentalities in modern life for the promotion of comfort among the people."

Many of the products being manufactured in factories in the late nineteenth and early twentieth centuries represented items previously made at home. Tinned meats and biscuits, "store-bought" bread, ready-made clothing, and soap all represented the impact of technology on the functions of the homemaker. Other products were new versions of things already being used. For example, the bathtub was designed solely for washing one's body, as opposed to the large bucket or tub in which one collected rainwater, washed clothes, and, every so often, bathed. Still other products and gadgets (such as the phonograph and the automobile) were completely new, the result of a fertile period of inventiveness (1860–1890) that saw more than ten times more patents issued than were issued during the entire period up to 1860 (only 36,000 patents were issued prior to the Civil War, but 440,000 were granted during the next thirty years).

There was no question that American industry could produce new products and distribute them nationwide. But there *was* a problem: How could American industry overcome the traditional American ethic of thrift and create a demand for products that might not have even existed a few years earlier? It was this problem that the new field of advertising set out to solve.

America in 1865 was a country of widespread, if uneven, literacy and a vast variety of newspapers and magazines, all competing for readership. Businesses quickly learned that mass production demanded a national, even an international, market, and money spent on national advertising in newspapers and magazines rose from $27 million in 1860 to more than $95 million in 1900. By 1929, the amount spent on advertising had climbed to more than $1 billion. Brand names and catchy slogans vied with one another to capture the consumer's interest. Consumers could choose from among many biscuit manufacturers, as the president of National Biscuit Company reported to his stockholders in 1901: "We do not pretend to sell our standard goods cheaper than other manufacturers of biscuits sell their goods. They always undersell us. Why do they not take away our business?" His answer was fourfold: efficiency, quality goods, innovative packaging, and advertising. "The trademarks we adopted," he concluded, "their value we created."

Advertising not only helped differentiate one brand of a product from another, but it also helped break down regional differences as well as differences between rural and urban lifestyles. Women living on farms in Kansas could order the latest "New York–style frocks" from a mail-order catalogue, and people in small towns in the Midwest or rural areas in the South could find the newest furniture styles, appliances, and automobiles enticingly displayed in mass-circulation magazines. In this era, more and more people abandoned the old ways of doing things and embraced the new ways of life that resulted from the application of modern technology, mass production, and efficient distribution of products. Thus, some historians have argued that advertising accelerated the transition of American society from one that emphasized production to one that stressed consumption.

The collective mentality, ideas, mood, and values of the rapidly changing society were reflected in nearly everything the society created, including its architecture. During the period from approximately 1865 to 1900, American architects designed public buildings, factories, banks, apartment houses, offices, and residential structures, aided by technological advances that allowed them to do things that had been impossible in the past. For instance, as American cities grew in size and population density, the value of real estate soared. Therefore, it made sense to design higher and higher buildings, taking advantage of every square foot of available land. The perfection of central heating systems; the inventions of the radiator, the elevator, and the flush toilet; and the use of steel framing allowed architects such as William Le Baron Jenney, Louis Sullivan, and others of the Chicago school of architecture to erect the modern skyscraper, a combined triumph of architecture, engineering, ingenuity, and construction.

At the same time, the new industrial elite were hiring these same architects to build their new homes—homes that often resembled huge Italian villas, French châteaux, and even Renaissance palaces. Only the wealthy, however, could afford homes individually designed by professional architects. Most people relied on contractors, builders, and carpenters who adapted drawings from books or magazines to suit their clients' needs and tastes. Such "pattern books," published by such men as Henry Holly, the Palliser brothers, Robert Shoppell, and the Radford Architectural Company, were extremely popular. It is estimated that in the mid-1870s, at least one hundred homes a year were being built from plans published in one women's magazine, *Godey's Lady's Book,* and thousands of others were built from pamphlets provided by lumber and plumbing fixture companies and architectural pattern books. Eventually, a person could order a complete home through the mail; all parts of the prefabricated house were shipped by railroad for assembly by local workers on the owner's site. George Barber of

Knoxville, Tennessee, the Aladdin Company of Bay City, Michigan, and even Sears Roebuck & Company were all prospering in mail-order homes around the turn of the century.

From the historian's viewpoint, both advertising and architecture created a wealth of evidence that can be used to reconstruct our collective past. By looking at and reading advertisements, we can trace Americans' changing habits, interests, and tastes. And by analyzing the kinds of emotional appeals used in the advertisements, we can begin to understand the aspirations and goals as well as the fears and anxieties of the people who lived in the rapidly chang-

ing society of the late nineteenth and early twentieth centuries.

Unfortunately, most people, including professional historians, are not used to looking for values and ideas in architecture. Yet every day we pass by houses and other buildings that could tell us a good deal about how people lived in a particular time period, as well as something about the values of the time. In this chapter, you will be examining closely both advertisements and house plans to reconstruct partially how middle-class Americans of the late nineteenth and early twentieth centuries lived.

✦

The Method

No historian would suggest that the advertisements of preceding decades (or today's advertisements, for that matter) speak for themselves—that they tell you how people actually lived. Like almost all other historical evidence, advertisements must be carefully analyzed for their messages. Advertisements are intended to make people want to buy various products and services. They can be positive or negative. Positive advertisements show the benefits—direct or indirect, explicit or implicit—that would come from owning a product. Such advertisements depict an ideal. Negative or "scare" advertisements demonstrate the disastrous consequences of not owning the product. Some of the most effective advertisements combine both negative

and positive approaches ("I was a lonely 360-pound woman before I discovered Dr. Quack's Appetite Suppressors—now I weigh 120 pounds and am engaged to be married!"). Advertisements also attempt to evoke an emotional response from potential consumers that will encourage the purchase of a particular product or service.

Very early advertisements tended to be primarily descriptive, simply picturing the product. Later advertisements often told a story with pictures and words. In looking at the advertisements in the Evidence section of this chapter, first determine whether the approach used in each one is positive, negative, or a combination of both factors. What were the expected consequences of using (or not using) the product? How did the advertisement try to sell the product or service? What emotional responses were expected?

The preceding evaluation is not too difficult, but in this exercise you must go even further with your analysis. You are trying to determine what each advertisement can tell you about earlier generations of Americans and the times in which they lived. Look at (and read) each advertisement carefully. Does it reveal anything about the values of the time period in which the advertisement appeared? about the roles of men and women? about attitudes concerning necessities and luxuries? about people's aspirations or fears?

House plans also must be analyzed if they are to tell us something about how people used to live. At one time or another, you have probably looked at a certain building and thought, "That is truly an ugly, awful-looking building! Whatever possessed the lunatic who built it?" Yet when that building was designed and built, most likely it was seen as a truly beautiful structure and may have been widely praised by its occupants as well as by those who merely passed by. Why is this so? Why did an earlier generation believe the building was beautiful?

All of us are aware that the standards for what is considered good art, good music, good literature, and good architecture change over time. What may be pleasing to the people of one era might be considered repugnant or even obscene by those of another time. But is this solely the result of changing fads, such as the sudden rises and declines in the popularity of movie and television stars, rock 'n' roll groups, or fashionable places to vacation?

The answer is partly yes, but only partly. Tastes do change, and fads such as the Hula-Hoop and the yo-yo come and inevitably go. However, we must still ask why a particular person or thing becomes popular or in vogue at a certain time. Do these changing tastes in art, music, literature, and architecture *mean* something? Can they tell us something about the people who embraced these various styles? More to the point, can they tell us something about the *values* of those who embraced them? Obviously, they can.

In examining these middle-class homes, you should first look for common exterior and interior features. Then look at the interior rooms and their functions, comparing them with rooms in American homes today. You also must try to imagine what impression these houses conveyed to people in the late nineteenth and early twentieth centuries. Finally, you will be thinking about all the evidence—the advertisements and the house plans—as a whole. What is the relationship between the material culture (in this case, the advertisements and the house plans) and the values and concerns of Americans in the late nineteenth and early twentieth centuries?

The Evidence

Sources 1 through 3 from Sears Roebuck & Company catalogues, 1897 and 1902.

1. Children's Reefer Jackets (1897) and Children's Toys (1902).

SEARS ROEBUCK & CO. INC.

85¢

$1.50

24171

24172

REEFER JACKETS FOR CHILDREN FROM 1 TO 5 YEARS OLD.

Do not forget to mention age and color desired when ordering.

Reefer Jackets for little toddlers, from one to four years, nobby, stylish little coats at little bits of prices. As usual S. R. & Co. will save you money on these goods.

DRESSED SAILOR DOLLS.
Sailor Girl Dolls.

No. 29R735 Sailor Girl Doll, bisque head, flowing hair, solid eyes, dressed to represent a girl in sailor costume. A very pretty doll. Length, 13 inches.
Price, each.................50c

Sailor Boy Dolls.

No. 29R739 Sailor Boy Doll, dressed to represent a boy in sailor costume, companion doll to sailor girl. Length, 13 inches.
Price, each........................50c

The Penny Saver.

No. 29R147 A perfect registering bank; no key, no combination. Each time a cent is dropped into the bank the bell rings and the register indicates. Opens automatically at each 50 cents. The total always in sight. They are attractive and interesting to children. The mechanism is made of steel, and will not break or get out of order. It is highly interesting to children, and for this reason will encourage them to save. Shipping weight, 5 pounds. Price, each.........85c

BOYS' WASH SUITS.

The extraordinary value we offer in Boys' Wash Suits can only be fully appreciated by those who order from this department. A trial order will surely convince you that we are able to furnish new, fresh, up to date, stylish and well made wash suits at much lower prices than similar value can be had from any other house.

NOTE.—Boys' wash suits can be had only in the sizes as mentioned after each description. Always state age of boy and if large or small of age.

Boy's Wash Crash Suit, 35 Cents.

38R2128
98c

38R2130
$1.39

38R2131 es.
$1.48

Navy Blue and White Percale Wash Suit, 40 Cents.

GIRLS' WASH DRESSES.

AGES FROM 4 TO 14 YEARS.

WHEN ORDERING please state Age, Height, Weight and Number of Inches around Bust.

SCALE OF SIZES, SHOWING PROPORTION OF BUST AND LENGTH TO THE AGE OF CHILD

Age	4	6	8	10	12	14
Bust	24	27	28	29	30	31
Skirt length	18	20	22	24	26	28

No. 38R2126 GIRLS' DRESS. Some made of Madras and some made of ginghams in fancy stripes and plaids, round yokes, "V" shape yokes, some trimmed with braid, ruffles and embroidery. We show no illustration of this number on account of the differ-

---

3. *Wash suits* and *wash dresses* were washable, casual clothing.

3. Hip Pad and Bustle, 1902.

Parisienne Hip Pad and Bustle.

No. 18R4880 The Parisienne Hip Pad and Bustle, made of best tempered, black enameled, woven wire with hip pads of padded cloth. Perfect in shape, and light in weight. Very durable.

Price, each...**40c**

If by mail, postage extra, each, 10 cents.

Sources 4 through 7 and 10 through 26 may also be found in Edgar R. Jones, *Those Were the Good Old Days: A Happy Look at American Advertising 1880–1930* (New York: Simon & Schuster, 1959).

Source 4 from an 1893 advertisement.

4. Corsets.

DOCTORS RECOMMEND REAST'S PATENT

INVIGORATOR CORSETS.

FOR LADIES, MAIDS, BOYS, GIRLS, AND CHILDREN.

Dr. M. O. B. NEVILLE, L.R.C.P., Edin. Medical Officer of Health, says, Nov. 1st, 1890:—

" From a scientific point of view, I am of opinion that your Corset is the only one that gives support without unduly compressing important organs. Its elasticity, in a great measure, prevents this. I am satisfied, by its support of back and shoulders, that it is a material help to expanding the chest."

"Mrs. WELDON'S FASHION JOURNAL," says July '90:—

" Undoubtedly supplies a long-felt want for ensuring an upright form and graceful carriage, COMBINES ELEGANCE of FORM WITH COMFORT. It renders a corset what it should be, comfort, and support to the wearer, strengthening the spine, expanding the chest, and giving necessary support without tight lacing or undue pressure."

PRICES.

Child's under 5 years, 3/4; Boys' and Girls' over 5 years, 4/6; Maids, 5/6; Ladies', 6/6, 8/6, 12/9, 18/6, 22/6, 63/-.

SOLD BY ALL DRAPERS, OR SEND P.O. TO

REAST, 15, CLAREMONT, HASTINGS, ENGLAND.

FOR LICENSE FOR MANUFACTURING, OR SALE OF AMERICAN PATENT APPLY AS ABOVE.

Source 5 from a 1912 advertisement.

5. Massage Cream for the Skin.

Source 6 from 1895, 1888, and 1912 advertisements.

6. Croup Remedy (1895), Garment Pins (1888), and *American Boy* Magazine (1912).

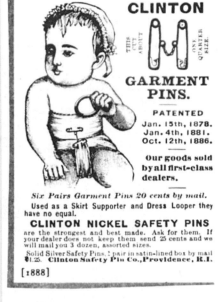

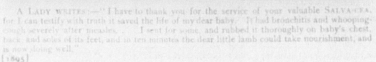

Source 7 from an 1893 advertisement.

7. Shaving Soaps.

WILLIAMS' SHAVING SOAPS have enjoyed an unblemished reputation for excellence—for over HALF A HUNDRED YEARS—and are to-day the *only* shaving soaps—of absolute purity, with well-established claims for healing and antiseptic properties.

"CHEAP" and impure Shaving Soaps—are composed largely of refuse animal fats—abound in scrofulous and other disease germs—and if used—are almost sure to impregnate the pores of the skin—resulting in torturing cutaneous eruptions and other forms of blood-poisoning.

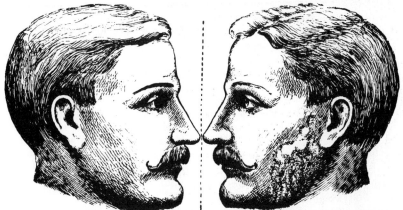

This view shows face—as shaved daily for years—with the famous WILLIAMS' Shaving Soap—always soft—fresh—bright and healthy.   Not a sore or pimple in over 20 years of Shaving Experience.

This view shows the effect of being shaved ONCE with an impure—so-called "Cheap" Shaving Soap.   Blood-poison—caused by applying impure animal fats to the tender cuticle of the face.

MR. CHAS. A. FOSTER,

34 SAVIN STREET,

BOSTON, MASS., writes :

"Never again will I allow a Barber to shave me unless he is using the only safe and reliable shaving soap made—namely **WILLIAMS'.**   The other day—being in a hurry—I went into a shop near the Boston and Maine depot—to get a shave.

"I noticed a rank odor when the lather was put on my face, and asked the Barber if he used WILLIAMS' Shaving Soap.   He said, 'No—I do not—because it costs a little more than other kinds.'

"A few days after this experience—my face was all broken out—terribly sore and smarting like fire.

"I consulted my Physician who told me it was a bad case of 'BARBER'S ITCH'—caused by the use of the Cheap Shaving Soap—containing diseased animal fats.

"I have suffered the worst kind of torture for two weeks—but I have learned a lesson."

Qu–?

Ask your Barber if *he* uses **WILLIAMS'.**   Take no chances.   Blood-poisoning—in some form or other is the almost sure result of using a cheaply made and impure Shaving Soap.   While shaving—the pores of the Skin are open—and quickly drink in—any of the disease germs which may be contained in the diseased animal fats—so largely used in all "cheap"—inferior Toilet and Shaving Soaps.

Ask for **WILLIAMS'**—and *insist* that you have it—and enjoy a feeling of SECURITY—as well as of comfort—while shaving or being shaved.

In providing for the **safety and comfort of visitors**—it has been officially ordered that

WILLIAMS' SHAVING SOAPS

shall be used EXCLUSIVELY—in all of the Barber Shops located on the Grounds of the World's Columbian Exposition.   Thus AT THE VERY START—it receives the highest possible Honor.

WILLIAMS' "JERSEY CREAM" TOILET SOAP.

Something new with us.   The result of 50 years of costly and laborious experiment.   Send for circular.

A most exquisite—healing and beautifying toilet soap.   Containing the rich yellow cream of *our own herd* of imported Jersey Cattle.   A full size cake mailed to any address for 25c. in stamps.

Do not fail to try it.   Ask your Druggist—or send to us.—Address,

The J. B. Williams Co., Glastonbury, Conn., U. S. A.

"WILLIAMS' SOAPS have for a foundation—over half a hundred years of unblemished reputation."

Source 8 from a 1908 advertisement.

8. Safety Razor.

Source 9 from a 1916 advertisement.

9. Colt Revolver.

Source 10 from an 1891 advertisement.

10. One-Volume Book Collection.

NONE ARE TOO BUSY TO READ

IN ONE VOLUME.

"The Best Fifty Books of the Greatest Authors."

CONDENSED FOR BUSY PEOPLE.

BENJAMIN R. DAVENPORT, EDITOR.

NO EXCUSE FOR IGNORANCE.

THIS WORK of 771 pages covers the whole range of Literature from Homer's Iliad, B. C. 1200 to Gen. Lew. Wallace's Ben Hur, A. D. 1880, including a Brief Biographical Sketch and FINE FULL-PAGE PORTRAIT OF EACH AUTHOR. Every one of the Fifty Books being so thoroughly reviewed and epitomized, as to enable the READERS OF THIS VOLUME TO DISCUSS THEM FULLY, making use of Familiar Quotations properly, and knowing the connection in which they were originally used by their Great Authors.

THIS BOOK is made from material furnished by Homer, Shakespeare, Milton, Bunyan, Dickens, Stowe, Gen. Lew. Wallace. and the other great authors of thirty centuries.

BY IT A LITERARY EDUCATION MAY BE ACQUIRED WITHIN ONE WEEK, ALL FROM ONE VOLUME.

A BOOK FOR BUSY AMERICANS.
TIME SAVED. MONEY SAVED.
KNOWLEDGE IN A NUTSHELL.

NEW YORK WORLD, March 15th.—"The book is one destined to have a great sale, because it supplies, IN THE FULLEST SENSE, A LONG FELT LITERARY WANT."

Born 1504.   William Shakespeare.   Died 1616.

Opinions expressed by practical, busy and successful self-made men, as to the great value and merit of Mr. Davenport's condensations:

Mr. PHILIP D. ARMOUR writes: "I am pleased to own 'Fifty Best Books.' It certainly should enable the busy American, at small expenditure of time, to gain a fairly comprehensive knowledge of the style and scope of the authors you have selected."

GEN. RUSSELL A. ALGER writes: "I have received the beautiful volume. It is surely a very desirable work."

GOV. JOSEPH E. BROWN, of Georgia, writes: "You have shown great power of condensation. This is eminently a practical age; men engaged in the struggle for bread have no time to enter much into details in literature. What the age wants is to get hold of the substance of a book. This work entitles you to be understood as a benefactor."

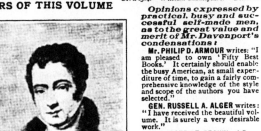

Born 1783.   Washington Irving.   Died 1859.

BOSTON DAILY GLOBE, April 2, 1891.—"Men of the present generation have not time to wade through from 2,000 to 3,000 pages of any of literature's standard volumes, and as a result they do not undertake it at all, and are often placed in an embarrassing position."

BUFFALO EXPRESS, March 1st.—"The Best Fifty Books of the Greatest Authors. Condensed for Busy People," edited by Benjamin R. Davenport, deserves high praise. It not only gives busy people an introduction to literature, but takes them to its very sanctum sanctorum and bids them be at home. The editor has selected his best fifty books with the advice of the most eminent literary men in England and America. These masterpieces, from Homer's 'Iliad' to Lew. Wallace's 'Ben Hur,' he has condensed into one volume of 771 pages, working in all of the famous passages and supplying a narrative in good, straightforward, unpretentious English. The story of each book is accompanied with a brief biographical sketch and a portrait of each author. No matter how familiar one is with any of these fifty books, be it for instance, 'Don Quixote,' 'Rasselas,' 'Les Miserables,' 'Paradise Lost,' or any other, he will be forced to admit, after reading the dozen pages devoted to each one in this condensation, that there is little, if anything, to add, either with regard to plot, characters, scenes, situations, quotations, or anything else that is ever discussed by people. The result of days or weeks of reading will be the possession of hardly one single bit of information or one tangible idea concerning the book in hand that is not to be acquired by reading the dozen pages in this condensation within a half hour."

Born 1812.   Charles Dickens.   Died 1870.

SOLD BY SUBSCRIPTION ONLY.   AGENTS WANTED EVERYWHERE.

CANVASSERS who desire to represent a book which sells rapidly and without argument should send for CIRCULARS. Books forwarded, postage paid, to any address upon receipt of price.

Fine English Muslin, Sprinkled Edges, $3 75.   Full Sheep, Library Style, Marbled Edges, $4.75.
Seal Russia, Gilt Edges, $5.75.

19th CENTURY BOOK CONCERN, 40 Exchange St., Buffalo, N. Y.

[1891]

Source 11 from a 1906 advertisement.

11. Correspondence School.

What are You Worth

From The
NECK
UP?

It is estimated that the average man is worth $2.00 a day from the neck *down*—what is he worth from the neck *up?*

That depends entirely upon training. **If you** are trained so that you can plan and direct work you are worth ten times as much as the man who can work only under orders.

The **International Correspondence Schools** go to the man who is struggling along on small pay and say to him, "We will train you for promotion right where you are, or we will qualify you to take up a more congenial line of work at a much higher salary."

What the I. C. S. says it can do, it *will* do. It has already done it for others and will do it for *you,* if you only show the inclination.

Thousands of ambitious men, realizing this fact, have marked the I. C. S. coupon, and multiplied their wages many times. During March, 403 students voluntarily reported an increase in salary and position as the direct result of **I. C. S.** training.

In this day of demand for leaders, a young man ought to be ashamed to be satisfied with small wages when he has the I. C. S. ready to qualify him for a higher salary.

Mark the coupon at once and mail it. You need not leave your present work, or your own home, while the I. C. S. prepares you to advance.

Back your *trained hand* with a *trained head!* It pays big. This coupon is for you. *Will you use it?*

International Correspondence Schools,
Box 815, SCRANTON, PA.
Please explain without further obligation on my part, how I can qualify for a larger salary in the position before which I have marked X

Bookkeeper	Mechanical Draftsman
Stenographer	Telephone Engineer
Advertisement Writer	Elec. Lighting Supt.
Show Card Writer	Mechan. Engineer
Window Trimmer	Surveyor
Commercial Law	Stationary Engineer
Illustrator	Civil Engineer
Civil Service	Building Contractor
Chemist	Architec'l Draftsman
Textile Mill Supt.	Architect
Electrician	Structural Engineer
Elec. Engineer	Bridge Engineer
	Mining Engineer

Name_____

Street and No._____

City_____ State_____

Source 12 from a 1908 advertisement.

12. Life Insurance Club.

Don't Depend on Your Relatives When You Get Old

If you let things go kind o' slip-shod *now*, you may later have to get out of the 'bus and set your carpet-bag on the stoop of some house where your arrival will hardly be attended by an ovation.

If you secure a membership in the Century Club this sad possibility will be nipped in the bud. It is very, very comfortable to be able to sit under a vine and fig-tree of your own.

The Club has metropolitan headquarters and a national membership of self-respecting women and men who are building little fortunes on the monthly plan. Those who have joined thus far are a happy lot—it would do your heart good to read their letters.

We would just as soon send our particulars to you as to anybody else, and there is no reason in the world why you shouldn't know all about everything. You'll be glad if you do and sorry if you don't.

Be kind to those relatives—*and to yourself.*

Address, stating without fail your occupation and the exact date of your birth,

Century Life-Insurance Club
Section O

5, 7 and 9 East 42d Street, New York

RICHARD WIGHTMAN, Secretary

Source 13 from 1896 and 1914 advertisements.

13. Gramophone (1896) and Victrola (1914).

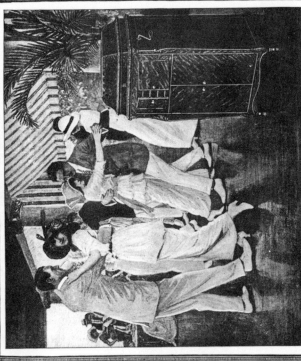

Source 14 from 1907 and 1912 advertisements.

14. Ford Automobile (1907) and Inter-State Electric Car for Women (1912).

FORD RUNABOUT
"Built for Two"

Two's company and a crowd frequently spoils a motoring trip.

When you have a large car you feel like filling up the seats—seems stingy for two to usurp so much luxury; so your tonneau is always full. Everybody's happy but—

Did you ever feel as if you'd just like to go alone—you and she—and have a day all your own? Go where you please, return when you please, drive as fancy dictates, without having to consult the wishes or the whims of others?

Ford Runabouts are ideal for such trips. Just hold two comfortably; ride like a light buggy, control easily and you can jog along mile after mile and enjoy the scenery.

Of course you can scorch if you want to—40 miles an hour easily—but you won't want to. You'll get used to the soft purr of the motor and the gentle motion of the car over the rolling country roads and—well, it's the most luxurious sensation one can imagine.

"We've enjoyed motoring more since we've had the Ford Runabout than we ever did before," says one lady whose purse can afford anything she desires. "Got the big car yet, but 'two's company,' and most times that's the way we go."

$600, F.O.B. Detroit

Model N. 4 Cyl. 15 H.P.

FORD MOTOR COMPANY,
25 Piquette Ave., - Detroit, Mich.

BRANCH RETAIL STORES—New York, Philadelphia, Boston, Chicago, Buffalo, Cleveland, Detroit and Kansas City. Standard Motor Co., San Francisco, Oakland and Los Angeles, distributors for California. Canadian trade supplied by Ford Motor Company of Canada, Walkerville, Ont.

The Automobile for Women

Electrically Started and Lighted

Controls Itself Pumps Its Own Tires

THE advent of the Inter-State, with its marvelously simple mechanism, its electrical self-starter and its self-controller has brought a revolution in motoring. Now the powerful and magnificent Inter-State starts and obeys the will of the woman driver as readily, as easily and as simply as an electric coupe. Without moving from the driver's seat or shifting gears she starts the engine by a turn of the switch — regulates the mixture by a simple movement of the lever on the steering column, and the magnificent Inter-State is under way

No labor to start the Inter-State

and under perfect and absolute control, with no more trouble than turning on an electric light. The Inter-State electric self-starter is **part of the system** and **built into** it, and the motor dynamo turns the engine itself until it picks up under its own power.

Electric Lights as in Your Own Home

Any or all lights on by turning switch

ONE of the greatest features of the Inter-State is its electric light system—not a single light or two—but an entire and reliable system, front—side—rear, all correlated and so arranged that by a turn of the switch, without leaving the driver's seat, any or all of the lights may be turned on in all their brilliancy. No more gas tanks, no more oil filling, no more lamp trimming or adjusting. The system is simply perfect. The front headlights are provided with a dimming feature so that driving in city streets may be done with a medium diffused light.

Write Today for Art Catalog

This describes fully the six 40 and 50 H. P. completely equipped Models which cost from $2,400 to $3,400. Gives complete details of all the equipment and features, and also shows the Inter-State Models 30-A and 32-B, 40 H. P., costing $1,750 and $1,700 respectively.

THAT greatest nuisance of motoring—tire pumping—is *totally eliminated* with the Inter-State equipment. Any woman can attach the valve to the tire, turn on the pump and in a few minutes have tires just as solid and as perfectly filled as if done by the greatest tire expert in the world.

The Inter-State *does* the work. You *direct* it. There is nothing to it at all and you are forearmed for any emergency with the complete and thorough equipment of the Inter-State.

Inter-State Tire Pumping—No Work

Motoring Now All Pleasure

THIS great car performs all the labor itself—electrically self-started—electric lights and ignition, tire pumping and the automatic regulation of fuel consumption.

For the first time in the history of the automobile, electricity plays its *real part* in the entire mechanism. The Inter-State Electric System is really the *nerve system* commanding the energy and motion of the powerful steel muscles that make the Inter-State such a masterpiece of construction. Every conceivable accessory and feature is built into or included in the Inter-State. The Inter-State is truly the *only complete car* in this country or abroad —and this statement is made advisedly.

The Only Complete Car—Equipment and Features Unequalled

INTER-STATE AUTOMOBILE COMPANY, Dept. X, Muncie, Indiana
Boston Branch: 153 Massachusetts Avenue   *Omaha Branch:* 310 South 18th Street

15. Musical Automobile Exhaust Horn.

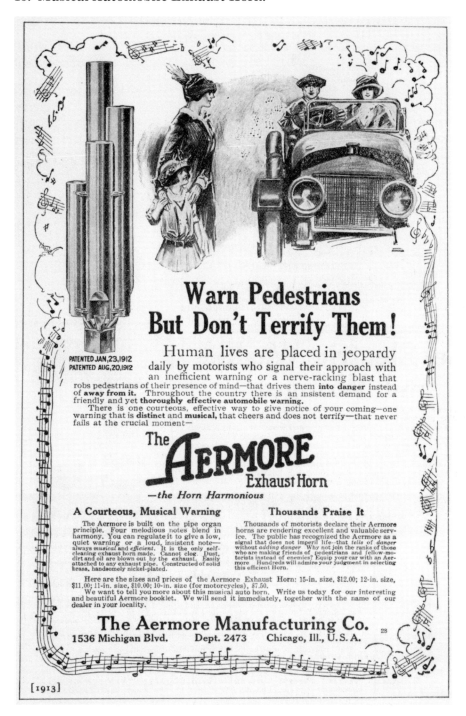

Source 16 from 1884 and 1908 advertisements.

16. Cooking Stove (1884) and Electric Washer and Wringer (1908).

ASK YOUR DEALER FOR THE
"GLENWOOD"

WITH PATENT MAGIC GRATE.

There is nothing more essential to the healthy happy home than well cooked food—which you may always be sure of by using the **Glenwood Range. 100 styles!** Illustrated Circular and Price List sent free.
WEIR STOVE CO., Taunton, Mass.

The Electric Washer and Wringer

Washing

YOU can now have your washings done by electricity. The 1900 Electric Washer Outfit (Washer, Wringer and Motor complete) does all the heavy work of washing and wrings out the clothes.

Any electric light current furnishes the power needed. You connect up the washer the same way you put an electric light globe into its socket. Then all there is to do to start the washer is—turn on the electricity. The motion of the tub (driven by the electricity) and the water and soap in the tub wash the clothes clean. Washing is done quicker and easier, and more thoroughly and economically this way than ever before.

30 Days' FREE Trial—Freight Prepaid

Wringing

Servants will stay contented—laundry bills will be saved—clothes will last twice as long—where there is a 1900 Electric Washer to do the washing.

These washers save so much work and worry and trouble, that they *sell themselves.* This is the way of it—

We ship you an Electric Washer and *prepay the freight.*

Use the washer a month. Wash your linens and laces—wash your blankets and quilts—wash your rugs.

Then—when the month is up, if you are not convinced the washer is all we say—don't keep it. Tell us you don't want the washer and that will settle the matter. We won't charge anything for the use you have had of it.

This is the *only* washer outfit that does *all* the drudgery of the washing—*washes* and *wrings* clothes—saves them from wear and tear—and keeps your servants contented.

Our Washer Book tells how our washers are made and how they work. Send for this book today.

Don't mortgage your pleasure in life to dread of wash-day and wash-day troubles with servants. Let the 1900 Electric Washer and Wringer shoulder your wash-day burden—save your clothes and money, and keep your servants contented.

Write for our Washer Book at once. Address—

The 1900 Washer Co. 3133 Henry Street, Binghamton, N. Y. (If you live in Canada, write to the Canadian 1900 Washer Co., 355 Yonge Street, Toronto, Ont.)

Source 17 from 1909 and 1913 advertisements.

17. Vacuum Cleaner (1909) and Bathroom Closet (1913).

Why stir up the Dust Demon to Frenzy like this?

The Man

always wonders why some way of cleaning can't be found without tormenting him with choking clouds of dust.

You can Escape all this for $25

EVERY MAN AND WOMAN

The Woman

thinks she is performing praiseworthy and necessary work in an unavoidable manner.

should now realize that such laborious and tormenting "cleaning" methods, are **a relic of barbarism, a mockery and a farce.** "Cleaning" with broom and carpet-sweeper merely scatters more of the dirt over a wider area. Old dirt has to be *raked again and again*, to clear the room thoroughly. The germs are never removed; they are left to multiply, then are sent flying to infect all those whose powers of resistance may be lowered.

THE IDEAL VACUUM CLEANER

(Fully Protected by Patents)

Operated by Hand puts no tax on the strength. **Price $25**

Or by Electric Motor, at a cost of 2 cents per hour. **Price $55 or $60**

"IT EATS UP THE DIRT" literally sucks out all the dust, grit, germs, moths and eggs of vermin that are *on* the object as well as *in* it—gobbles them down into its capacious maw, never to trouble you again.

This machine places in your hands a method of cleaning carpets, rugs, curtains, upholstery, wall decorations, etc., that hitherto has been limited to the very rich. It does exactly the same work as the Vacuum Cleaning systems that cost from $500 up—*and does it better and with more convenience.* The Ideal Vacuum Cleaner is the perfection of the Vacuum Cleaning principle.

OPERATED BY HAND

Weighs only 20 pounds. Anybody can use it. Everybody can afford it. Compared with sweeping

It is ease itself.

It is absolutely dustless.

Every machine guaranteed.

Our free Illustrated Booklet tells an interesting story of a remarkable saving in money, time, labor, health, and strength. Send for it to-day.

The American Vacuum Cleaner Company

225 Fifth Avenue, New York City

PRICE $55-$60

[1909]

The Noiselessness of the Siwelclo Is an Advantage Found in No Other Similar Fixture.

This appeals particularly to those whose sense of refinement is shocked by the noisy flushing of the old style closet. The Siwelclo was designed to prevent such embarrassment and has been welcomed whenever its noiseless feature has become known. When properly installed it cannot be heard outside of its immediate environment.

SIWELCLO Noiseless Siphon Jet CLOSET

Every sanitary feature has been perfected in the Siwelclo—deep water seal preventing the passage of sewer gas, thorough flushing, etc.

The Siwelclo is made of Trenton Potteries Co. Vitreous China, with a surface that actually repels dirt like a china plate. It is glazed at a temperature 1000 degrees higher than is possible with any other material.

The most sanitary and satisfactory materials for all bathroom, kitchen and laundry fixtures are Tepeco Solid Porcelain and Trenton Potteries Co. Vitreous China and Solid Porcelain. Your architect and plumber will recommend them. If you are planning a new house or remodeling, you ought to see the great variety and beauty of design such as are shown in our new free booklet S13 "Bathrooms of Character." Send for a copy now.

The Trenton Potteries Co.

Trenton, N.J., U.S.A.

The largest manufacturers of sanitary pottery in the U.S.A.

Source 18 from an 1882 advertisement.

18. Musical Organ.

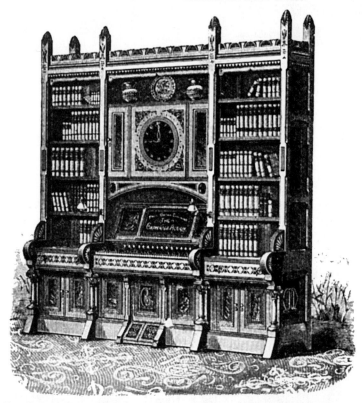

THIS effective and beautiful design in the modern Queen Anne Style is intended to meet the demands of those desiring an instrument of special elegance, and in harmony with the fittings and furnishings of the Study or Library Room, combining as it does, in a substantial and tasteful manner, the Organ, the Library cases, and the cabinet for bric-a-brac and articles of virtu.

It is well adapted to find favor in homes of culture and refinement, and will be championed by the music lover and connoisseur.

The composition is one of well balanced proportions, chaste subordination of ornamentation, and of artistic arrangement in constructive details, imparting to the design a rich simplicity and substantial worth

This beautiful organ contains the Celebrated Carpenter Organ Action. The action is to an Organ what the works are to a watch. The merits of the Carpenter Organ were fully proved on page 158 of the YOUTH'S COMPANION of April 20th, to which special attention is directed.

A beautiful 80-page Catalogue, the finest of its kind ever published, is now ready and will be sent free to all applying for it.

Nearly all reliable dealers sell the Carpenter Organs, but if any do not have them to show you, write to us for a Catalogue and information where you can see them. DO NOT BUY ANY ORGAN UNTIL YOU HAVE EXAMINED "THE CARPENTER." In writing for a Catalogue always state that you saw this advertisement in the *Youth's Companion.*

Address or call on E. P. CARPENTER, Worcester, Mass., U. S. A.

19. Houses in New York (1887) and Tennessee (1892): Exterior Views and Floor Plans.

* * * This marvelous house has been built more than 300 times from our plans; *it is so well planned* that it affords ample room even for a large family. 1st floor shown above; on 2d floor are 4 bedrooms and in attic 2 more. Plenty of Closets. The whole warmed by one chimney.

Large illustrations and full description of the above as well as of 39 other houses, ranging in cost from $400 up to $6,500, may be found in "SHOPPELL'S MODERN LOW-COST HOUSES," a large quarto pamphlet, showing also how to select sites, get loans, &c. Sent postpaid on receipt of 50c. Stamps taken, or send $1 bill and we will return the change. Address, BUILDING PLAN ASSOCIATION. (Mention this paper.) 24 Beekman St. (Box 2702,) N. Y.

Source 20 from a *Ladies' Home Journal* advertisement, 1909.

20. Advice for Couples Buying a Home.

This is the house the young couple saved and paid for in five years.

A Young Couple
Were Married 5 Years Ago

He had a moderate salary. They started simply and saved. But they didn't skimp. They gave little dinners and heard the best lectures. In five years they had saved enough to pay for the house at the head of this page.

Another Young Couple Were Married, Too

They put by $7 a week, and the house at the bottom of this page is now theirs, —entirely paid for. A third young couple's income was $16 per week. They saved $8 of it, and bought and paid for the house at the bottom of this page.

How these and 97 others did it, step by step, dollar by dollar, is all told in the great series, "*How We Saved For a Home*,"— 100 articles by 100 people who saved for and now own their own homes on an

Average Salary of $15 a Week: None Higher Than $30

This great series will run for an entire year in

The Ladies' Home Journal

For ONE DOLLAR, for a year's subscription, you get the whole series.

THE CURTIS PUBLISHING COMPANY, PHILADELPHIA, PA.

This is the house saved for on $7 a week and now all paid for.

This is the house paid for out of a salary of $16 per week, saving $8.

Sources 21 through 24 from *Palliser's Model Homes,* 1878.

21. Cottage for a Mill Hand at Chelsea, Massachusetts (cost $1,200), 1878.

This is a very attractive design, and intended to give ample accommodation at a low cost for an ordinary family.

The cellar is placed under the Kitchen and Hall, which was thought in this instance to be sufficient to meet all requirements, though it is generally considered, in the Eastern States at least, to be poor economy not to have a cellar under the whole house, as it only requires about one foot in depth of additional stone work to secure a cellar, it being necessary to put down the stone work in any case, so that it will be beyond the reach of frost. The Kitchen is without a fire-place, the cooking to be done by a stove, which, if properly contrived, is a very effective ventilator, and preferred by many housekeepers for all Kitchen purposes.

The Parlor and Dining-room or general Living-room are provided with the healthy luxury of an open fire-place, and we know of no more elegant, cleanly and effective contrivance for this purpose than the one adopted in this instance; they are built of buff brick, with molded jambs and segment arch, and in which a basket grate or fire dogs can be placed for the desired fire, and in this way large rooms are kept perfectly comfortable in cold weather without heat from any other source. These fire-places are also provided with neat mantels constructed of ash, and which are elegant compared with the marbelized slate mantel, which is a sham, and repulsive to an educated taste.

On entering nearly every house in the land we find the same turned walnut post at the bottom of the stairs with tapering walnut sticks all the way up, surmounted with a flattened walnut rail having a shepherd's crook at the top; however, in this instance it is not so, but the staircase is surmounted with an ash rail, balusters and newel of simple, though unique design; and now that people are giving more attention to this important piece of furniture, we may look for a change in this respect.

This house is supplied with a cistern constructed with great care, the Kitchen sink being supplied with water by a pump, and there is no more easy method of procuring good water for all purposes of the household.

For a compact, convenient Cottage with every facility for doing the work with the least number of steps, for a low-priced elegant Cottage, we do not know of anything that surpasses this. Cost, $1,200.

Mr. E. A. Jones of Newport, Ohio, is also erecting this Cottage with the necessary changes to suit points of compass. Such a house as this if tastefully furnished, and embellished with suitable surroundings, as neat and well-kept grounds, flowers, etc., will always attract more attention than the uninviting, ill-designed buildings, no matter how much money may have been expended on them.

It is not necessary that artistic feeling should have always a large field for its display; and in the lesser works and smaller commissions as much art may find expression as in the costly façades and more pretentious structures.

22. Floor Plan and Exterior View of Cottage for a Mill Hand, 1878.

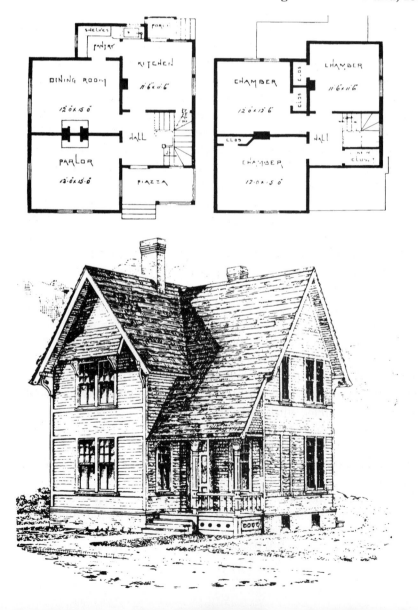

23. Residence of Rev. Dr. Marble, Newtown, Connecticut (cost $2,925), 1878.

This house commands a particularly fine view from both sides and the front, and is situated in one of the pleasantest country towns in New England, the hotels of this town being crowded during the summer months with people from the cities.

The exterior design is plain, yet picturesque, and at once gives one an idea of ease and comfort. The roofing over the Hall and Sitting-room is a particularly fine feature, and the elevation of the rear is very striking, the roof over the porch being a part of the main roof.

The interior arrangements are very nice, the Hall being very spacious, and in it we have a very easy and handsome stair-case of plain design, constructed of Georgia pine; the newel extends up to ceiling of first floor, while the other two posts extend up to ceiling of second floor. In all country houses one of the first things to be aimed at is to secure ample stair-cases, and until a man can afford space for an easy ascent to a second floor he should stay below; and to-day we find in houses, where there is no necessity for it, stairs that are little better than step-ladders, making a pretence of breadth at the bottom with swelled steps, and winding the steps on approaching the floor above, thus making a trap for the old and for the children.

The corner fire-place between Parlor and Dining-room is a feature we indulge in to a great extent in these days of economy, sliding doors and fire-places, although we sometimes have clients who object to this, thinking it would not look as well as when placed in center of side wall; but when they are asked how this and that can be provided for with the best and most economical results, they readily give in.

There is no water-closet [toilet] in the house, but an Earth-Closet is provided in the rear Hall, which is thoroughly ventilated.

The Dining-room is a very cheerful room and the Kitchen is reached through a passage also connecting with side veranda. The pantry is lighted with a window placed above press; each fire-place is furnished with a neat hard-wood mantel, and the Hall is finished in Georgia pine, the floor being laid with this material, and finished in natural color.

The exterior is painted as follows: Ground, light slate; trimmings, buff; and chamfers, black. Cost, $2,925.

The sight of this house in the locality in which it is built is very refreshing, and is greatly in advance of the old styles of rural box architecture to be found there. When people see beautiful things, they very naturally covet them, and they grow discontented in the possession of ugliness. Handsome houses, other things equal, are always the most valuable. They sell quickest and for the most money. Builders who feign a blindness to beauty must come to grief.

24. Floor Plan and Exterior View of a Clergyman's Residence, 1878.

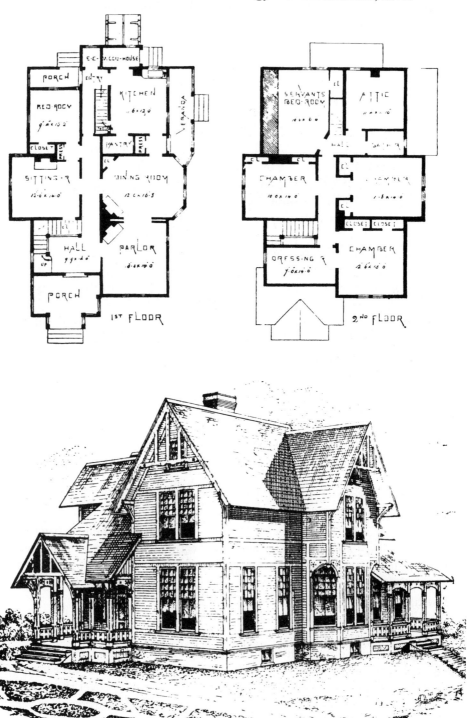

25. Exterior View and Floor Plan for a Suburban Middle-Class Home (cost $3,600), 1900.

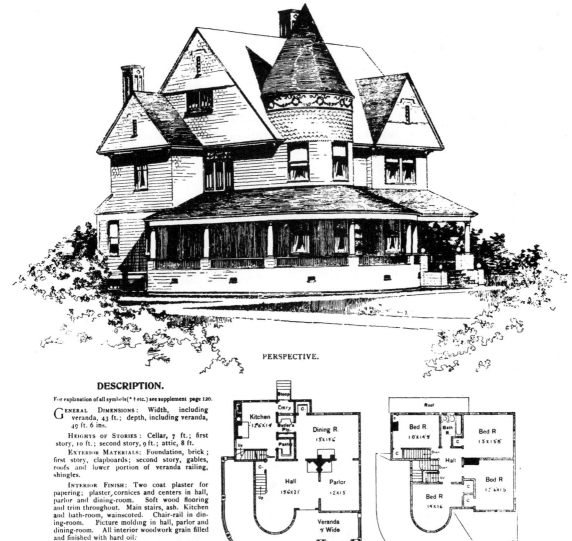

PERSPECTIVE.

DESCRIPTION.

For explanation of all symbols(* † etc.) see supplement page 120.

GENERAL DIMENSIONS: Width, including veranda, 43 ft.; depth, including veranda, 49 ft. 6 ins.

HEIGHTS OF STORIES: Cellar, 7 ft.; first story, 10 ft.; second story, 9 ft.; attic, 8 ft.

EXTERIOR MATERIALS: Foundation, brick; first story, clapboards; second story, gables, roofs and lower portion of veranda railing, shingles.

INTERIOR FINISH: Two coat plaster for papering; plaster cornices and centers in hall, parlor and dining-room. Soft wood flooring and trim throughout. Main stairs, ash. Kitchen and bath-room, wainscoted. Chair-rail in dining-room. Picture molding in hall, parlor and dining-room. All interior woodwork grain filled and finished with hard oil.

COLORS: All clapboards, first story, Colonial yellow. Trim, including water-table, corner boards, casings, cornices, bands, veranda posts and rails, outside doors, conductors, etc., ivory white. Veranda floor and ceiling, oiled. Shingles on side walls and gables stained dark yellow. Roof shingles, dark red.

ACCOMMODATIONS: The principal rooms, and their sizes, closets, etc., are shown by the floor plans. Cellar under whole house with inside and outside entrances and concrete floor. One room finished in attic, remainder of attic floored for storage. Double folding doors between parlor and hall and parlor and dining-room. Direct communication from hall with dining-room, parlor and kitchen. Bathroom, with complete plumbing, in second story. Open fire-places in dining-room, parlor and hall. Wide veranda. Bay-window in hall and bedroom over. Two stationary wash-tubs in cellar under kitchen.

COST: $3,600, including mantels, range and heater. The estimate is based on † New York prices for labor and materials.

Price of working plans, specifications, detail drawings, etc., $35.
Price of †† bill of materials, ... 10.

FEASIBLE MODIFICATIONS: General dimensions, materials and colors may be changed. Cellar may be decreased in size or wholly omitted. Sliding doors may be used in place of folding doors. Portable range may be used instead of brick-set range. Servants' water-closet could be introduced in cellar. Fireplaces may be reduced in number.

The price of working plans, specifications, etc., for a modified design, varies according to the alterations required and will be made known upon application to the Architects.

Address, CO-OPERATIVE BUILDING PLAN ASSOCIATION, Architects, 203 Broadway and 164–6–8 Fulton Street, New York, N. Y.

26. Excerpts on the New Business of Advertising, 1898–1927.

From "Photographs in Advertising," *Printers' Ink*, August 17, 1898, p. 18.

It may have been noticed that the trend of modern magazine advertising is toward the use of photographs. . . . An advertisement that contains the photograph of a beautiful woman is certain to be attractive, and consequently its success is largely guaranteed. . . . But there are a host of articles on the market that can be advertised to great advantage by the introduction of a lady into the picture, and many advertisers have already seen this. . . .

But though the photographs of pretty women are only supposed to be attractive to the male sex, the picture of a baby or "cute" child will immediately captivate ninety-nine per cent of humanity. . . . Whatever he or she is supposed to advertise, we feel kindly toward, even if it is only for introducing us to the baby.

From Earnest Elmo Calkins, *The Business of Advertising* (1915; reprint, New York: D. Appleton and Co., 1920), pp. 1, 9.

It is hard to find a satisfactory definition of advertising. A picturesque way of putting it is to call it business imagination, an imagination that sees in a product possibilities which can be realized only by appealing to the public in new ways to create a desire where none existed before. . . .

Advertising modifies the course of the people's daily thoughts, gives them new words, new phrases, new ideas, new fashions, new prejudices and new customs. In the same way it obliterates old sets of words and phrases, fashions and customs. It may be doubted if any other one force, the school, the church and the press excepted, has so great an influence as advertising. To it we largely owe the prevalence of good roads, rubber tires, open plumbing, sanitary underwear, water filters, hygienic waters, vacuum cleaners, automobiles, kitchen cabinets, pure foods. These are only a few of the things which the public has been taught by advertising to use, to believe in, and to demand.

From S. Roland Hall, *The Advertising Handbook: A Reference Work Covering the Principles and Practice of Advertising* (New York: McGraw-Hill, 1921), pp. 79–80, 101–103.

In other words, certain thoughts have become fixed in our minds in connection with certain other thoughts, and when we bring up one end of the connection the other is likely to follow. . . .

There is a motive, and a good one, in calling an automobile the "Lincoln," for that suggests sturdy, honest qualities.

No writer would undertake to make a real hero out of a character known as "Percy," for this name suggests "sissiness." . . .

Man is the stronger, as a rule. He is the bread-winner, to a large extent. His job is more in the outside world. He grows up to severer tasks, as a rule. He is more accustomed to rebuffs.

Though woman has progressed a long way in taking her place on an equal plane with that of man in business, politics and the professions, yet she is still to a large extent more sheltered than man. Her affairs are more within the home. Her sex makes her interest in clothes, home-furnishings, and the like keener than man's as a general thing. . . .

Because of her years of comparative non-acquaintance with mechanical matters, woman is generally less apt in understanding mechanical description and directions, and such advertisers must use greater care when appealing to women. . . .

On the other hand it is generally admitted that men are more democratic, more gregarious, than women—that women move more within their own circle or "clique."

A man is not likely to care if several other men in his circle have a hat exactly like his own. A woman would hardly care to buy a hat exactly like one worn by several other women in her town or community. A woman ordinarily will think nothing of shopping at several places to look at hats. A man is likely to visit only one shop.

From Claude C. Hopkins, *My Life in Advertising* (1927), reprinted as Claude C. Hopkins, *My Life in Advertising and Scientific Advertising* (Chicago: Advertising Publications, 1966), pp. 8–9, 119.

I am sure that I could not impress the rich, for I do not know them. I have never tried to sell what they buy. . . . But I do know the common people. I love to talk to laboring-men, to study housewives who must count their pennies, to gain the confidence and learn the ambitions of poor boys and girls. Give me something which they want and I will strike the responsive chord. My words will be simple, my sentences short. Scholars may ridicule my style. The rich and vain may laugh at the factors which I feature. But in millions of humble homes the common people will read and buy. They will feel that the writer knows them. And they, in advertising, form 95 per cent of our customers. . . .

People are like sheep. They cannot judge values, nor can you and I. We judge things largely by others' impressions, by popular favor. We go with the crowd. So the most effective thing I have ever found in advertising is the trend of the crowd.

◆

Questions to Consider

For convenience, the evidence is divided into three sections. Sources 1 through 18 are advertisements from popular magazines and the 1897 and 1902 Sears Roebuck & Company catalogues. The prices probably seem ridiculously low to you, but these items were reasonably priced and affordable—although not really cheap—for most middle-class Americans in cities and towns and on farms. Sources 19 through 25 all deal with houses and buying a house, including house plans readily available by mail and through pattern books. Again, the prices seem very low, but working-class homes could be built for less than $1,000 (excluding the cost of the land) and middle-class homes for as little as $2,000 during this period. Source 26 focuses on the business of advertising.

As you read each advertisement, you will find it helpful to jot down notes. First, try to determine the message of the ad. What is the advertiser trying to sell? What emotion(s) does the ad appeal to? What fears? What hopes? Then ask what the ad tells you about society during that time. Does it tell you anything about men's roles? about women's roles? about the relationships between men and women? Does it tell you anything about children or young people? about adults' concerns about young people? about elderly people? Finally, do you see any changes occurring during the time period—for exam-

ple, in the ads for the Gramophone and the Victrola (Source 13) or in the ads for automobiles (Sources 14 and 15)? If so, what do these changes tell you about the roles of men, women, and young people between the 1880s and 1917?

Source 19 contains two advertisements for houses. Source 20 is an advertisement for a magazine series giving advice on how to buy a home. What do they tell you about people's needs and wants with regard to housing? What advice is offered to young married people? What values are emphasized by these advertisements for housing? Sources 21 through 25 consist of house plans and descriptions from architectural pattern books from 1878 and 1900. Look carefully at the exterior features of these houses. How would you describe them to a student who had not seen the pictures? Next, look at the interior rooms and their comparative sizes. What use or uses would each room probably have had? What rooms did these houses have that our own modern houses do not have? Do modern houses have rooms that these houses lacked? What similarities do you find in all the houses, from the mill hand's cottage ($1,200) in Sources 21 and 22 to the suburban middle-class home ($3,600) in Source 25? What differences are there? Finally, what kinds of things seemed to be important to the owners of these houses? What kind of impression did they wish to make on other people?

The excerpts in Source 26 are drawn from an advertising journal, two textbooks, and the autobiography of a famous advertising pioneer. *Printers' Ink* was a weekly journal of advertising founded in the second half of the nineteenth century. What kinds of photographs does the author recommend using? Why? What is the relationship between the photographs and the item being sold? Earnest Calkins first published a book on "modern" advertising in 1895, which he later rewrote as a textbook, *The Business of Advertising*. How does he define advertising? In what ways does he believe that advertising affects people?

S. Roland Hall had worked in advertising and later taught both salesmanship and advertising. Why does he believe that the names of products are important? What does he think are the major differences between men and women? How might these differences affect people who wrote advertisements? Finally, Claude Hopkins was a self-made man who became one of the highest-paid advertising copywriters of the late nineteenth and early twentieth centuries, at one time earning over $100,000 a year. In this excerpt from his autobiography, he explains the basic elements in his approach to advertising. To what factors does he attribute his success?

To conclude, consider what you have learned from the evidence as a whole. Can you describe how white middle-class Americans lived during this period? How the new business of advertising promoted material goods and houses? What these advertisements reveal about white middle-class values, hopes, and fears during this era of rapid change?

Epilogue

Of course, not all Americans could live like the middle-class families you just studied. The poor and the immigrants who lived in the cities were crowded into windowless, airless tenement buildings that often covered an entire block. Poor rural black and white sharecroppers in the South lived in one- or two-room shacks, and many farmers in the western plains and prairies could afford to build only sod houses. During the Great Depression of the 1930s, many people, including middle-class families, lost their homes entirely through foreclosure, and the 1960s and 1970s saw the price of houses increase so rapidly that many families were priced out of the housing market. Even today, the problem of the homeless has not been solved.

The early twentieth century saw the captains of industry come under attack for what many came to believe were excesses. Evidence of their disdain for and defiance of the public good, as well as of their treatment of workers, their political influence, and their ruthless business practices, came more and more to light due to the efforts of reformers and muckraking journalists. The society that once had venerated the industrial barons began to worry that they had too much power and came to believe that such power should be restricted.

Architecture also was undergoing a rapid transformation. Neoclassical, Georgian, colonial, and bungalow styles signaled a shift toward less ostentation and increased moderation in private dwellings. Perhaps the most striking work was done by Chicago architect Frank Lloyd Wright, who sought to give functional and social meaning to his designs and to make each structure blend into its unique landscape. According to Wright's concepts, there was no standard design for the "perfect house." Wright's ideas formed the basis for a series of movements that ultimately changed the perspective and direction of American architecture.

Progressive muckrakers also criticized advertising, particularly the claims of patent medicine advertisements. Such salesmanship, however, was described as "the brightest hope of America" by the 1920s. Bruce Barton, a talented salesman and founder of a huge advertising agency, even discovered "advertisements" in the Bible, which he described as the first "best seller." Although its image was slightly tarnished by the disillusionment accompanying the Great Depression, advertising helped "sell" World War II to the American public by encouraging conservation of scarce resources, and it emerged stronger and more persuasive than ever in the 1950s. Americans were starved for consumer goods after wartime rationing, and their rapid acceptance of a new entertainment medium—television—greatly expanded advertising opportunities.

But advertising still had (and has) its critics. Writing in 1954, historian David Potter, in *People of Plenty,* characterized advertising as the basic "institution of abundance." Advertising, he maintained, had become as powerful as religion or education had been in earlier eras. Advertising, he said, now actually *created* the standards and values of our society. Because advertising lacked social goals or social responsibility, however, he believed that its power was dangerous. We must not forget, Potter warned, "that it ultimately regards man as a consumer and defines its own mission as one of stimulating him to consume."

Progressives and the Family: The Redefinition of Childhood, 1880–1920

◆

The Problem

In 1890, former New York City police reporter and photographer, Jacob Riis, published *How the Other Half Lives.* The book was enormously popular among middle-class readers and generally received very favorable reviews. Combining stories, commentary, and pictures, Riis took his readers into slum neighborhoods, tenement blocks, cheap lodging houses and saloons, and dangerous alleyways. With interior and evening photographs using the new "flashlight powder," Riis both illuminated the lives of the urban poor and inspired middle-class reformers in their efforts to improve—as they saw it—the slums and their inhabitants.

As a young Danish immigrant, Riis himself had been poor and homeless. After drifting into a series of jobs as a laborer and salesman, he became a reporter, an editor, and, eventually, the owner of a newspaper. After he married, he sold his newspaper and returned to journalism as a police reporter. An early supporter of tenement-house reform, Riis was gradually drawn into other Progressive-era activities, eventually becoming a full time reformer.

For more than thirty years he wrote books and articles, lectured, gave magic lantern slide shows of his photographs, and took politicians and celebrities such as Theodore Roosevelt on tours of the slum neighborhoods. Jacob Riis was especially sympathetic toward the plight of poor, urban children. Using both posed and candid photos, he showed children in their homes, at their jobs, and on the streets. In his book *Children of the Tenements* (1903), Riis included stories of impoverished Christmas celebrations, drunken parents, hunger, harsh punishments, and the deaths of babies and small children from illness and accidents.

Riis's work encouraged the many middle-class white women who were reformers and members of social improvement clubs, and whose activities already focused on issues related to the well-being of women and their families. To these women, the conditions under which the children of the urban poor lived and worked were shocking and appalling. Their own middle-class children lived far more sheltered and protected lives, and middle-class women believed that this was, or should be, the

◆ CHAPTER 4

Progressives and
the Family:
The Redefinition
of Childhood,
1880–1920

"normal" situation for all children. As a result, ideas about children and childhood were gradually redefined through reform efforts aimed at dramatically changing children's lives.

In this problem, you will be studying some of these reform efforts, to understand exactly *how* and *why* children's lives were changing during the Progressive era. You will also be identifying the new Progressive-era ideas about the nature of "normal" childhood.

◆

Background

Progressivism has sometimes been described as a spirit of reform that swept through the United States in the late nineteenth and early twentieth centuries. Usually associated with the presidencies of Theodore Roosevelt and Woodrow Wilson, progressivism probably began gradually in the 1880s, peaked in the period between 1900 and 1914, and declined gradually throughout the 1920s. Both political parties contained progressives, although both parties also contained those who believed in a kind of popularized social Darwinism. Such political and social conservatives thought that the "fittest" people would survive and reformers should not interfere with the natural course of things. Progressive reformers, on the other hand, were optimists who believed that although the United States was basically a sound country, it could be even better if certain economic, political, and social problems were solved.

Who were the progressives and what did they believe? Historians have shown that Progressive reformers were generally from Anglo-Saxon, Protestant backgrounds—people who had been born in small towns but often lived their adult lives in cities. They had faith in the ability of individuals, especially when acting through organizations, to bring about change. But first, the public had to be educated about the problems in American life. Experts such as social scientists, social workers, and specialists would collect information and data, and then circulate it to the general public in a form that could be easily understood by all. Public opinion, once made aware of the situation, would naturally support whatever actions, laws, or even constitutional amendments were necessary to solve the problem.

The Progressive agenda was very broad and included a variety of reforms: women's suffrage; pure food and drugs; tenement-housing reform; educational curriculum changes; the referendum, initiative, and recall; a graduated income tax; efficiency in government and in the workplace; lower tariffs; better wages and working conditions; the Americanization of immigrants; and some limited regulation of large corporations. The National Association of Colored Women and the National Association for the Advancement of Colored People (NAACP) were both Progressive organizations that worked to improve conditions for African Americans.

Although white, middle-class women were active in the whole gamut of Progressive reforms, many of these women, and some Progressive men, were especially interested in issues concerning the vulnerable, poverty-stricken women and children who lived in the urban slums described by Jacob Riis and others. Social settlement houses, like Jane Addams's Hull House in Chicago or Lillian Wald's Henry Street Settlement in New York, were located in poor, immigrant neighborhoods and served as residences for the social workers. Public-health nurses and field investigators usually called directly on their immigrant neighbors, visiting them in their homes to give advice and guidance to mothers about their children.

In the colonial period in America, once children became toddlers they were considered as miniature adults-in-the-making. In other words, childhood was not a separate, prolonged period with special characteristics of its own, but rather a period in which children gradually took on the chores and responsibilities of adults. Children entered the work force in stages, and it was not unusual for a six- or seven-year-old child to be hired out or apprenticed to a relative or neighbor to learn a trade or, if female, to further develop necessary domestic skills. Asa Sheldon of Massachusetts began to hire himself out for jobs at age seven; at age nine he was apprenticed by his father as a manservant. Another New England boy, Moses Pierce, went into a textile mill in 1819 at age eleven; at age

fourteen he was working in various factory stores. As historian Joseph Kett has noted, throughout the early years of the nineteenth century, "youths" (ages ten to twenty-one) were in a state of "semidependence," with poor children leaving home earlier and more often than more well-to-do children.[1] However, socioeconomic class differences were not as great as they would become in the latter part of the nineteenth century.

Urbanization, becoming noticeable in the pre–Civil War era and increasing rapidly and dramatically in the postwar period, highlighted the plight of poor children. At first, orphans were included with adults in the almshouses, or poorhouses; only later were special institutions—orphanages—set aside for children. It has been estimated that in the late nineteenth century, only about 20 percent of the children in such institutions were really orphans; the rest had one or two living parents who were unable to care for them because of extreme poverty, alcoholism, illness, or having too many other children. "We wuz six . . . and we ain't got no father. Some of us had to go," a twelve-year-old boy who shined shoes for a living told Jacob Riis.[2] The boy, along with other younger boys, paid a total of eighteen cents a day for his bed and two meals at the Newsboys' Lodging House in New York City. These boys were among the more fortunate; many other children slept out-

1. Joseph F. Kett, *Rites of Passage: Adolescence in America, 1790 to the Present* (New York: Basic Books, 1977), pp. 21, 25, 29–31.
2. Jacob Riis, *How the Other Half Lives,* edited and with an introduction by David Leviatin (Boston: Bedford Books, 1996), 191.

◆ CHAPTER 4

Progressives and
the Family:
The Redefinition
of Childhood,
1880–1920

side in doorways, boxes, wheelbarrows, or on street grates.

In a campaign to "save" apparently homeless or abandoned children during the late nineteenth and early twentieth centuries, Charles Loring Brace and the Children's Aid Society of New York City rounded up more than 200,000 children and put them on "orphan trains" to the nearby countryside or to the West and the South. During the early twentieth century, the Society relocated as many as 2,000 children each year, prosecuted both parents and employers for physically abusing children, and helped finance foundling hospitals for abandoned infants. Unfortunately, the foundling hospitals had very high death rates.

Some of the relocated children did have better lives in the rural areas, especially if they were younger. However, many others were exploited by farm families and ran away as soon as they could. Relatively few children were legally adopted. In this period, adoption procedures varied greatly from state to state, and private adoptions, involving an exchange of money, were still common. The concept of foster care had just been introduced and was too new and unorganized to provide a real alternative for homeless children.

Another late-nineteenth-century campaign to "save the babies" involved providing pure milk and vital information on infant nutrition to poor families. Malnutrition and diarrhea caused by poor diets killed large numbers of infants and toddlers. Children in the countryside drank raw milk containing dangerous bacteria, but they were actually better off than city children. Milk sent to the cities was often wa-

tered down, spoiled from not being kept cool, and then adulterated with sweeteners to cover the bad taste. In 1900, over 90 percent of American women gave birth at home; only half of them had a doctor available and the rest depended on midwives or neighbors. The maternal death rate between 1900 and 1920 was thirty times higher than it is now, primarily from post-childbirth infections. Poor women who survived childbirth frequently could not nurse their babies or could provide only partial nourishment for them, and had to supplement with cows' milk. Poor women fed their babies the same table food—mashed up or chewed up—that the adults in the family ate. Women with large families or who worked depended on their female children, whom the reformers called "little mothers," to care for infants. One in six children died before reaching five years old.

In 1912, after years of effort, the Progressives were able to persuade the federal government to establish a Children's Bureau. Headed first by Julia Lathrop and then by Grace Abbot, both talented women with extensive reform backgrounds, the Bureau tried to educate mothers by providing free pamphlets such as *Infant Care*. Instrumental in establishing better standards for birth and death registration of children, the Bureau collected the first reliable statistics on the reasons for infant mortality. Small and underfunded, the Children's Bureau depended upon huge numbers of women volunteers from such organizations as those included in the General Federation of Women's Clubs to interview mothers and collect information to be analyzed later by the Bureau's small staff.

Progressive reformers saw a direct connection between the increase in child labor and the declining opportunities for poor children to obtain an education. Although by 1918 all states had compulsory school attendance laws, they were often ignored or inadequate. In North Carolina, for example, children between the ages of eight and thirteen had to attend school at least four months each year. The Children's Bureau advocated school laws that raised the age of compulsory attendance and encouraged the movement to provide playgrounds and parks for urban children. Although it was very controversial, the Bureau also worked actively with the National Child Labor Committee and other organizations to abolish or regulate the work of children. Concentrating on the dangerous jobs that children performed in the canning industry, coal mines, and textile mills, Progressive reformers also focused on children who worked with their mothers doing piece work in their tenement homes and those who worked in the street trades, such as newsboys, bootblacks, messenger boys, and peddlers.

All of these reforms were intended to change the lives of urban poor children in the late nineteenth and early twentieth centuries. Although there was some concern with industrial child labor in the South, Progressives tended to idealize life on family farms where, in fact, children often did heavy physical work for long hours and had limited opportunities for education or recreation. Additionally, white Progressive reformers were not free from the prejudices of their times; most of them did little or nothing to ameliorate the conditions of Native American or African American children, urban or rural. There was also a tendency for Progressives to underestimate the impact of poverty on the choices available to immigrant and working families, and to assume that middle-class standards and ideals should be the norm. In spite of their limitations, however, the Progressives were in many ways beginning to redefine the nature of childhood.

The Method

It is important to remember that the meanings of words and concepts are not absolute and fixed, but rather are dynamic and changeable. Thus, a word such as "equality" may be defined very differently at various times in our history. Certainly, Americans in the seventeenth and eighteenth centuries would not have believed that all people were literally "equal." Men and women were not always equal, white Americans and African Americans were not always equal, and men who did not own property were not always equal to those who did. In the twenty-first century, however, we like to think that everyone is equal, or at least should have equal *opportunity*. Conceptions

✦ CHAPTER 4

Progressives and
the Family:
The Redefinition
of Childhood,
1880–1920

also change their meanings in different time periods or even in different regions of the country. The concept of Southern "honor" might be a good example of a regional understanding, whereas the concept of what it means to be "manly" or "womanly" not only changes over time but is also subject to regional variations, such as what it means to be "feminine" on the frontier.

The concept of childhood has also changed during our history, slowly perhaps, but significantly. We find it hard to believe that colonial Americans treated children as miniature adults who could, and should, begin independent work and responsibilities at about age seven. Today, Americans refer to unmarried college students and di-vorced people who move back in with their parents as "adult children," a phrase that would mystify Americans of a hundred years ago. The key to examining the changing concept of childhood is to realize that attitudes toward and ideas about children are *socially constructed*—that is, they are formed by certain aspects of our society at a particular point in history. One of the crucial changes in our understanding of what it means to be a child is clearly located in the Progressive era, between 1880 and 1920, and this is where your focus will be in this chapter. *How* and *why* did attitudes toward children change? *What* was the emerging Progressive concept of childhood?

The Evidence

VISUAL EVIDENCE

Source 1 from Bary Cross, *The Cute and the Cool: Wondrous Innocence and Modern American Children's Culture* (New York: Oxford University Press, 2004), p. 55. Photo: Allison-Shelley Collection, Special Collections, Pattee Library, Pennsylvania State University.

1. Teddy Bear Storybook.

◆ CHAPTER 4

Progressives and
the Family:
The Redefinition
of Childhood,
1880–1920

Source 2 from Robert H. Bremner, ed., *Children and Youth in America: A Documentary History* (Cambridge; Harvard University Press, 1971), Vol. II, 1866–1932, Parts 1–6, ff. p. 14. Photo: New-York Historical Society, New York City.

2. Middle-Class Girls Playing with Dolls.

Source 3 from David I. Macleod, *The Age of the Child: Children in America, 1890–1920* (New York: Twayne Publishers, 1998), p. 68. Photo: Library of Congress.

3. Young Boy with His Toys.

✦ CHAPTER 4

Progressives and
the Family:
The Redefinition
of Childhood,
1880–1920

Source 4 photograph by Lewis W. Hine. Photo: © CORBIS.

4. Three Newsboys.

Source 5 from Elliot West, *Growing Up in Twentieth Century America: A History and Reference Guide* (Westport, Conn.: Greenwood Press, 1996), p. 50. Photo: Library of Congress.

5. Slum Children Playing in the Street.

Source 6 photograph by Lewis W. Hine, from Bremner, ed., *Children and Youth in America*, ff. p. 686. Photo: Art Institute of Chicago.

6. Boys Working at a Coal Mine.

Source 7 photograph by Lewis W. Hine, from West, *Growing Up in Twentieth Century America*, p. 14. Photo: George Eastman House.

7. Young Girl in an Orphanage.

✦ CHAPTER 4

Progressives and
the Family:
The Redefinition
of Childhood,
1880–1920

Source 8 from Jacob A. Riis, *How the Other Half Lives*, David Leviatin, ed. (Boston: Bedford/St. Martin's, 1996), p. 94. Photo: Library of Congress.

8. A Poor Italian Mother and Her Baby.

Source 9 from Winfield Scott Hall, M.D., and Jeannette Winter Hall, *Counsel to Parents* (Chicago: Howard-Severance Company, 1913, 1917), ff. p. 114.

9. A Middle-Class Couple and Their Baby.

◆ CHAPTER 4

Progressives and
the Family:
The Redefinition
of Childhood,
1880–1920

Source 10: Photo from CORBIS; poster from Richard A. Meckel, *Save the Babies:
American Public Health Reform and the Prevention of Infant Mortality, 1850–1929*
(Baltimore: Johns Hopkins Press, 1990), ff. p. 158.

10. A Pure Milk Station (Cincinnati, c. 1908) and Poster (Chicago).

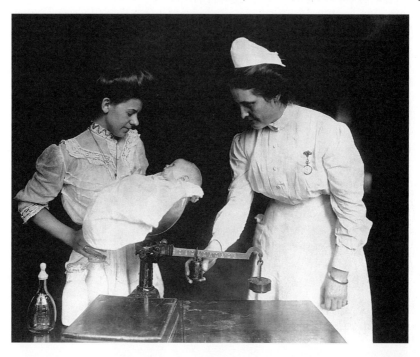

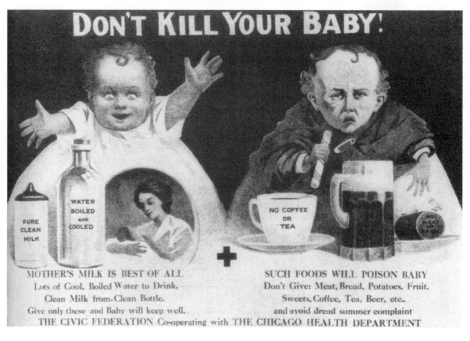

INFORMATION GATHERING

Source 11 from John Spargo, *The Bitter Cry of the Children* (New York: Johnson Reprint Corporation, 1969 [original published 1906]), p. 93.

11. School Children's Meals.

Family	No. of School Children	Breakfast	Lunch	Supper
1	2	Bread and tea only.	None.	Bread and tea.
2	1	None.	Soup from charity.	Coffee and bread.
3	1	Coffee and rolls (no butter or jam).	Coffee and bread.	Tea and bread.
4	3	Bread and tea only.	None.	Bread and tea only.
5	2	None.	Soup with the soup-meat.	Piece of bread.
6	1	Bread and jam with coffee.	None.	Tea and bread with jam.

Source 12 from Massachusetts Society for the Prevention of Cruelty to Children, *Twenty-First Annual Report* (Boston, 1901), pp. 23–25. Found in Bremner, ed., *Children and Youth in America*, pp. 211–212.

12. Child Neglect Cases.

23705. Parents and six children, ages from one year to twelve. Both parents drink badly. A girl of four was suffering from an injured knee, and could not leave her bed. The city physician was notified, but was refused admittance by the parents, who were drinking at the time. Our agent visited, and removed the injured child at once to the hospital. The baby, which appeared in a dying condition, was taken by an aunt to her home, also two of the other children. . . .

13321. A mother and four children. The youngest, a babe of five months, was found very emaciated and apparently dying from starvation. The mother had offered to give the child to any one who would take it. Its body was completely raw from neglect. A boy of three was nearly naked. . . .

15278. The father worked steadily, and yet the house was as desolate as it was possible for a house to be. Filth reigned everywhere. There was but one bed for the entire family. . . . Neighbors testified that the children were in the habit of eating from their swill barrels. Children were in a terrible condition,—with heads sore from vermin, and with little clothing. A warrant was

◆ CHAPTER 4

Progressives and
the Family:
The Redefinition
of Childhood,
1880–1920

secured, and the children promptly removed. The family bed was black with dirt, the floors looked as though water had never touched them; and the breakfast table dirty, and with no food, was a sad sight. . . .

20735.   Father earning $3 per day, and with his wife and four children living in the utmost condition of filth. But one bed, the children burrowing in a pile of feathers on the floor. They were so foul that, when they went to school, the teacher had to burn sticks to fumigate the room. A complaint of neglect was made.

ADVICE

Source 13 from Molly Ladd-Taylor, *Raising a Baby the Government Way: Mothers' Letters to the Children's Bureau, 1915–1932* (New Brunswick, N.J.: Rutgers University Press, 1986), pp. 49, 52, 53, 116–117, 128, 133–134, 135.

13. Letters to the Children's Bureau.

Mrs. A.P., Wyoming (October 19, 1916)

Dear Miss Lathrop,

. . . I live sixty five miles from a Dr. and my other babies (two) were very large at birth, one 12-lbs the other 10½ lbs. I have been *very* badly torn each time, through the rectum the last time. My youngest child is 7½ (and when I am delivered this time it will be past 8½ yrs). I am 37 years old and I am so worried and filled with perfect horror at the prospects ahead. So many of my neighbors die at giving birth to their children. I have a baby 11 months old in my keeping now whose mother died—when I reached their cabin last Nov., it was 22 below zero and I had to ride 7 miles horse back. She was nearly dead when I got there and died after giving birth to a 14 lb. boy. It seems awfull to me to think of giving up all my work and leaving my little ones. . . .

Will you please send me all the information for the care of my self before and after and at the time of delivery.

Mrs. H.R., Georgia (June 14, 1920)

Dear Madame

I need advise. I am a farmers wife, do my household duties and a regular field hand too. The mother of 9 children and in family way again. I am quar[re]lsome when tired & fatigued. . . .

What shall I do? My Husband wont sympathise with me one bit but talks rough to me. . . . Does it make a Mother unvirtuous for a man physician to wait on her during confinement? Is it Safe for me to go through it Without aid from any one? Please give me Some advise. There isent any mid wives near us now. I am not friendless but going to you for advise too keep down gossip. Yours.

Mrs. C.T., Tennessee (June 29, 1921)

I am a farmers wife only thirty three years of age, the mother of seven children. This is the eighth pregnancy, and I am in real bad health and am quite unable to have proper medicine, diet or clothing.

My husband does not see any necessity of any extra care of my health now, and says it is only foolishness. So I am quite at a loss to know what to do. [I] have been in bed most of the time for 6 or 7 weeks without much care, as it takes quite all my little girl's (who is fifteen years old) time to do the housework and care for the smaller little one. Please send me any reading matter that might help me as I like to read. Your friend.

Mrs. W.D., Brooklyn, New York (September 10, 1917)

My Dear Mrs. M. West.

A year ago last Mar. I gave birth to a beautiful fat boy and it lived but 3 days. The Drs. claimed the baby had a leaking heart; he died in convulsions. I would like to know if the injection the *woman* gave him of soap & water threw him in these convulsions as he just moaned like a pigeon & his whole body shook after that & at night he was dead. This was the first time I became pregnant in 4 yrs and you can imagine how glad & happy I was, only instead of having him at my breast, the third day they brought him to the door in his little casket. My heart was broke. I wish that I too was taken, as I suffer terrible with my head during the 9 mths and then I am always in labor from 10 to 12 hrs at a stretch before I can bear my babies. It was only 3 mts again until I was to become a mother again, so I had another babe the next Feb., this making 2 in 1 yrs. I raised him until he was 1 yr and 11 days. He was an angel, never cried, to[o] good I guess to be left on earth. I washed and put his night drawers on and put him to bed well & healthy. He played about the floor that night, laughing and as happy as could be. I nursed him at 3 o'clock in the morning and I awoke at 7 am and found him dead along side of me. You can think how I feel. I cry night and day for my big fat baby, [taken] from me like that.

I try and live a good honest life and my home is my heaven and babies are my idols. I love them but I am afraid something will happen to this one again. I am stout and as a rule healthy. I can't understand why my babies should

◆ CHAPTER 4

Progressives and
the Family:
The Redefinition
of Childhood,
1880–1920

have weak hearts; that is why I am asking for your books. Maybe I can be spared that terrible long labor and my babies will be spared.

Mrs. M.T., Texas (June 23, 1916):

I have had nine children, but there is much in these booklets I never heard, no, nor even thought of. I have one little girl nearly 10, but I do not know how or what to teach her hardly: in fact, I have so much to do, I have no time to teach, only to scramble through some way. If you have booklets which will be helpful to me, I would thank you to tell me of them or just send them. My mother taught *me nothing.* I am *still* paying the penalty of ignorance. Thanking you again, I am yours sincerely.

Mrs. M.R., Idaho (January 4, 1916)

Dear Madame.

I would like to know if your people can give me a answer on this. What I am to do I dont know. I am living 25 miles away from any Doctor. We have 4 small children, my Husband is only making 1.35 a day, and every thing is so high it takes all he makes to keep our babys in cloth[e]s and food, as we have ev[e]ry thing we put in our mouths to buy. I am looking for the stork about the 19 of aprial. . . . How am I going to get 35 dollar to have a doctor, for he will not come for less and not unless we have the cash. Talk about better babys, when a mother must be like some cow or mare when a babys come. If she lives, all wright, and if not, Just the same.

So please answer me if you can. You may send me a copie of Bulletin and if I live [through] it, then I will try to [follow] it as close as I can.
Yours truly, answe[r] at [once].

Mrs. W.S., Brooklyn, New York (January 30, 1918)

Dear Madam,

I read this mornings article in the New York American about the campaign to save babies. I fear my baby will be born too soon to have such wonderful help as you propose. My babies come fast and where I am going to meet the Doctors bills I cannot see. I have a daughter one year old this Jan. . . . I can and would gladly do sewing to earn some money but can find no work like that in these times. Can you show me a way out or a way I can help my self? I expect my baby the first of March. I hope I have not done anything wrong in writing to you like this. I am very respectfully.

Source 14 from Hall and Winter Hall, *Counsel to Parents,* pp. 61, 63, 65–66, 106, 238.

14. Advice to Middle-Class Parents.

The problem of securing pure air for the baby to breathe and at the same time having this air sufficiently warm for a very young child, and of securing free access of the air to the room in which the child is kept without causing draughts, is really a very delicate and serious problem of domestic hygiene. . . .

Quiet should pervade the household where a very young child is. . . .

If the mother is nursing her child at the breast, it goes without saying that her own health is a matter of the greatest importance for the well-being of her child. Not only should the nursing mother be in as nearly perfect health, and should maintain as nearly a perfect state of nutrition, as is possible, but it is a matter of no small importance that the mother maintains a happy frame of mind. . . .

At this place we need only call attention to the general importance of cleanliness as a matter of household hygiene, and emphasize the fact that the infant is especially sensitive to uncleanliness. Not only its person and its food, but also its clothing and bedding, and everything that comes in any way in contact with the child, should be kept spotlessly clean. . . .

Not infrequently conditions are such that the caretaker of the child or children is subject to frequent calls during the night. In such cases there must be provision for turning on the light with as little loss of time and energy as possible. The most convenient and at the same time the most hygienic night light is the electric lamp. A push button may be located where the mother or nurse may reach it without getting up, or an extension lamp may be placed on a stand where it may be easily turned on, or a special electric night lamp may be installed. . . .

[*Dr. Hall, like many Progressives, also advocated sex education by parents—mothers explaining to their daughters and fathers to their sons. Here he gives an example of what to tell preadolescent girls who ask questions about human reproduction.*]

"Well, daughter, it isn't a very long story; it's a very short little story, but Mamma thinks it's a very sweet and beautiful story. Edward and Philip were getting to be pretty big boys. Philip was six and Edward was four and Mamma didn't have any little daughter. She kept wishing, wishing, that God would send her a little daughter. Then after a while Mamma knew that a little new baby was going to come to her. You see, Miriam, every little baby grows within its Mamma's body, and for nearly a year it has to grow slowly from a tiny little

◆ CHAPTER 4

Progressives and
the Family:
The Redefinition
of Childhood,
1880–1920

speck, getting larger and larger until it is ready to be born. Then it leaves the
Mamma's body."

"In what part of the Mamma's body does it grow?" asks Miriam.

"Why, there's a little sort of nest in the Mamma's body and the baby grows
from a little egg that comes into this nest. This little nest lies deep down in
Mamma's body below her heart."

"And what is the little baby made of?" Miriam asks again, wonderingly.

And the mother replies, "Baby was made out of very precious material that
is drawn out of Mamma's blood. So you see, little daughter, why it is that the
mother loves her baby so, because she has given her own life blood for it."

"And is that where you got me, too?"

"Yes, daughter. . . . Do you wonder, now that you know this story, that every
Mamma loves her baby more than she loves her own life?"

LEGISLATION AND THE COURTS

Source 15 from Ch. 432, U.S. Statutes at Large, XXXIX, Part I, pp. 675–676. Found in
Bremner, ed., *Children and Youth in America*, pp. 703–704.

15. Keating Owen Act.

*Be it enacted by the Senate and House of Representatives of the United States
of America in Congress assembled,* That no producer, manufacturer, or dealer
shall ship or deliver for shipment in interstate or foreign commerce any article or commodity the product of any mine or quarry, situated in the United
States, in which within thirty days prior to the time of the removal of such
product therefrom children under the age of sixteen years have been employed or permitted to work, or any article or commodity the product of any
mill, cannery, workshop, factory, or manufacturing establishment, situated
in the United States, in which within thirty days prior to the removal of such
product therefrom children under the age of fourteen years have been employed or permitted to work, or children between the ages of fourteen years
and sixteen years have been employed or permitted to work more than eight
hours in any day, or more than six days in any week, or after the hour of
seven o'clock postmeridian, or before the hour of six o'clock antemeridian. . . .

SEC. 3. That for the purpose of securing proper enforcement of this Act the
Secretary of Labor, or any person duly authorized by him, shall have authority to enter and inspect at any time mines, quarries, mills, canneries, workshops, factories, manufacturing establishments, and other places in which
goods are produced or held for interstate commerce; and the Secretary of La-

bor shall have authority to employ such assistance for the purposes of this Act as may from time to time be authorized by appropriation or other law.

Source 16 from 247 U.S. 251, 268–281. Found in Bremner, ed., *Children and Youth in America*, pp. 712–714.

16. *Hammer v. Dagenhart.*

Opinion of the Court, delivered by MR. JUSTICE DAY, as follows:

A bill was filed in the United States District Court for the Western District of North Carolina by a father in his own behalf and as next friend of his two minor sons, one under the age of fourteen years and the other between the ages of fourteen and sixteen years, employees in a cotton mill at Charlotte, North Carolina, to enjoin the enforcement of the act of Congress intended to prevent interstate commerce in the products of child labor. . . .

The District Court held the act unconstitutional and entered a decree enjoining its enforcement. This appeal brings the case here.

The controlling question for decision is: Is it within the authority of Congress in regulating commerce among the States to prohibit the transportation in interstate commerce of manufactured goods, the product of a factory in which, within thirty days prior to their removal therefrom, children under the age of fourteen have been employed or permitted to work, or children between the ages of fourteen and sixteen years have been employed or permitted to work more than eight hours in any day, or more than six days in any week, or after the hour of seven o'clock P.M. or before the hour of six o'clock A.M.? . . .

In interpreting the Constitution it must never be forgotten that the Nation is made up of States to which are entrusted the powers of local government. And to them and to the people and the powers not expressly delegated to the National Government are reserved. . . .

To sustain this statute would not be in our judgment a recognition of the lawful exertion of congressional authority over interstate commerce, but would sanction an invasion by the federal power of the control of a matter purely local in its character, and over which no authority has been delegated to Congress in conferring the power to regulate commerce among the States. . . .

. . . if Congress can thus regulate matters entrusted to local authority by prohibition of the movement of commodities in interstate commerce, all free-

◆ CHAPTER 4

Progressives and
the Family:
The Redefinition
of Childhood,
1880–1920

dom of commerce will be at an end, and the power of the States over local matters may be eliminated, and thus our system of government be practically
destroyed.

For those reasons we hold that this law exceeds the constitutional authority
of Congress.

◆

Questions to Consider

The evidence in this problem is
grouped into four sections, each representing a common approach that Progressives used in nearly all their reform efforts. *Visual* displays were
perhaps the most important to the era,
often taking the form of photographs illustrating written material, posters,
cartoons, and magic lantern shows. In
Sources 1 through 3, you have examples showing middle-class children and
their playthings. How would you describe these children and their toys?
Sources 4 through 7 are images of poor
children from the same time period.
Compare their appearance and activities with those of the middle-class children. In Sources 8 and 9, note the differences between the images of the two
mothers and their babies. The final
piece of visual evidence (Source 10)
consists of a photograph of nurses at a
pure milk station and a poster promoting pure milk. What messages do they
each convey?

Sources 11 and 12 represent some of
the *information gathering* activities of
the reformers. What does Source 11 tell
you about the nutrition of poor school-
children? Source 12 is based on investi-
gations of the Massachusetts Society
for the Prevention of Cruelty to
Children. In what ways did parents neglect their children? Can you see any
evidence of middle-class bias in the reports of these field agents?

Advice or prescriptive literature was
also important to the reformers' efforts
to change the attitudes and behaviors
of the middle class as well as the poor.
During the Progressive era, the
Children's Bureau received thousands
of letters from women asking for advice
about pregnancy and childrearing.
Each letter was answered personally by
Mrs. West, the author of *Infant Care;*
female doctors who worked for the bureau; or by the director, Julia Lathrop,
herself. What kinds of concerns did
these letter writers express to the Bureau? Winfield Scott Hall was a doctor
whose medical and general advice was
aimed solely at middle-class parents.
What did he advise them about nursing
and sex education? Why wouldn't this
advice help the urban poor?

Finally, the Progressives usually
turned to *legislation and the courts,*
sometimes on the state level but more
often on the federal level, to provide
remedies for the problems they had
identified. Laws and court decisions
dealing with children proliferated during this period; those presented in this
section are just a small sampling.
Source 15 is an excerpt from an important piece of Progressive federal legislation, the Keating Owen Act of 1916.

What was the intent of this law? Source 16 is taken from the U.S. Supreme Court decision that declared the act unconstitutional. Why did the Court strike it down?

Look back through the evidence and summarize the specific changes that Progressives tried to make through the dissemination of information, advice, and laws. Review the visual evidence to help you compare the lives of middle-class and poor children. How did the Progressive reformers redefine the meaning of childhood?

Epilogue

Many of the Progressive reforms were partially or totally achieved during the period from 1880 to 1920, and other reforms were implemented during the New Deal of the 1930s. For example, the Sixteenth, Seventeenth, Eighteenth, and Nineteenth amendments to the Constitution instituted a national income tax, provided for the direct election of senators, gave women the vote, and established national prohibition of alcoholic beverages. Although the Keating Owen Act was declared unconstitutional by the Supreme Court, child labor in manufacturing and mining declined significantly during the twenties. Influenced by public reaction to the Progressive efforts to document the harmful effects on child workers, states raised the age of compulsory school attendance and prohibited child labor in the most dangerous industries. In the South, however, less progress was made, and throughout the nation there were still "invisible" child workers in door-to-door sales, home production, domestic service, and farm and migrant agriculture. It was not until the New Deal of the 1930s that federal legislation prohibiting most child labor was enacted.

In 1921, Progressives were successful in their efforts to get federal government help for poor mothers and babies. The Sheppard Towner Act appropriated money to be used by the states for the improvement of maternal and child welfare. Although the act was always controversial and expired in 1929, the number of infant deaths declined greatly during the 1920s. The use of pasteurized milk became widespread by the 1930s, and better understanding of the role of vitamins improved the nutritional advice given to mothers. Finally, the Progressive idea about "mothers' pensions" to help poor women support their children was enacted in a slightly different form, aid to dependent children, as part of the Social Security Act of the 1930s.

In spite of the Progressives' faith that all the problems involving children could be solved, however, there are still homeless children, children without access to proper medical care, poor children living in dangerous environments, abused children, and child workers in agriculture. Nevertheless, today a network of state and federal laws protects most children, and the general public accepts the idea of childhood as a distinct, sheltered time of life.

5

Homogenizing a Pluralistic Nation: Propaganda During World War I

The Problem

One week after Congress approved the war declaration that brought the United States into World War I,[1] President Woodrow Wilson signed Executive Order 2594, which created the Committee on Public Information, a government agency designed to mobilize public opinion behind the war effort. Wilson selected forty-one-year-old journalist and political ally George Creel to direct the committee's efforts. Creel immediately established voluntary press censorship, which essentially made the committee the overseer of all war-related news.

The Committee on Public Information also produced films, engaged some seventy-five thousand lecturers (called "Four Minute Men") who delivered approximately 7.5 million talks (each of which was to last no longer than four minutes), commissioned posters intended to aid recruitment and sell war bonds (seven hundred poster designs

were submitted to the committee and more than 9 million posters were printed in 1918 alone), and engaged in numerous other propaganda activities.

Why did the federal government believe that the Committee on Public Information was necessary? For one thing, there appears to have been considerable concern in the Wilson administration that American public opinion, which had supported the nation's neutrality and noninvolvement, would not support the war effort. More important, however, was the fear of many government officials that large ethnic blocs of Americans would not support the United States' entry into the conflict. In 1917, the Census Bureau had estimated that approximately 4.7 million people living in the United States had been born in Germany or in one of the other Central Powers.[2] It was also known that the nation con-

---

1. Wilson delivered his war message on April 2, 1917. The Senate declared war on April 3 and the House of Representatives followed suit on April 6.

2. The actual figure was closer to 4.27 million people. See U.S. Bureau of the Census, *Historical Statistics of the United States* (Washington, D.C.: U.S. Government Printing Office, 1975), pt. I, p. 117.

tained a large number of Irish Americans, many of whom were vehemently anti-British and thus might be expected to side with the Central Powers.[3] Could such a heterogeneous society be persuaded to support the war effort voluntarily? Could Americans of the same ethnic stock as the enemies be rallied to the cause?

The purpose of the Committee on Public Information was to use every means at its disposal to garner support for the United States' war effort. Not only did the committee create its own propaganda, but it also either discouraged or banned outright speeches, news reports, editorials, and films that expressed conflicting opinions.

Although examples of propaganda probably are nearly as old as society itself, by World War I the combination of government propaganda and modern communications technology made the manipulation of collective attitudes and opinions considerably more pervasive and doubtless more effective than earlier efforts. Indeed, some liberal intellectuals began to fear that propaganda techniques exploited latent prejudices, created a kind of mob psychology, and used lies and half-truths to sway the crowd. For these increasingly concerned individuals, the word *propaganda* itself began to take on sinister connotations. Thus Socialist leader Eugene V. Debs was not completely alone when he recognized the "irony of free speech suppressed by a nation allegedly fighting for democracy." Yet these doubters and worriers were in the dis-

tinct minority, and the Committee on Public Information for the most part not only successfully marshaled American public opinion in support of the war effort, but in doing so helped create a climate of mass fear and suspicion.[4]

In this chapter, you will be examining and analyzing the propaganda techniques of a modern nation at war. The Evidence section contains material sponsored or commissioned by the Committee on Public Information (posters, newspaper advertisements, excerpts from speeches by Four Minute Men) as well as privately produced works (song lyrics and commercial film advertisements) that either were approved by the committee or tended to parallel its efforts. After examining the evidence, you will work to answer the following questions:

1. How did the government attempt to mobilize the opinion of a diverse American public in support of a united war effort?

2. What were the consequences—positive and negative—of this effort?

On a larger scale, you should be willing to ponder other questions as well, although they do not relate directly to the evidence you will examine. To begin with, is government-sponsored

3. According to the U.S. census of 1920, there were 1.04 million Americans who had been born in Ireland and 3.12 million native-born Americans who had one or both parents of Irish birth.

4. For three especially interesting studies of propaganda during World War I, see J. Michael Sproule, *Propaganda and Democracy: The American Experience of Media and Mass Persuasion* (Cambridge: Cambridge University Press, 1997), esp. pp. 1–14; Brett Gary, *The Nervous Liberals: Propaganda Anxieties from World War I to the Cold War* (New York: Columbia University Press, 1999), esp. pp. 1–23; and Philip M. Taylor, *Munitions of the Mind: A History of Propaganda from the Ancient World to the Present Era* (Manchester, U.K.: Manchester University Press, 2003), esp. pp. 177–185.

propaganda during wartime a good thing? When it comes into conflict with the First Amendment's guarantees of freedom of speech, which should prevail? Finally, is there a danger that government-sponsored propaganda can be carried too far? Why do you think that was (or was not) the case during World War I?

◆

Background

By the early twentieth century, the United States had worldwide economic interests and even had acquired a modest colonial empire, but many Americans wanted to believe that they were insulated from world affairs and impervious to world problems. Two great oceans seemed to protect the nation from overseas threats, and the enormity of the country and comparative weakness of its neighbors appeared to secure it against all dangers. Let other nations waste their people and resources in petty wars over status and territory, Americans reasoned. The United States should stand above such greed or insanity, and certainly should not wade into foreign mud puddles.

To many Americans, European nations were especially suspect. For centuries, European nations had engaged in an almost ceaseless round of armed conflicts—wars for national unity, territory, or even religion or empire. Moreover, in the eyes of many Americans, these bloody wars appeared to have solved little or nothing, and the end of one war seemed to be but a prelude to the next. Ambitious kings and their plotting ministers seemed to make Europe the scene of almost constant uproar, an uproar that many Americans saw as devoid of reason and morality. Nor did it appear that the United States, as powerful as it was, could have any effect on the unstable European situation.

For this reason, most Americans greeted news of the outbreak of war in Europe in 1914 with equal measures of surprise and determination not to become involved. They applauded President Wilson's August 4 proclamation of neutrality, his statement (issued two weeks later) urging Americans to be impartial in thought as well as in deed, and his insistence that the United States continue neutral commerce with all the belligerents. Few Americans protested German violation of Belgian neutrality. Indeed, most Americans (naively, as it turned out) believed that the United States both should and could remain aloof from the conflict in Europe.

But many factors pulled the United States into the conflict that later became known as World War I.[5] America's economic prosperity to a large extent rested on commercial ties with Europe. In 1914, U.S. trade with the Allies (England, France, Russia) exceeded $800 million, whereas trade with the Central Powers (Germany,

5. Until the outbreak of what became known as World War II, World War I was referred to as the Great War.

Austria, Turkey) stood at approximately $170 million. Much of the trade with Great Britain and France was financed through loans from American banks, something President Wilson and Secretary of State William Jennings Bryan openly discouraged because both men believed that those economic interests might eventually draw the United States into the conflict. Indeed, Wilson and Bryan probably were correct. Nevertheless, American economic interests were closely tied to those of Great Britain and France. Thus a victory by the Central Powers might damage U.S. trade. As Wilson drifted to an acceptance of this fact, Bryan had to back down.

A second factor pulling the United States into the war was the deep-seated feelings of President Wilson himself. Formerly a constitutional historian (Wilson had been a college professor and university president before entering the political arena as a reform governor of New Jersey), Wilson had long admired the British people and their form of government. Although technically neutral, the president strongly, though privately, favored the Allies and viewed a German victory as unthinkable. Moreover, many of Wilson's key advisers and the people close to him were decidedly pro-British. Such was the persuasion of the president's friend and closest adviser, Colonel Edward House, as well as that of Robert Lansing (who replaced Bryan as secretary of state)[6] and Walter Hines Page (ambassador to England). These men and others helped strengthen Wilson's strong political opinions and influence the president's changing position toward the war in Europe. Hence, although Wilson asked Americans to be neutral in thought as well as in deed, in fact he and his principal advisers were neither. More than once, the president chose to ignore British violations of America's neutrality. Finally, when it appeared that the Central Powers might outlast their enemies, Wilson was determined to intercede. It was truly an agonizing decision for the president, who had worked so diligently to keep his nation out of war.

A third factor pulling the United States toward war was the strong ethnic ties of many Americans to the Old World. Many Americans had been born in Europe, and an even larger number were the sons and daughters of European immigrants. Although these people considered themselves to be, and were, Americans, some retained emotional ties to Europe that they sometimes carried into the political arena—ties that could influence America's foreign policy.

Finally, as the largest neutral commercial power in the world, the United States soon became caught in the middle of the commercial warfare of the belligerents. With the declaration of war, both Great Britain and Germany threw up naval blockades. Great Britain's blockade was designed to cut the Central Powers off from war materiel. American commercial vessels bound for Germany were stopped, searched, and often seized by the British navy. Wilson protested British policy many

6. Bryan resigned in 1915, in protest over what he considered Wilson's too sharp note to Germany over the sinking of the passenger liner *Lusitania*. Wilson called the act "illegal and inhuman." Bryan sensed that the Wilson administration was tilting away from neutrality.

times, but to no effect. After all, giving in to Wilson's protests would have deprived Britain of its principal military asset: the British navy.

Germany's blockade was even more dangerous to the United States, partly because the vast majority of American trade was with England and France. In addition, however, Germany's chief method of blockading the Allies was the use of the submarine, a comparatively new weapon in 1914. Because of the nature of the submarine (lethal while underwater, not equal to other fighting vessels on the surface), it was difficult for the submarine to remain effective and at the same time adhere to international law, such as the requirement that sufficient warning be given before sinking an enemy ship.[7] In 1915, hoping to terrorize the British into making peace, Germany unleashed its submarines in the Atlantic with orders to sink all ships flying Allied flags. In March, a German submarine sank the British passenger ship *Falaba.* Then on May 7, 1915, the British liner *Lusitania* was sunk with a loss of more than 1,000 lives, 128 of them American. Although Germany had published warnings in American newspapers specifically cautioning Americans not to travel on the *Lusitania,* and although it was ultimately discovered that the *Lusitania* had gone down so fast (in only eighteen minutes) because the British were shipping ammunition in the hold of the passenger ship, Americans were shocked by the Germans' actions on

the high seas. Most Americans, however, continued to believe that the United States should stay out of the war and approved of Wilson's statement, issued three days after the *Lusitania* sank to the bottom, that "there is such a thing as a man being too proud to fight."

Yet a combination of economic interests, German submarine warfare, and other events gradually pushed the United States toward involvement. In early February 1917, Germany announced a policy of unrestricted submarine warfare against all ships—belligerent and neutral alike. Ships would be sunk without warning if found to be in what Germany designated as forbidden waters. Later that month, the British intercepted a secret telegram intended for the German minister to Mexico, stationed in Mexico City. In that telegram, German Foreign Secretary Arthur Zimmermann offered Mexico a deal: Germany would help Mexico retrieve territory lost to the United States in the 1840s if Mexico would make a military alliance with Germany and declare war on the United States in the event that the United States declared war on Germany. Knowing the impact that such a telegram would have on American public opinion, the British quickly handed the telegram over to Wilson, who released it to the press. From that point on, it was but a matter of time before the United States would become involved in World War I.

On March 20, 1917, President Wilson called his cabinet together at the White House to advise him on how to proceed in the deteriorating situation with Germany. Wilson's cabinet officers unanimously urged the president to call Congress into session immedi-

---

7. International laws governing warfare at sea, as well as neutral shipping during wartime, were written in the mid-eighteenth century, more than one hundred years before the submarine became a potent seagoing weapon.

ately and ask for a declaration of war against Germany. When the last cabinet member had finished speaking, Wilson said, "Well, gentlemen, I think there is no doubt as to what your advice is. I thank you," and dismissed the meeting without informing the cabinet of his own intentions.

Yet even though Wilson had labored so arduously to keep the United States out of the war in Europe, by March 20 (or very soon after) his mind was made up: The United States must make war on Germany. Typing out his war message on his own Hammond portable typewriter, Wilson was out of sorts and complained often of headaches. The president, devoted to peace and Progressive reform, was drafting the document he had prayed he would never have to write.

On April 2, 1917, President Wilson appeared in person before a joint session of Congress to deliver his war message. Congress was ready. On April 4, the Senate approved a war declaration (the vote was 82–6). The House of Representatives followed suit two days later (by a vote of 373–50).[8]

As noted earlier, at the outset of the United States' entry into the war, the Wilson administration feared that the ethnically diverse American public might not unite in support of the nation's involvement in the Great War. Without a decisive event to prompt the war declaration (some Americans even suspected the Zimmermann telegram was a British hoax), would the American people support the war with sufficient unanimity? No firing on Fort Sumter or blowing up of the battleship *Maine* would force America's entrance into this war, nor would the *Lusitania* sinking, which had occurred two years before the 1917 war declaration. Without the obvious threat of having been attacked, would the American people rally to the colors to defeat a faraway enemy? Could isolationist and noninterventionist opinion, very strong as late as the presidential election of 1916, be overcome? Could an ethnically heterogeneous people stand together in time of war? To bind together a diverse people behind the war effort, President Wilson created the Committee on Public Information.

The Method

For George Creel and the Committee on Public Information, the purposes of propaganda were very clear:

1. Unite a multiethnic, pluralistic society behind the war effort.

2. Attract a sufficient number of men to the armed services and elicit universal civilian support for those men.

3. Influence civilians to support the war effort by purchasing war bonds or by other actions (such as limiting

8. The fifty-six votes in the Senate and House against the declaration of war essentially came from three separate groups: senators and congressmen with strong German and Austrian constituencies, isolationists who believed the United States should not become involved on either side, and some Progressive reformers who maintained that the war would divert America's attention from political, economic, and social reforms.

personal consumption or rolling bandages).

4. Influence civilians to put pressure on other civilians to refrain from antiwar comments, strikes, antidraft activities, unwitting dispersal of information to spies, and other public acts that could hurt the war effort.

To achieve these ends, propaganda techniques had to be used with extreme care. For propaganda to be effective, it would have to contain one or more of the following features:

1. Portrayal of American and Allied servicemen in the best possible light.
2. Portrayal of the enemy in the worst possible light.
3. Portrayal of the American and Allied cause as just and the enemy's cause as unjust.
4. Message to civilians that they were being involved in the war effort in important ways.
5. Communication of a sense of urgency to civilians.

In this chapter, you are given the following six types of World War I propaganda to analyze, some of it produced directly by the Committee on Public Information and some produced privately but examined and approved by the committee:

1. One popular song, perhaps the most famous to come out of World War I, performed in music halls and vaudeville houses (Source 1). Although the Committee on Public Information did not produce this kind of material, it could—and did—discourage performances of "unpatriotic" popular songs.
2. Three newspaper and magazine advertisements produced directly by the Committee on Public Information (Sources 2 through 4).
3. Nine posters either commissioned or approved by the committee and used for recruiting, advertising liberty loans,[9] and other purposes (Sources 5 through 13).
4. Two cartoons, one an editorial cartoon and the other a prize-winning cartoon in a contest sponsored by a U.S. Army camp publication (Sources 14 and 15).
5. Two excerpts of speeches by Four Minute Men and one poem by a Four Minute Man. (Sources 16 through 18).
6. Material concerning American-made feature films, including suggestions to theater owners on how to advertise the film *Kultur* ("Culture"), two film advertisements, and one still photograph used in advertising a feature film (Sources 19 through 22).

As you examine the evidence, you will see that effective propaganda operates on two levels. On the surface, there is the logical appeal for support to help win the war. On another level, however, certain images and themes are used to excite the emotions of the people for whom the propaganda is designed. As you examine the evidence, ask yourself the following questions:

1. For whom was this piece of propaganda designed?
2. What was this piece of propaganda trying to get people to think? to do?

9. Liberty loans were loans made by U.S. citizens to the government to finance the war effort. They were repaid with interest and were similar to liberty bonds.

3. What logical appeals were being made?
4. What emotional appeals were being made?
5. What might have been the results—positive and negative—of these kinds of appeals?

In songs, speeches, advertisements, and film reviews, are there key words or important images? Where there are illustrations (ads, posters, cartoons), what facial expressions and images are used? Finally, are there any common logical and emotional themes running through government-sponsored propaganda during World War I? How did the United States use propaganda to mobilize public opinion during the war?

The Evidence

Source 1 is a popular song by George M. Cohan, 1917.

1. "Over There."

Johnnie, get your gun,
Get your gun, get your gun,
Take it on the run,
On the run, on the run.
Hear them calling you and me,
Every son of liberty.
Hurry right away,
No delay, no delay.
Make your daddy glad
To have had such a lad.
Tell your sweetheart not to pine,
To be proud her boy's in line.

Chorus (repeat chorus twice)
Over there, over there,
Send the word, send the word over there—
That the Yanks are coming,
The Yanks are coming,
The drums rum-tumming
Ev'rywhere.
So prepare, say a pray'r,
Send the word, send the word to beware.
We'll be over, we're coming over,
And we won't come back till it's over
Over there.

Sources 2 through 4 from James R. Mock and Cedric Larson, *Words That Won the War: The Story of the Committee on Public Information* (Princeton: Princeton University Press, 1939), pp. 64, 169, 184. Photos: The National Archives.

2. "Spies *and* Lies" Advertisement Urging Americans to Report the Enemy.

Spies *and* Lies

German agents are everywhere, eager to gather scraps of news about our men, our ships, our munitions. It is still possible to get such information through to Germany, where thousands of these fragments — often individually harmless—are patiently pieced together into a whole which spells death to American soldiers and danger to American homes.

But while the enemy is most industrious in trying to collect information, and his systems elaborate, he is *not* superhuman—indeed he is often very stupid, and would fail to get what he wants were it not deliberately handed to him by the carelessness of loyal Americans.

Do not discuss in public, or with strangers, any news of troop and transport movements, or bits of gossip as to our military preparations, which come into your possession.

Do not permit your friends in service to tell you—or write you—"inside" facts about where they are, what they are doing and seeing.

Do not become a tool of the Hun by passing on the malicious, disheartening rumors which he so eagerly sows. Remember he asks no better service than to have you spread his lies of disasters to our soldiers and sailors, gross scandals in the Red Cross, cruelties, neglect and wholesale executions in our camps, drunkenness and vice in the Expeditionary Force, and other tales certain to disturb American patriots and to bring anxiety and grief to American parents.

And do not wait until you catch someone putting a bomb under a factory. Report the man who spreads pessimistic stories, divulges—or seeks—confidential military information, cries for peace, or belittles our efforts to win the war.

Send the names of such persons, even if they are in uniform, to the Department of Justice, Washington. Give all the details you can, with names of witnesses if possible—show the Hun that we can beat him at his own game of collecting scattered information and putting it to work. The fact that you made the report will not become public.

You are in contact with the enemy *today*, just as truly as if you faced him across No Man's Land. In your hands are two powerful weapons with which to meet him—discretion and vigilance. *Use them.*

COMMITTEE ON PUBLIC INFORMATION
8 JACKSON PLACE, WASHINGTON, D. C.

George Creel, Chairman
The Secretary of State
The Secretary of War
The Secretary of the Navy

Contributed through Division of Advertising   *United States Gov't Comm. on Public Information*

3. "Bachelor of Atrocities" Advertisement for Fighting the Enemy by Buying Liberty Bonds.

Bachelor *of* Atrocities

IN the vicious guttural language of Kultur,[10] the degree A. B. means Bachelor of Atrocities. Are you going to let the Prussian Python strike at your Alma Mater, as it struck at the University of Louvain?[11]

The Hohenzollern[12] fang strikes at every element of decency and culture and taste that your college stands for. It leaves a track so terrible that only whispered fragments may be recounted. It has ripped all the world-old romance out of war, and reduced it to the dead, black depths of muck, and hate, and bitterness.

You may soon be called to fight. But you are called upon right now to buy Liberty Bonds. You are called upon to economize in every way. It is sometimes harder to live nobly than to die nobly. The supreme sacrifice of life may come easier than the petty sacrifices of comforts and luxuries. You are called to exercise stern self-discipline. Upon this the Allied Success depends.

Set aside every possible dollar for the purchase of Liberty Bonds. Do it relentlessly. Kill every wasteful impulse, that America may live. Every bond you buy fires point-blank at Prussian Terrorism.

BUY U. S. GOVERNMENT BONDS FOURTH LIBERTY LOAN

Contributed through Division of Advertising

United States Gov't Comm. on Public Information

This space contributed for the Winning of the War by
A. T SKERRY, '84, and CYRILLE CARREAU, '04.

Appeal to the Symbols of Education

Two Graduates of New York University Contributed the Space for This CPI Advertisement in Their "Alumni News"

10. Germans often asserted that they had *Kultur,* or a superior culture, in contrast to *civilization,* which they viewed as weak and effeminate.

11. The *University of Louvain,* in Belgium, was pillaged and partially destroyed by German troops. Some professors were beaten and others killed, and the library (containing 250,000 books and manuscripts, some irreplaceable) was totally destroyed. The students themselves were home for summer vacation.

12. *Hohenzollern* was the name of the German royal family since the nation's founding in 1871. It had been the Prussian royal family since 1525.

4. Advertisement Appealing to History Teachers, April 4, 1917.

The Committee on Public Information

Established by Order of the President, April 4, 1917

Distribute free *except as noted* the following publications:

I. Red, White and Blue Series:

No. 1. How the War Came to America (English, German, Polish, Bohemian, Italian, Spanish and Swedish).

No. 2. National Service Handbook (primarily for libraries, schools, Y. M. C. A.'s, Clubs, fraternal organizations, etc., as a guide and reference work on all forms of war activity, civil, charitable and military).

No. 3. The Battle Line of Democracy. Prose and Poetry of the Great War. Price 25 cent. Special price to teachers. Proceeds to the Red Cross. Other issues in preparation.

II. War Information Series:

No. 1. The War Message and Facts Behind it.

No. 2. The Nation in Arms, by Secretaries Lane and Baker.

No. 3. The Government of Germany, by Prof. Charles D. Hazen.

No. 4. The Great War from Spectator to Participant.

No. 5. A War of Self Defense, by Secretary Lansing and Assistant Secretary of Labor Louis F. Post.

No. 6. American Loyalty by Citizens of German Descent.

No. 7. Amerikanische Bürgertreue, a translation of No. 6.

Other issues will appear shortly.

III. Official Bulletin:

Accurate daily statement of what all agencies of government are doing in war times. Sent free to newspapers and postmasters (to be put on bulletin boards). Subscription price $5.00 per year.

Address Requests to

Committee on Public Information, Washington, D. C.

What Can History Teachers Do Now?

You can help the community realize what history should mean to it.

You can confute those who by selecting a few historic facts seek to establish some simple cure-all for humanity.

You can confute those who urge that mankind can wipe the past off the slate and lay new foundations for civilization.

You can encourage the sane use of experience in discussions of public questions.

You can help people understand what democracy is by pointing out the common principle in the ideas of Plato, Cromwell, Rousseau, Jefferson, Jackson and Washington.

You can help people understand what German autocracy has in common with the autocracy of the Grand Mogul.

You can help people understand that democracy is not inconsistent with law and efficient government.

You can help people understand that failure of the past to make the world safe for democracy does not mean that it can not be made safe in the future.

You can so teach your students that they will acquire "historical mindedness" and realize the connection of the past with the present.

You can not do these things unless you inform yourself, and think over your information.

You can help yourself by reading the following:
"History and the Great War" bulletin of Bureau of Education.
A series of articles published throughout the year in THE HISTORY TEACHER'S MAGAZINE.

You can obtain aid and advice by writing to

The National Board for Historical Service, 1133 Woodward Building, Washington, D. C.

United States Bureau of Education, Division of Civic Education, Washington, D. C.

Committee on Public Information, Division of Educational Co-operation, 10 Jackson Place, Washington, D. C.

The Committee on Patriotism through Education of the National Security League, 31 Pine Street, New York City.

Carnegie Endowment for International Peace, 2 Jackson Place, Washington, D. C.

National Committee of Patriotic and Defense Societies, Southern Building, Washington, D. C.

The World Peace Foundation, 40 Mount Vernon St., Boston, Mass.

American Association for International Conciliation, 407 West 117th Street, New York City.

The American Society for Judicial Settlement of International Disputes, Baltimore, Md.

The Editor, THE HISTORY TEACHER'S MAGAZINE, Philadelphia.

4

Source 5 from *The James Montgomery Flagg Poster Book*, introduction by Susan E. Meyer (New York: Watson-Guptill Publications, 1975). Photo: Library of Congress.

5. The Famous Uncle Sam Poster.

Source 6 from Peter Stanley, *What Did You Do in the War, Daddy?* (Melbourne: Oxford University Press, 1983), p. 55. Photo: Imperial War Museum.

6. Poster Portraying Germany as a Raging Beast.

Source 7 from *The James Montgomery Flagg Poster Book.*

7. United States Marines Recruiting Poster.

Source 8 from Anthony Crawford, *Posters in the George C. Marshall Research Foundation* (Charlottesville: University of Virginia Press, 1939), p. 30. Photo: Culver Pictures.

8. **"Women of America, Save Your Country" Poster.**

Source 9 from Library of Congress, Prints and Photographs Division #POS-US. C66, no. 1.

9. "The Government asks you to do your Xmas Shopping Early" Poster.

Source 10 from Walton Rawls, *Wake Up, America! World War I and the American Poster* (New York: Abbeville Press, 1988), p. 232.

10. "Americans All!" Poster.

Sources 11 and 12 from Special Collections, University of Tennessee.

11. "See Him Through" Poster, Knights of Columbus, 1918.

12. Jewish Welfare Board Poster, 1918.

Source 13 from a private collection. Used with permission.

13. "Colored Man Is No Slacker" Poster.

Source 14 from John Higham, *Strangers in the Land: Patterns of American Nativism,
1860–1925* (New Brunswick, N.J.: Rutgers University Press, 1955), p. 210.

**14. *New York Herald* Editorial Cartoon: German American Dr. Karl
Muck, Conductor of the Boston Symphony Orchestra, Needed a
Police Escort When He Conducted a Concert in March 1918 in New
York City.**

Source 15 from *New York Times,* January 6, 1918.

15. Hines's Prize-Winning Cartoon in the 1918 *Trench and Camp* Cartoon Contest.[13]

13. *Trench and Camp* was a weekly publication of the United States Army for its thirty-two training centers in the United States. For this prize-winning cartoon, Frank Hines won a wristwatch. In the cartoon, the American soldier is holding a *pickelhaube,* a German spiked helmet.

Sources 16 through 18 from Alfred E. Cornbise, *War as Advertised: The Four Minute Men and America's Crusade, 1917–1918* (Philadelphia: American Philosophical Society, 1984), pp. 72–73, 122, 60. Reprinted by permission of the American Philosophical Society.

16. Excerpt of a Speech by a Four Minute Man.

Ladies and Gentlemen:

I have just received the information that there is a German spy among us— a German spy watching *us*.

He is around here somewhere, reporting upon you and me—sending reports about us to Berlin and telling the Germans just what we are doing with the Liberty Loan. From every section of the country these spies have been getting reports over to Potsdam[14]—not general reports but details—where the loan is going well and where its success seems weak, and what people are saying in each community.

For the German government is worried about our great loan. Those Junkers[15] fear its effect upon the German *morale*. They're raising a loan this month, too.

If the American people lend their billions now, one and all with a hip-hip-hurrah, it means that America is united and strong. While, if we lend our money half-heartedly, America seems weak and autocracy remains strong.

Money means everything now; it means quicker victory and therefore less bloodshed. We are *in* the war, and now Americans can have but *one* opinion, only *one* wish in the Liberty Loan.

Well, I hope these spies are getting their messages straight, letting Potsdam know that America is *hurling back* to the autocrats these answers:

For treachery here, attempted treachery in Mexico, treachery everywhere—*one billion*.

For murder of American women and children—*one billion more*.

For broken faith and promise to murder more Americans—*billions and billions more*.

And then we will add:

In the world fight for Liberty, our share—*billions and billions and billions and endless billions*.

Do not let the German spy hear and report that *you* are a slacker.

14. *Potsdam* (a suburb of Berlin) was where the Kaiser lived.
15. *Junkers* were the Prussian nobility.

17. Part of a Speech by a Four Minute Man.

German agents are telling the people of this . . . race[16] through the South that if they will not oppose the German Government, or help our Government, they will be rewarded with Ford automobiles when Germany is in control here. They are told that 10 negroes are being conscripted to 1 white man in order that the Negro race may be killed off; and that the reason Germany went into Belgium was to punish the people of that country for the cruel treatment of the negroes in the Congo.

18. "It's Duty Boy," a Poem Read by Four Minute Men.

My boy must never bring disgrace to his immortal sires—
At Valley Forge and Lexington they kindled freedom's fires,
John's father died at Gettysburg, mine fell at Chancellorsville;
While John himself was with the boys who charged up San Juan Hill.
And John, if he was living now, would surely say with me,
"No son of ours shall e'er disgrace our grand old family tree
By turning out a slacker when his country needs his aid."
It is not of such timber that America was made.
I'd rather you had died at birth or not been born at all,
Than know that I had raised a son who cannot hear the call
That freedom has sent round the world, its precious rights to save—
This call is meant for you, my boy, and I would have you brave;
And though my heart is breaking, boy, I bid you do your part,
And show the world no son of mine is cursed with craven heart;
And if, perchance, you ne'er return, my later days to cheer,
And I have only memories of my brave boy, so dear,
I'd rather have it so, my boy, and know you bravely died
Than have a living coward sit supinely by my side.
To save the world from sin, my boy, God gave his only son—
He's asking for MY boy, to-day, and may His will be done.

16. At the front lines in France, Germans barraged America's African American soldiers with leaflets urging them to desert (none did). One of those propaganda leaflets said, in part, "Do you enjoy the same rights as the white people do in America . . . or are you rather not treated over there as second-class citizens?" As to the charge of discrimination against African Americans by draft boards, there were numerous complaints that African Americans found it almost impossible to get exemptions from military service. In the end, about 31 percent of the African Americans who registered were called into service, as opposed to 26 percent of the registered whites. To counteract German propaganda, prominent African Americans were sent to France to lecture to the African American troops.

Source 19 from *The Moving Picture World*, September 28, 1918.

19. Promotional Tips to Theater Managers, 1918.

ADVERTISING AIDS FOR BUSY MANAGERS
"KULTUR."

William Fox Presents Gladys Brockwell in a Typical Example of the Brutality of the Wilhelmstrasse to Its Spy-slaves.

Cast.

Countess Griselda Von Arenburg,
                         Gladys Brockwell
Eliska ....Georgia Woodthorpe
René de Bornay................William Scott
Baron von Zeller ....Willard Louis
Archduke Franz Ferdinand ....Charles Clary
Danilo ....Nigel de Brullier
The Kaiser ....William Burress
Emperor Franz Josef..........Alfred Fremont

Directed by Edward J. Le Saint.

The Story: The Kaiser decides that the time is ripe for a declaration of war, and sends word to his vassal monarch of Austria. René de Bornay is sent by France to discover what is being planned. He meets the Countess, who falls in love with him. She sickens of the spy system and declares that she is done with it, but is warned that she cannot withdraw. She is told to secure René's undoing, but instead procures his escape and in her own boudoir is stood against the wall and shot for saving the man whom she loves better than her life.

Feature Gladys Brockwell as Countess Griselda Von Arenburg and William Scott as René de Bornay.

Program and Advertising Phrases: Gladys Brockwell, Star of Latest Picture, Exposing Hun Brutality and Satanic Intrigue.
How An Austrian Countess Gave Her All for Democracy.
She Was an Emperor's Favorite Yet She Died for World Freedom.
Story of an Emperor's Mistress and a Crime That Rocked the World.
Daring Exposure of Scandals and Crimes in Hun Court Circles.
Astonishing Revelations of Hun Plots to Rape Democracy.

Advertising Angles: Do not offer this as a propaganda story, but tell that it is one of the angles of the merciless Prussian spy system about which has been woven a real romance. Play up the spy angle heavily both in your newspaper work and through window cards with such lines as "even the spies themselves hate their degradation." Miss Brockwell wears some stunning and daring gowns in this play, and with these special appeal can be made to the women.

Source 20 from the National Archives.

20. Advertisement for the Feature Film *The Kaiser, the Beast of Berlin* (1918), Described by Some as the Most Famous "Hate Picture."

21. **Still Photograph from *The Kaiser, the Beast of Berlin* (1918). Used in Advertising.**

Source 22 from Fox Film Corporation, 1918.

22. Advertising Poster for *The Prussian Cur* (1918).

✦

Questions to Consider

Source 1, George M. Cohan's enormously popular song, "Over There," was familiar to almost every American in 1917 to 1918 and has been since. What is the song urging young men to do? What emotions are the song's lyrics trying to arouse? How would you interpret the lines, "Make your daddy glad" and (speaking of sweethearts) "To be proud her boy's in line"? Recordings of the song "Over There" are readily available. As you listen to the song, how does it make you feel?

The advertisements shown in Sources 2 through 4 were produced by the Committee on Public Information. How are the Germans portrayed in the "Spies *and* Lies" ad (Source 2)? in the "Bachelor of Atrocities" ad (Source 3)? Source 4 is an appeal to history teachers. Did the Committee on Public Information ask history teachers to "tilt" their treatments of the past? If so, how? Were there any dangers inherent in the kinds of activities the committee was urging on patriotic Americans?

In some ways, poster art (Sources 5 through 13) is similar to editorial cartoon art (Sources 14 and 15), principally because the artist has only one canvas or frame on which to tell his or her story. Yet the poster must be more arresting than the cartoon, must convey its message rapidly, and must avoid ambiguities and confusion. Posters commissioned or approved by the Committee on Public Information were an extremely popular form of propaganda during World War I. Indeed, so popular were the posters of James Montgomery Flagg (1877–1960) that he helped sell

$1,000 of liberty bonds by performing (in his case, painting posters) in front of the New York Public Library.

Source 5, Flagg's Uncle Sam poster, probably is the most famous poster ever created. The idea was taken from a British poster by Alfred Leete, and Flagg was his own model for Uncle Sam. The poster is still used by the United States Army. What feeling did the poster seek to elicit?

Sources 6 and 7 are military recruiting posters, urging men to enlist in the armed services. What innuendoes are common to both posters? How are the Germans portrayed? What feelings are the posters intended to elicit? How are the appeals of these recruiting posters different from the appeals of the song in Source 1?

The posters in Sources 8 and 9 focus on women. How are women portrayed in each poster? In Source 9, what are American women asked to do to contribute to the war effort? What does this poster by artist Haskell Coffin tell you about World War I–era gender roles and stereotypes? How might women in 1917 respond to this poster? How might American women today react to a similar appeal?

Sources 10 through 13 are extremely interesting in light of the government's fears and the role President Wilson assigned to the Committee on Public Information. What emotion does the extraordinary "Americans All!" poster (Source 10) attempt to elicit? What is the poster's intended "message"? How do Sources 11 through 13 seek to bolster that message? If the goal of the committee was to *unite* Americans behind the war effort, why do you think it chose to target appeals to specific groups?

Speaking of cartoons, nineteenth-century New York political boss William Marcy ("Boss") Tweed once exclaimed, "Let's stop these damn pictures. I don't care so much what the papers say about me—my constituents can't read; but damn it, they can see the pictures!" The editorial cartoon from the *New York Herald* (Source 14) is fairly self-explanatory. What emotions does the cartoon seek to elicit? What actions, intended or unintended, might have resulted from those emotions? Karl Muck, incidentally, was deported. Frank Hines's prize-winning cartoon (Source 15) seeks to elicit very different emotions. Compare this cartoon with Cohan's lyrics (Source 1).

Sources 16 through 18, by Four Minute Men, were also published in the Committee on Public Information's *Bulletin,* which was distributed to all volunteer speakers. Several of the Four Minute Men were women. Speakers received certificates from President Wilson after the war. What appeals are made in Source 16? How are appeals to African Americans (Source 17) the same or different? The poem in Source 18 is particularly painful to read. Why is that so? How can this poem be compared with Sources 1 and 15?

From 1917 to 1918, the American film industry and the Committee on Public Information produced over 180 feature films, 6 serials, 72 short subjects, 112 documentaries, 44 cartoons, and 37 liberty loan special films. Unfortunately, the vast majority of those motion pictures no longer are available,

principally because the nitrate film stock on which the films were printed was extremely flammable and subject to decomposition.[17]

No sound films were produced in the United States before 1927. Until that time, a small orchestra or (more prevalent) a piano accompanied a film's showing. What dialogue there was— and there was not much—was given in subtitles.

The advertising tips for the film *Kultur* (Source 19) suggest a number of phrases and angles designed to attract audiences. What are the strongest appeals suggested to theater owners? Do those same appeals also appear in the song, advertisements, posters, cartoons, and speeches?

Sources 20 through 22 are advertisements for two films produced in 1918: *The Kaiser, the Beast of Berlin* (Sources 20 and 21) and *The Prussian Cur* (Source 22). What appeal is made to prospective viewers in Source 20? How are Germans depicted in Source 21? How can Source 21 be compared with Sources 6 and 7? How can Source 22 be compared with those sources as well?

You must now summarize your findings and return to the central questions: How did the United States use propaganda to mobilize public opinion in support of the nation's par-

---

17. In 1949, an improved safety-based stock was introduced. Those films that do survive, except in private collections, are in the Library of Congress; the American Film Institute Library in Beverly Hills, California; the Academy of Motion Picture Arts and Sciences in Los Angeles; the Museum of Modern Art in New York; the National Archives in Washington, D.C.; the New York Public Library; and the Wisconsin Center for Theater Research in Madison.

ticipation in World War I? What were the consequences—positive and negative—of the mobilization of public opinion?

Epilogue

The creation of the Committee on Public Information and its subsequent work show that the Wilson administration had serious doubts concerning whether the American people, multi-ethnic and pluralistic as they were, would support the war effort with unanimity. And, to be sure, there was opposition to American involvement in the war, not only from socialist Eugene Debs and the left but also from reformers Robert La Follette, Jane Addams, and others. As it turned out, however, the Wilson administration's worst fears proved groundless. Americans of all ethnic backgrounds overwhelmingly supported the war effort, sometimes rivaling each other in patriotic ardor. How much of this unanimity can be attributed to patriotism and how much to the propaganda efforts of the Committee on Public Information will never really be known. Yet, for whatever reason, it can be said that the war had a kind of unifying effect on the American people. Women sold liberty bonds, worked for agencies such as the Red Cross, rolled bandages, and cooperated in the government's effort to conserve food and fuel. Indeed, even African Americans sprang to the colors, reasoning, as did the president of Howard University, that service in the war might help them achieve long-withheld civil and political rights.

However, this homogenization was not without its price. Propaganda was so effective that it created a kind of national hysteria, sometimes with terrible results. Vigilante-type groups often shamefully persecuted German Americans, lynching one German American man of draft age for not being in uniform (the man was physically ineligible, having only one eye) and badgering German American children in and out of school. Many states forbade the teaching of German in schools, and a host of German words were purged from the language (sauerkraut became liberty cabbage, German measles became liberty measles, hamburgers became liberty steaks, frankfurters became hot dogs). The city of Cincinnati even banned pretzels from saloons. In such an atmosphere, many Americans lived in genuine fear of being accused of spying or of becoming victims of intimidation or violence. In a society intent upon homogenization, being different could be dangerous.

During such hysteria, one would expect the federal government in general and the Committee on Public Information in particular to have attempted to dampen the more extreme forms of vigilantism. However, it seemed as if the government had become the victim of its own propaganda. The postmaster general (Albert Burleson), empowered to censor the mail, looking for examples of treason, insurrection, or forcible resistance to laws, used his power to suppress all socialist publications, all anti-British and pro-Irish mail, and anything that he believed threatened the war effort. One movie producer, Robert Goldstein, was sentenced to ten years in prison for releasing his film *The Spirit of '76* (about the American Revolution) because it portrayed the British in an unfavorable light.[18] Socialist party leader Eugene Debs was given a similar sentence for criticizing the war in a speech in Canton, Ohio.[19] The left-wing Industrial Workers of the World (IWW) was broken. Freedom of speech, press, and assembly were violated countless times, and numerous lynchings, whippings, and tar-and-featherings occurred. Excesses by both government and private individuals were as effective in *forcing* homogeneity as were the voluntary efforts of American people of all backgrounds.

Once the hysteria had begun, it is doubtful whether even President Wilson could have stopped it. Yet Wilson showed no inclination to do so, even stating that dissent was not appreciated by the government. Without the president to reverse the process, the hysteria continued unabated.

Before the outbreak of World War I, anti-immigrant sentiment had been growing, although most Americans seem to have believed that the solution was to Americanize the immigrants rather than to restrict their entrance.

18. This gave rise to a court case with the improbable title *United States v. The Spirit of '76.*
19. Debs, indicted the day before he made his speech, spent three years in prison.

But the drive toward homogenization that accompanied America's war hysteria acted to increase cries for restricting further immigration and to weaken champions of the "melting pot." As restriction advocate Madison Grant wrote in 1922, "The world has seen many such [racial] mixtures and the character of a mongrel race is only just beginning to be understood at its true value. . . . Whether we like to admit it or not, the result of the mixture of two races . . . gives us a race reverting to the more ancient, generalized and lower type." Labor leaders, journalists, and politicians called for immigration restrictions, and a general immigration restriction (called the National Origins Act) became law in 1924.

This insistence on homogenization also resulted in the Red Scare of 1919, during which Attorney General A. Mitchell Palmer violated many people's civil liberties in a series of raids, arrests, and deportations directed largely against recent immigrants. As seen, the efforts to homogenize a pluralistic nation could have an ugly side.

As noted in the Problem section of this chapter, some liberal intellectuals were both shocked and frightened by the relative ease with which the Committee on Public Information was able to manipulate public opinion and create a climate of mass patriotic hysteria. How, they asked, could "the people" be trusted if they could be swayed and stampeded so easily? And yet, open criticism of the government or the American people themselves still could be dangerous. As one minor example, noted historian Charles Beard resigned from Columbia University in protest over the firings of antiwar faculty members. As a result, sales of Beard's books plummeted.[20]

As Americans approached World War II, some called for a revival of the Committee on Public Information. Yet President Franklin Roosevelt rejected this sweeping approach. The Office of War Information was created, but its role was a restricted one. Even so, Japanese Americans were subjected to relocation and humiliation in one of the most shameful episodes of recent American history. And although propaganda techniques were sometimes more subtle, they nevertheless displayed features that would cause Americans to hate their enemies and want to destroy them. Japanese people especially were portrayed as barbaric.

A good example of this is seen in Source 23 (on the next page). In general, however, a different spirit pervaded the United States during World War II, a spirit generally more tolerant of American pluralism and less willing to stir Americans into an emotional frenzy.

And yet the possibility that propaganda will create mass hysteria and thus endanger the civil rights of some Americans is present in every national crisis, especially in wartime. In the "total wars" of the twentieth century, in which civilians played as crucial a role as fighting men (in factories, in training facilities for soldiers, and in shipping soldiers and materiel to the front), the mobilization of the home front was a necessity. But could that kind of mobilization be carried too far?

20. On liberals' fear, see Walter Lippmann's columns in the November and December 1919 issues of *Atlantic Monthly,* cited in Gary, *Nervous Liberals,* p. 2. On Beard, see Sproule, *Propaganda and Democracy,* p. 14.

Source 23 from Library of Congress.

23. United States Army Poster from World War II.

6

The "New" Woman: Social Science Experts and the Redefinition of Women's Roles in the 1920s

◆

The Problem

In 1920, the Nineteenth Amendment to the Constitution, granting women the right to vote, was finally ratified. "Few people live to see the actual and final realization of hopes to which they have devoted their lives," announced Carrie Chapman Catt to the two thousand women attending the National American Woman Suffrage Association (NAWSA). "That privilege is ours." After more than an hour of singing, parading, and waving banners, the delegates turned their attention to the business of converting the NAWSA into the League of Women Voters (LWV). After some initial uncertainty about its purpose, the LWV became a nonpartisan organization dedicated to educating voters about issues and candidates and encouraging citizens to get out and vote. "A dream has come true," exulted the new league president and former suffragist, Maude Wood Park.[1]

Little did these women realize what lay ahead. As the decade of the 1920s progressed, more and more of the former suffragists became discouraged and disillusioned. In spite of the passage of some important pieces of federal legislation for women, a succession of Republican presidents—Warren Harding, Calvin Coolidge, and Herbert Hoover—seemed to practice politics as usual, very much as things had been before women gained the right to vote. Nor did women vote as a bloc, although they did come together occasionally on certain issues of special interest to them. For most of the decade, however, women were divided by their party affiliations and by their support for or opposition to the Equal Rights Amendment.

Even more disappointing were the attitudes of the new generation of women who came of age during this

1. Barbara Stuhler (ed.), *For the Public Record: A Documentary History of the League of* *Women Voters* (Westport, Conn: Greenwood Press, 2000), pp. 31, 43.

era. These "new" women, the flappers and their imitators, refused to identify with serious-minded reform efforts, criticized feminism as old-fashioned, and rejected what they described as Victorian attitudes toward sex and sexuality. The "new" women also argued that they were already equal to men and that they would be the first generation of women to have it all: education, career, marriage, and children. For advice on how to gain personal fulfillment, they turned to the experts, primarily social scientists such as sociologists, psychologists, economists, political scientists, home economists, and anthropologists. However, creating real change in such institutions as colleges and universities, the family, and the economy proved extremely difficult, and the experts were not in agreement about *how* or even *whether* such changes should occur.

In this chapter, you will read several selections from some of the vast social science literature of the 1920s, in order to identify and understand the issues surrounding the redefinition of "new" (or modern) women's roles. What were these issues? What assumptions and recommendations did social scientists make?

◆

Background

The struggle for woman suffrage had, indeed, been very long and hard, beginning with the demand for the vote at the Seneca Falls Convention in 1848, and culminating in the exhausting, state-by-state ratification campaigns of 1920. Issues of race, class, and tactics had often badly divided the suffragists: Should they reach out to immigrant women? What role, if any, should working women have in the movement? And what about African American women? Wouldn't their inclusion in the suffrage movement alienate both southern white women and southern legislators? Should the suffragists focus on amending state constitutions, or should they work only for a federal amendment? Should they use aggressive protest tactics in Washington, D.C., to influence the president (as Alice Paul and the Constitutional Union had done), or should they try to persuade male legislators of both parties through more traditional lobbying techniques (as Catt and the NAWSA had done)?

In some northern industrial cities, suffragists did reach out to immigrants and working women. In a few of these cities, middle-class African American women were also included in suffrage activities through the affiliation of their clubs and the "colored" Young Women's Christian Association (YWCA). However, the national leaders were always aware of the "race question" and were willing to placate southerners on this issue. Suffragists worked both for state voting rights and, increasingly after 1910, for the federal woman suffrage amendment. The National American Woman Suffrage Association and the Congressional Union coexisted uneasily until the latter became the National Woman's Party (NWP) under Alice Paul's leadership.

✦ CHAPTER 6

The "New" Woman:
Social Science
Experts and the
Redefinition of
Women's Roles
in the 1920s

In general, it is fair to say that both the NAWSA and the NWP remained white, upper- and middle-class women's organizations dedicated to winning the vote for women like themselves.

Moreover, because the fight for suffrage had been so long and difficult, many women came to believe that the struggle for women's rights and the recognition of women's abilities were completed by the passage of the Nineteenth Amendment. The LWV's membership was much smaller than that of the NAWSA, and membership in women's reform organizations, such as the Consumer's League and the Women's Trade Union League, declined drastically during the 1920s.

Although women's reform initiatives were generally weaker in the 1920s than in the pre–World War I era, they did continue with some success throughout the decade. Passage of the federal Sheppard-Towner Maternity Act, in effect from 1921 to 1928, provided funding to states for improved maternal and infant health care measures. Another breakthrough came in the form of the Cable Act (1930), which allowed American women who married foreign citizens to retain their own U.S. citizenship, rather than losing it as they had previously. Many women were also politically active on the municipal and state levels, as well as working to create female networks and a "place" for themselves within national party politics. But in a discouraging setback, the effort to pass a federal amendment outlawing child labor failed in the 1920s, in spite of the combined support and diligent work of several women's organizations.

Furthermore, former suffragists who remained politically active during the 1920s were badly divided. Shocked at the remaining civil inequalities of women, the National Woman's Party proposed an Equal Rights Amendment (ERA) to the Constitution in 1923. The proposed amendment declared that "men and women shall have equal rights throughout the United States and every place subject to its jurisdiction." The NWP argued that the ERA would eliminate laws that discriminated against women, such as those that granted automatic guardianship of children to husbands, established different grounds for divorce for men and women, excluded women from certain occupations, barred them from running for certain political offices and serving on juries, and sanctioned different pay scales for men and women. The Equal Rights Amendment, the NWP feminists argued, would complete the legal equalization of men and women.

The League of Women Voters—and most other women's groups of the 1920s—opposed the ERA. The amendment was so broad, they maintained, that it would remove certain essential, hard-earned protections that women already had in the law. Although there was some concern about alimony and service in the armed forces, the real problem lay in protective labor laws for women in the various states. These laws were based on women's physical differences from men, especially their reproductive functions. Such laws kept women out of dangerous trades or job situations, restricted the amount of weight that women were expected to lift, required seats or rest periods for women on the job, limited the number of hours and shifts that women could work, and so forth. Whereas the NWP saw such laws as *restrictive* of women's rights, the LWV viewed them as *protective* of women's special nature. Thus, the former suffragists battled each other over the Equal Rights Amendment throughout the decade.

Suffrage was only one of women's many interlinked reform activities during the Progressive era, most of which had been supported by innovative approaches to studying society. Beginning in the late nineteenth century as a response to massive immigration, rapid industrialization, and widespread urbanization, researchers began investigating and documenting the problems associated with these social changes. Borrowing some of their methods from natural science and taking their general field of study as society, new social scientists began to emerge in the universities and government service. Sociologist Thorstein Veblen wrote *The Theory of the Leisure Class* (1899) while teaching at the University of Chicago; Richard Ely was head of the Economics Department at the University of Wisconsin when he wrote *Monopolies and Trusts* (1900). Both men were interested in the analysis of the formation and functions of great wealth during the period. In contrast, anthropologist Elsie Clews Parsons was teaching part time at Columbia University when she wrote *The Family* (1906), followed by five other books during the next ten years in which she compared contemporary American social attitudes and conventions to those of other, preindustrial cultures.

Progressive reformers were generally optimistic, believing that people were basically good. If Americans were properly educated about social problems, reformers believed, they could and would find solutions to the problems. The new social sciences—especially sociology, political science, psychology, economics, and home economics—fit into this orientation very well. Gathering data, interviewing individuals, and compiling statistics provided the material with which reformers could educate people, formulate social policy, and convince government officials of the need for corrective ordinances or laws. In this era, there seemed to be little personal conflict for most social scientists between the need for objectivity in their research and the reformist convictions that guided their choice of subject matter and methodology. In the natural sciences, well-known sociologist Robert Lynd pointed out, one might be motivated by pure curiosity, but it was "the *interested* desire to know in order to do something about problems that has predominantly motivated social science. . . ."[2] In other words, social scientists saw themselves as practical researchers and writers whose work could form the basis for important social and economic reforms.

During World War I, social scientists gained even more prestige as they cooperated with the government in a series of studies of the backgrounds, intelligence, and physical health of army recruits. The dramatic changes of the postwar decade, nearly all of which had their origins in pre–World War I Amer-

2. Robert S. Lynd, *Knowledge for What? The Place of Social Science in American Culture* (Princeton: Princeton University Press, 1939), pp. 114–115.

✦ CHAPTER 6

The "New" Woman:
Social Science
Experts and the
Redefinition of
Women's Roles
in the 1920s

ica, provided a fertile field of study for the new social scientists. Widely accepted as experts in their specialized fields, they published their research findings and recommendations in popular middle-class books and magazines as well as in scholarly journals during the 1920s. For the first half of the decade, political scientists were very interested in the impact of the newly enfranchised women voters. That interest waned, however, as the decade progressed, and political questions were replaced by questions about women's roles in the work force and the family.

To most economists, the 1920s appeared to be a time of enormous prosperity. There were, nevertheless, some troubling trends: the growth of consumer debt fueled by the new advertising, the increase in corporate mergers, the development of a kind of corporate paternalism to counteract labor unionism, and the gross inflation of the unregulated stock market. In addition, farming, mining, and some other sectors of the economy were not sharing in the economic good times at all. Home economists were especially aware of the rates at which women were entering high schools and universities, preparing for professions, and entering the work force, especially in the expanding service sector. Although the typical woman worker was single, there was a definite increase in married women (and married women with children) in the work force. As more women pursued jobs and careers, the role of homemaker seemed to become less important. This in turn raised important questions about women's traditional roles in the home and family,

questions that home economists, psychologists, and sociologists all tried to answer.

There is no doubt that this decade was characterized by serious social and cultural strains. Anti-immigrant sentiment increased, culminating in a new quota system that drastically limited immigration from southern and eastern Europe. The decade also saw the rise of a new Ku Klux Klan, for the first time popular in urban areas and outside the South, dedicated to "100 percent Americanism" and devoted to enforcing the values of nineteenth-century rural America. Two famous trials of the decade—the Sacco and Vanzetti case against Italian anarchists convicted of committing a murder during a payroll robbery, and the Scopes case involving a teacher found guilty of breaking state law by teaching about evolution—highlighted the social and cultural strains inherent in the conflict between the older values of rural and small-town America and the newer values of twentieth-century modernism.

These were especially difficult times for African Americans. A series of race riots occurred immediately after World War I, followed by episodes of lynching throughout the South. The migration to northern cities had already begun, Garveyism promoted pride in the African heritage for northern migrants, and the Harlem Renaissance showcased black writers, artists, and intellectuals. But racial ghetto formation was also well under way in northern cities, and most blacks still lived in abject poverty in the rural South. White sociologists studied immigrants far more frequently than they studied African Americans. Although sociologist

W. E. B. Du Bois had written about the effects of racial oppression in the pre–World War I era, other famous African American sociologists E. Franklin Frazier and Charles S. Johnson were still studying and doing research during the 1920s and thus did not publish their major studies of the African American community and family until the 1930s and 1940s.

Perhaps nowhere were the cultural and social strains of the decade more evident than in the confusion and debates about the proper place and roles of white women. There was no doubt in the minds of contemporary observers that women's experiences were changing, and there was a great deal of public concern about the modern or "new" women. Fashions in clothing and hairstyles had altered dramatically, and the movies, department stores, and mail-order catalogues made this "new look" available to women across the country. Smoking and drinking in public, dating casually, and dancing all night to the new jazz music, the young women known as flappers embodied the most extreme, sometimes shocking, changes in behavior. But many other women were also affected by these new standards. What impact would these changes have on the home and family, long considered the basis of American society?

In this chapter, you will read some selections from the social science literature of the 1920s about the roles of modern women in order to answer several questions: What did these researchers identify as the major social and economic issues surrounding the roles of modern women? What ethnic groups and social classes most concerned researchers? What assumptions did the social scientists make? What were their recommendations, and to what degree did they suggest redefining women's roles?

The Method

Historians who use evidence such as social science literature from the early twentieth century do so with caution. Although these writers and researchers believed themselves truly to be objective (unbiased) "scientists," they were influenced by who they were and the times in which they lived. The great majority of these social scientists were from middle- or upper-class backgrounds; in addition, most were Protestants whose families had lived in the United States for many generations. Most of them were white and—an important point to note—most of them had been directly or indirectly involved in various urban reform activities.

The obvious problems of the 1920s were related to the major impacts of the immigration, industrialization, and urbanization that had begun in the late nineteenth century. However, the social scientists themselves *chose* which problems they would study. As noted earlier in the Background section, most social scientists of this decade chose to

♦ CHAPTER 6

The "New" Woman:
Social Science
Experts and the
Redefinition of
Women's Roles
in the 1920s

study the "problems" of the immi-grants rather than African American ghettos, lynchings, or segregation, for example. Thus, we certainly cannot say that the social science literature of this era was really objective.

However, this does not mean that such evidence is worthless to the histo-rian. In fact, much, perhaps most, of the evidence relied on by historians is imperfect or "tainted." Because of this, historians avoid taking any evidence literally or at face value; rather, they approach their evidence critically, aware of its imperfections and limits with regard to answering historical questions.

In analyzing the social science litera-ture presented in the Evidence section, you should focus on three specific tasks:

1. Briefly summarize the *message* of each excerpt. What does it describe, criticize or praise, or recommend? What issues are revealed?

2. Identify the underlying *assump-tions* of the author. Does the writer assume readers are male or female? of a working- or middle-class back-ground? Does the writer seem to have fixed or flexible beliefs about women's roles? How do these as-sumptions affect the author's mes-sage?

3. Determine what this piece of evi-dence reveals about the *dilemmas* surrounding the redefinition of women's roles during the 1920s.

Of course, social science literature is only one of several types of evidence that help us understand the degree to which women's roles were being redefined in the 1920s. We need to be very cautious about making generaliza-tions based on such limited evidence. Nevertheless, an analysis of the social science literature can give us insight into an important part of the story.

♦

The Evidence

SEX AND SEXUALITY

Sources 1 and 11 from *The Unadjusted Girl* by William Isaac Thomas, pp. 98, 230, 231. Copyright © 1923 by William I. Thomas. Copyright © renewed 1951 by William I. Thomas. By permission of Little, Brown and Co., Inc.

1. W. I. Thomas on Changing Standards of Morality.

The rôle which a girl is expected to play in life is first of all indicated to her by her family in a series of æsthetic-moral definitions of the situation. Civilized societies, more especially, have endowed the young girl with a character of so-cial sacredness. . . .

But we must understand that this sublimation of life is an investment. It requires . . . incessant attention and effort . . . and goes on best when life is economically secure. And there are families and whole strata of society where life affords no investments. There is little to gain and little to lose. Social workers report that sometimes overburdened mothers with large families complain that they have no "graveyard luck"—all the children live. In cases of great neglect the girl cannot be said to fall, because she has never risen. She is not immoral, because this implies the loss of morality, but a-moral—never having had a moral code.

Source 2 from Alyse Gregory, "The Changing Morality of Women," *Current History* 19 (1923): 298, 299. Reprinted with permission from Current History magazine. Copyright 1923, Current History, Inc.

2. Alyse Gregory on Sex and the New Woman.

Girls' New Habits

Then suddenly all was changed again. The war [World War I] was over and women were admonished to hurry once more home and give the men back their jobs. It was too late. The old discipline had vanished in the night. There was neither an avenging God nor an avenging father to coerce women back into their old places at the family board. They took flats or studios and went on earning their livings. They filled executive offices, they became organizers, editors, copywriters, efficiency managers, artists, writers, real estate agents, and even in rare instances brokers. . . . However unwilling one may be to acknowledge it, girls began to sow their wild oats. Women of the aristocratic upper classes and the poorest women had never followed too rigidly the cast-iron rules of respectability because in neither instance had they anything to lose by digressing. But for the first time in the memory of man, girls from well-bred, respectable middle-class families broke through those invisible chains of custom and asserted their right to a nonchalant, self-sustaining life of their own with a cigarette after every meal and a lover in the evening to wander about with and lend color to life. If the relationship became more intimate than such relationships are supposed to be, there was nothing to be lost that a girl could not well dispense with. Her employer asked no questions as to her life outside the office. She had her own salary at the end of the month and asked no other recompense from her lover but his love and companionship. Into the privacy of her own snug and pleasant rooms not even her mother or her oldest brother could penetrate, for she and she alone, unless perhaps one other, carried the only key that would fit the lock.

Profoundly shocking as such a state of affairs may seem to large numbers of

◆ CHAPTER 6

The "New" Woman:
Social Science
Experts and the
Redefinition of
Women's Roles
in the 1920s

people, there is no use pretending that it does not exist. There are too many signs abroad to prove that it does. Ministers may extol chastity for women from pulpit rostrums and quote passages from the Old and New Testaments to prove that purity and fidelity are still her most precious assets, but this new woman only shrugs her shoulders and smiles a slow, penetrating, secret smile.

Source 3 from Ernest Groves, *Personality and Social Adjustment* (New York: Longman, Green, 1925), pp. 204, 213, 214.

3. Ernest Groves on the Psychological Development of Girls.

The development of the girl's affection is not so simple as that of the boy's. It also has greater opportunities for emotional disturbances. The girl begins, as does the boy, with a fixation upon the mother. But this in the case of the girl is a homosexual experience and thus at the very start of the evolution of affection of the girl there is satisfaction in a relationship which does not require cognizance of sex differences. It is easier therefore for the girl to continue the expression of affection upon members of her own sex straight through childhood into the adult period. Even if the boy has only the dimmest of ideas of the differences between his mother and himself he nevertheless has some slight understanding that he belongs to the class to which his father belongs and not to that of his mother.

It is fortunate that most girls, as if by instinct, tend as they pass the first years of the infantile period to turn their affection to their fathers. . . .

The period that covers the daughter's greatest need of her father's help is necessarily brief. She normally passes quickly on to the next adventure in affection and her impulses turn all the deep interests of her life toward men of her own age. Her emotions and her thought are concentrated upon her new experiences in heterosexual association. It is easy for the adult to forget how tremendous these reactions are in the average girl. What she wears, where she goes, what she does, all her behavior is primarily related to "man." Her feeble efforts to conceal this fact frequently make it all the more noticeable. She is like an actress playing a part with her consciousness fixed upon her audience.

If her new attention to men receives a favorable response her emotional life is wont to flow smoothly. She may still err, to be sure, in her judgment and may consequently make an unwise choice for a life-mate, but she has at least passed through all the various phases of the love experience that precedes adulthood.

Source 4 from *The Nation*, July 6, 1927. Reprinted with permission.

4. John Watson on the Sex Adjustment of Modern Women.

. . . These women were too modern to seek happiness; they sought what? Freedom. So many hundreds of women I have talked to have sought freedom. I have tried to find out diplomatically but behavioristically what they mean. Is it to wear trousers? Is it to vote—to hold office—to work at men's trades—to take men's jobs away from them—to get men's salaries? Does their demand for this mystical thing called freedom imply a resentment against child-bearing—a resentment against the fact that men's sex behavior is different from women's (but not so much any more)? I rarely arrive at a reasonable answer. . . . When a woman is a militant suffragist the chances are, shall we say, a hundred to one that her sex life is not well adjusted? Marriage as such brings adjustment in only approximately 20 per cent of all cases, so poorly have men and women been taught about sex. Among the 20 per cent who find adjustment I find no militant women, I find no women shouting about their rights to some fanciful career that men—the brutes—have robbed them of. They work—they work like a man (than which nothing better can be said about work)—they often quietly achieve careers. Most of the terrible women one must meet, women with the blatant views and voices, women who have to be noticed, who shoulder one about, who can't take life quietly, belong to this large percentage of women who have never made a sex adjustment.

WOMEN'S WORK INSIDE AND OUTSIDE THE HOME

Source 5 from Gwendolyn Hughes, *Mothers in Industry* (New York: New Republic, 1925), pp. 1, 149, 180–181.

5. Gwendolyn Hughes on Working Mothers.

When the mother of young children leaves her traditional place in the home to earn money in a factory she becomes the subject of heated controversy. By some sincere observers she is regarded as a menace to the race and held accountable for the falling birthrate, declining parental responsibility and decadence in home and family life. To others, equally in earnest, her action is entirely commendable and she is regarded as a champion of woman's rights, establishing the greater personal freedom and financial independence of women. . . .

✦ CHAPTER 6

The "New" Woman:
Social Science
Experts and the
Redefinition of
Women's Roles
in the 1920s

Most of the mothers are working full time in industry. . . . The most common weekly schedule is nine and one-fourth hours or nine and three-fourths hours a day with five and one-fourth hours on Saturday, a total of 52½ or 54 hours. . . .

. . . Although most of these homes have running water in the kitchen, there are no stationary tubs, no washing machines, no mangles,[3] no electric irons. The wage-earning mother does not have the means to purchase these household appliances and must do the washing under conditions which most increase her two great disabilities, exhaustion and lack of time. . . .

On Saturday afternoon and Sunday these mothers who work full time clean house, scrub the steps, wash and iron, bathe the children and do the extra cooking. Practically without exception, they maintain that they give their families home cooking; some of them even bake bread.

Source 6 from Christine Frederick, *Efficient Housekeeping, or Household Engineering: Scientific Management in the Home* (Chicago: American School of Home Economics, 1925), pp. 17, 70, 384, 385.

6. Christine Frederick on Efficient Housekeeping.

I want you who take this course to feel that you are *not working alone* in your own home kitchen. I want you to feel that when you discover new methods of housework and better ways of management that you can receive the same recognition that a scientist or business investigator receives. Do not think you are working out the problem for your own home only. You are helping solve the problems of countless other women and homes, and *what you do will be passed on,* and help build up a great mass of proved knowledge on housekeeping. . . .

[Sample] Schedule for Family of Five

Monday

6:00– 6:30	Rise and dress; start water heater
6:30– 7:00	Prepare breakfast
7:00– 7:30	Breakfast
7:30– 8:30	Wash dishes; straighten kitchen; inspect icebox; plan meals for Monday and Tuesday

3. Machines for pressing fabrics by means of heated rollers.

8:30– 9:00	Prepare towards lunch
9:00–10:00	Bedrooms, bath and hall cleaned; sort and prepare soiled linen and laundry
10:00–11:00	Thorough downstairs cleaning
11:00–11:30	*Rest period*
11:30–12:00	Serve lunch
12:00– 1:00	Lunch
1:00– 3:00	Lunch dishes; prepare cooking for Monday and Tuesday; mop kitchen
3:00– 4:00	Sewing and mending
4:00– 4:30	Soak clothes and prepare for next day's washing
4:30– 5:30	*Rest period;* play with children; walk, recreation or market
5:30– 6:00	Prepare supper
6:00– 7:00	Supper
7:00– 7:30	Wash dishes

Tuesday

6:00– 6:30	Rise and dress; put on boiler [tub in which to boil dirty clothes]
6:30– 7:00	Prepare breakfast
7:00– 7:30	Breakfast
7:30– 8:00	Stack dishes; make beds
8:00–11:30	Washing
11:30–12:00	*Rest period*
12:00– 1:00	Lunch (prepared day before)
1:00– 2:30	Wash breakfast and lunch dishes; clear up laundry
2:30– 4:00	Take in clothes; fold, sprinkle [dampen clothes before ironing], lay away
4:00– 5:30	*Rest period*
5:30– 6:00	Prepare supper
6:00– 7:00	Supper
7:00– 7:30	Wash dishes

In some households where there is no permanent worker, it often happens that the homemaker looks to the husband as a kind of nursemaid, choreman or kitchen assistant. The author's feeling is very much against this view,—that the moment a man comes into the house he should be asked to carry out the slops, hold the baby or wash the dishes. If the father works hard and faithfully at his task of earning money during his work day, it is not more fair to

◆ CHAPTER 6

The "New" Woman:
Social Science
Experts and the
Redefinition of
Women's Roles
in the 1920s

ask him to turn choreman as soon as he comes home, than it would be to ask the woman who has cooked and cleaned all day to turn around and do office or business work after five o'clock. It is not fair to put on a father any housework duties; his hours at home should be hours of recuperation, or so that he can study *his own work,* become more proficient, and thus secure advancement or a better economic position.

There comes to mind the case of a gifted man starting a profession, who, because of his wife's poor management, spent his time after office hours caring for the children and doing chores. He never seemed to "get on" as far as people had expected. Would it not have been better to use his spare time studying and improving in his own profession and thus be eventually able to pay for more service to help his wife, than to neglect his own opportunities by doing the housework?

Source 7 from Lillian M. Gilbreth, *The Homemaker and Her Job* (New York: Appleton-Century, 1927), pp. vii, 50, 51.

7. Lillian M. Gilbreth on Making Housework Satisfying.

Home-making is the finest job in the world, and it is the aim of this book to make it as interesting and satisfying as it is important.

Waste of energy is the cause of drudgery in work of any kind. In industry the engineer and the psychologist, working together, have devised means of getting more done with less effort and fatigue and of making everything that is done more interesting. The worker not only spends his working hours more effectively and with more satisfaction, but has more time and more energy freed for other things.

This book applies to the home the methods of eliminating waste that have been successful in industry. To the home-maker it offers a philosophy that will make her work satisfying, a technic that will make it easy, and a method of approach that will make it interesting.

Source 8 from Alice Rogers Hager, "Occupations and Earnings of Women in Industry," in *The Annals: Women in the Modern World* (Philadelphia: Sage Publications, 1929), p. 72. Reprinted with permission of The American Academy of Political and Social Science.

8. Alice Rogers Hager on Men's and Women's Factory Pay in the Mid-1920s.

WEEK'S EARNINGS OF MALES AND OF FEMALES IN FACTORIES.
ILLINOIS, 1924 TO 1928

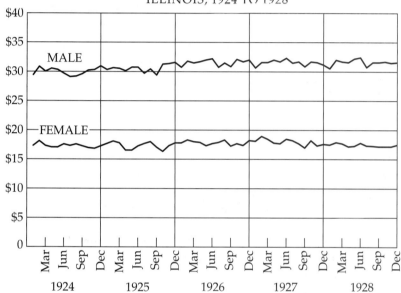

Source 9 from Benjamin R. Andrews, "The Home Woman as Buyer and Controller of Consumption," in *The Annals: Women in the Modern World*, pp. 47, 48. Reprinted by permission of The American Academy of Political and Social Science.

9. Benjamin R. Andrews on Ethical Duties of the Home Buyer, 1929.

What ethical duties has the private buyer? Some standards the buyer is recognizing as a code, and these, with other techniques, the new household buyer will be taught. She will not seek her personal advantage, when it means a loss to the dealer. This is the standard that she would demand of him, not to seek his advantage at her loss, and it is only fair that she practice it herself. She will not hold goods unnecessarily on approval and cause losses that have to be made up by higher prices. She will not take unnecessary time in examining goods in stores. She is willing to pay for all the services that

✦ CHAPTER 6

The "New" Woman:
Social Science
Experts and the
Redefinition of
Women's Roles
in the 1920s

she demands. She returns goods promptly, and in perfect condition. She does not abuse her credit privileges, or seek unusual advantages as a credit customer. She remembers that courtesy is equally binding upon customer and salesperson. . . .

The home buyer must realize that, to her family, she is the guardian of the treasury, and that her watch over expenditures makes, or mars, the quality of life which they achieve. She must seek the best that her income makes possible, and she is finding that controlled and planned spending pays.

Source 10 from Caroline Manning, *The Immigrant Woman and Her Job* (Washington, D.C.: U.S. Government Printing Office, 1930), pp. 40, 50, 59.

10. Caroline Manning on Immigrant Women Workers.

Care during mother's absence.—The families were large, the children young, and life was especially strenuous for the 500 employed mothers whose youngest child was less than 6. It was not customary for children to begin school before they were 6, and in more than half of the families with five, six, and seven or more children the youngest child was not yet 4 years old. . . .

The opinion was general among the families visited that children of 7 who were in school part of the time certainly knew enough to get something to eat at noon and to take care of themselves when not in school, and that children as old as 12 were quite able to care not only for themselves but for younger children; in fact, the care of a 12-year-old presented few problems. . . .

To the question as to why the women had returned to work after marriage there was repetition in the answers: "Times weren't so good." "Expenses so high." "We were getting behind in everything." "The men were laid off and we needed a slice of bread." "Never know when sickness comes how much it cost." "To pay for my home some day." All "needed to help a little out"— husbands ill, husbands out of work or on part time, rent to pay, and children to feed were indeed common to all. . . .

. . . Yet the conversation often drifted into channels that revealed deeper hopes and ambitions. Though the women did not give such desires as their definite reasons for working, they constituted perhaps the impelling force that directed the lives of these wage earners. At least 700 mothers referred to the plans they had for their children and the problems arising in regard to their education and the kinds of work in which they should be trained. Their comments speak for themselves: "I am still a greenhorn. My little girl must be smart." "She must not do stripping like me." "My boys must go to high school if they have good heads." "He must not work in the mill but be an American."

The children of an ambitious woman who was spending her days at the polishing wheel took music lessons. Another mother, recalling her days of "slavery" in the mill, was helping her daughter through a business college.

Women feeling the pinch of hard times were ready to make sacrifices: "We do by our children in school what we can afford." The goal of a widow who worked 10 hours a day was to see her daughter a graduate of the normal school: "I no care how long I work if she can teach in a school."

MARRIAGE AND THE FAMILY

Source 11 from W. I. Thomas, *The Unadjusted Girl*, pp. 72, 73.

11. W. I. Thomas, Case 37: A Married Woman's Despair, 1923.

My husband's career, upon which I spent the best years of my life, is established favorably; our children are a joy to me as a mother; nor can I complain about our material circumstances. But I am dissatisfied with myself. My love for my children, be it ever so great, cannot destroy myself. A human being is not created like a bee which dies after accomplishing its only task. . . .

Desires, long latent, have been aroused in me and become more aggressive the more obstacles they encounter. . . . I now have the desire to go about and see and hear everything. I wish to take part in everything—to dance, skate, play the piano, sing, go to the theatre, opera, lectures and generally mingle in society. As you see, I am no idler whose purpose is to chase all sorts of foolish things, as a result of loose ways. This is not the case.

My present unrest is a natural result following a long period of hunger and thirst for non-satisfied desires in every field of human experience. It is the dread of losing that which never can be recovered—youth and time which do not stand still—an impulse to catch up with the things I have missed. . . . If it were not for my maternal feeling I would go away into the wide world.

Source 12 from *The Nation*, July 6, 1927. Reprinted with permission.

12. John Watson on Married Women and Careers, 1926.

I have never believed that there were any unsuperable difficulties which keep women from succeeding. They have strength enough to paint, yet there has never been a great woman painter. They have strength enough to play the violin and yet there has never been a great woman violinist. They have endur-

◆ CHAPTER 6

The "New" Woman:
Social Science
Experts and the
Redefinition of
Women's Roles
in the 1920s

ance and strength enough to become great scientists and yet one can count on fewer than the fingers of one hand the women scientists who have achieved real greatness. During the past thirty years thousands of women have taken the degree of Ph.D. and yet scarcely a dozen have come to the front. . . .

Not being trained from infancy to the tradition of incessant manipulative work they drop out of the race as soon as they get comfortable. Marriage is usually the shady spot that causes them to lie down and rest. And when they fail in that, as 80 per cent do, restlessness again sets in, but now it is too late to go back and take up the threads of the old career. Most women who had aspirations for a career have tried to eat their cake and have it too. A career is a jealous all-consuming taskmaster.

Marriage as such should be no barrier to a career. Apartment hotels, which can be found in every town where a woman would have a career, have freed married women without children almost completely. The having of children is almost an insuperable barrier to a career. The rearing of children and the running of a home for them is a profession second to none in its demands for technique.

Source 13 from Ernest Groves and Gladys Hoagland Groves, *Wholesome Marriage*, pp. 100, 101, 206–209, 214. Copyright 1927 by Houghton Mifflin Company; copyright renewed © 1955 by Gladys Hoagland Groves. Reprinted by permission of Houghton Mifflin Company. All rights reserved.

13. Ernest and Gladys H. Groves on How to Have a Happy Marriage, 1927.

LIFE PARTNERSHIP.   What is the secret of those marriages in which the wedding day seems to be a turning-point that brings the man to the straightaway leading to business success? It would be well to know, if the knowledge could be used to help those for whom the marriage ceremony is but a milestone in a long, slow, uphill climb to financial security.

The answer lies in the reactions of the newly married couple to their new relationship. Normally the man is very proud of his responsibility for the welfare of his family. He takes his business much more seriously than he did before, for now he has two mouths to feed instead of one. It would never do to lose his job, or even to miss an expected promotion.

The young husband "settles down" to his work, determined to make good if it is in him. He is somewhat helped in the settling-down process by the strange, new fact that he is no longer in constant fear of losing his sweetheart.

She is his "for keeps" now, and his only anxiety is to be able to do his part well in the establishment of the home life they are entering upon.

This means money, a steady stream of it that can be depended on and promises to grow larger in time. So the young man throws himself into his work whole-heartedly, and the stuff he is made of shows. That is his side of the story. . . .

Of course the wife who helps her husband on to success makes the home life restful and refreshing. Dissatisfaction finds no quarters within the four walls of the house, be it two-room flat or rambling country homestead. Good housekeeping is not enough to turn the trick, but it is an indispensable card. Singleness of purpose, alertness of mind, and a broad outlook on life are all needed.

Then the wife does not put her embroidery, bridge, and tea parties above her husband's peace of mind. She does her best to keep the home life pleasant, that her man may be in tip-top condition for his work outside. Turning and twisting to save a penny, she sees to it that the family lives within its income, so that her husband will not be worried by unpaid bills, when he is trying to increase his earning capacity. Above all she has faith in her husband's ability to better his condition.

Source 14 from Lorine Pruette, "The Married Woman and the Part-Time Job," in *The Annals: Women in the Modern World*, pp. 302, 303, 306. Reprinted by permission of The American Academy of Political and Social Science.

14. Lorine Pruette on the Demoralizing Influence of the Home, 1929.

The worst thing that can be said for the American home is that it ruins so many of its members. It is a disheartening and disillusioning business to survey the middle-aged married women of the country. They have been permanently damaged as persons by the disintegrating influences of the modern home and family life. Conversely, they contribute to the further disintegration of the institution to which they have given their lives.

It is only the rare woman who can pass without deterioration through many years of uninterrupted domesticity. . . . Schemes for coördination and coöperation in women's activities appear predicated on the idea that wives, when freed from minor household responsibilities, will find their satisfactions in helping their husbands get ahead in their vocations. This implies a subordination of self unfashionable in an age where the emphasis is on self-expression and uncommon among the individualistic American women of to-day. . . .

Not only does part-time employment of the married woman offer the oppor-

✦ CHAPTER 6

The "New" Woman:
Social Science
Experts and the
Redefinition of
Women's Roles
in the 1920s

tunity for the development of a new home life, it lessens or destroys the appalling economic risk taken by every woman who today marries and devotes herself to the traditional rôle of wife. There is no security in domesticity. It is heart-breaking to see the middle-aged woman, trained for nothing except the duties of the home, venture out into the industrial world. Divorce, death or loss of money may put her in this position, where she has so little to offer organized industry and so much to suffer. The married woman who lets herself go upon the easy tide of domesticity is offering herself as a victim in a future tragedy.

Source 15 from Willystine Goodsell, *Problems of the Family* (New York: Century Company, 1928), pp. 281, 282.

15. Willystine Goodsell on the Frustration of Educated Wives, 1928.

Perhaps a concrete instance of the situation in which the trained woman often finds herself after marriage may serve to make the problem more real in the minds of the indifferent or the unsympathetic. In one of the issues of the *Journal of the Association of Collegiate Alumnae,* there appeared a few years ago a brief article entitled "Reflections of a Professor's Wife." With her husband, the writer had spent several years in the graduate school of a university where both had earned their doctors' degrees. Then the equality in work and the delightful companionship ceased. The man was appointed assistant professor in a state university at a small salary; and the woman, who had eagerly looked forward to a similar appointment in the same institution, was brought face to face with the ruling, by no means uncommon, which prohibited wives of faculty members from teaching in the university. The comments of the professor's wife, after years spent in housekeeping, are worth quoting, for they reflect the feelings of many other women caught in a similar net of circumstance:

"After an expenditure of several thousand dollars and the devotion of some of the best years of my life to special study, I was cut off from any opportunity to utilize this training. And unless I could earn enough money to pay some one else to do the housework, I was doomed to spend a large part of my time in tasks which a woman with practically no education could do. However, accepting the situation, I put on my apron and went into the kitchen, where for six years I have cooked a professor's meals and pondered over the policy of our university. Can it be in the divine order of things that one Ph.D. should wash dishes a whole life time for another Ph.D. just because one is a woman and the other a man?"

Source 16 from Ernest Mowrer, *Domestic Discord* (Chicago: University of Chicago Press, 1928), pp. 160, 169. Copyright © 1928 by the University of Chicago Press. Reprinted by permission.

16. Ernest Mowrer, Notes from Two Social Workers' Visits with Two Immigrant Families, 1928.

"Visited home. Mr. M and children at home. House and children very dirty and the babies half dressed. Mr. M said Mrs. M is working. Goes early in the morning and works ten hours. . . .

"Told him that if he would leave drink alone and work regularly that Mrs. M wouldn't have to work. Compared the neatness and cleanliness of the children when Mrs. M was home and the filth and dirt now. He said she wanted to work. I told him that was because she couldn't see the children without clothes and food."

Then four months later:

"I told the interpreter to explain very carefully to Mr. M that Mrs. M should not be working. That it was her job to stay at home and take care of the children. It is his job to support them, and if he does not do it, we will have to send him to the Bridewell [correctional institution]. . . . I am going to check up his pay every two weeks, and if he does not come up to the standard he will have to give me satisfactory reason, or we will have to bring him into court. . . ."

"Visited the B home. The house was in a terrible condition, the bed was unmade, everything was dusty and dirty, and the children were dirty and half-dressed.

Mrs. B still wishes to leave her husband as she feels that there will never be any harmony between them. She proposes to leave the two oldest children with Mr. B and take the baby with her. She knows that Mr. B is a dutiful father and will not abuse them. She states "she is still young and can make a living for herself at any time."

Mrs. B is selfish and is always thinking of her own comfort and pleasure. She has permitted her jealousy to overrule her and is constantly doubting her husband's fidelity. Also finding fault in the unimportant things.

Worker tried to make Mrs. B realize her responsibility as a wife and mother. Advised her that she ought to keep her house and children clean if she wishes to command the respect of her husband. Also advised her to have her husband's meals ready on time when he comes home from a hard day's work."

✦ CHAPTER 6

The "New" Woman:
Social Science
Experts and the
Redefinition of
Women's Roles
in the 1920s

THREE "NEW" WOMEN

First written passage in Source 17 from Margaret Sanger, *An Autobiography* (New York: W. W. Norton, 1938), pp. 192–193. Second written passage from Margaret Sanger, *Women and the New Race* (New York: Brentano's, 1920), pp. 93–95. Photo: Library of Congress.

17. Margaret Sanger.

[*While serving as a nurse-midwife in New York City, Sanger became concerned about the number of women, primarily married women, who submitted to dangerous, often fatal, abortions. When she opened a birth control clinic in 1916, however, she was arrested, tried, and convicted of violating a state law prohibiting the distribution of birth control devices and information. In a major victory for Sanger and her middle-class supporters, the appeals court ruled that licensed physicians could give such information and devices to their patients. From 1920 on, Margaret Sanger openly advocated birth control. She was one of the founders of the organization that later became Planned Parenthood. In her autobiography, Sanger recalls her feelings before giving her first public lecture on birth control in 1916.*]

The anxiety that went into the composition of the speech was as nothing to the agonies with which I contemplated its utterance. My mother used to say a decent woman only had her name in the papers three times during her life— when she was born, when she married, and when she died. Although by nature I shrank from publicity, the kind of work I had undertaken did not allow me to shirk it—but I was frightened to death. Hoping that practice would give me greater confidence, I used to climb to the roof of the Lexington Avenue hotel where I was staying and recite, my voice going out over the house tops and echoing timidly among the chimney pots.

[*In the 1920s, there was a large, middle-class audience for nonfiction. Sanger's book,* Women and the New Race, *set forth her basic arguments for birth control to receptive readers.*]

The problem of birth control has arisen directly from the effort of the feminine spirit to free itself from bondage. Woman herself has wrought that bondage through her reproductive powers and while enslaving herself has enslaved the world. The physical suffering to be relieved is chiefly woman's. Hers, too, is the love life that dies first under the blight of too prolific breeding. Within her is wrapped up the future of the race—it is hers to make or mar. All of these considerations point unmistakably to one fact—it is woman's duty as well as her privilege to lay hold of the means of freedom. Whatever men may do, she cannot escape the responsibility. For ages she has been deprived of the opportunity to meet this obligation. She is now emerging from her helplessness. Even as no one can share the suffering of the overburdened mother, so no one can do this work for her. Others may help, but she and she alone can free herself.

The basic freedom of the world is woman's freedom. A free race cannot be born of slave mothers. A woman enchained cannot choose but give a measure of that bondage to her sons and daughters. No woman can call herself free who does not own and control her body. No woman can call herself free until she can choose consciously whether she will or will not be a mother.

◆ CHAPTER 6

The "New" Woman:
Social Science
Experts and the
Redefinition of
Women's Roles
in the 1920s

Source 18 from David Stern, *Clara Bow: Runnin' Wild* (New York: Cooper Square Press, 2000), pp. 2, 68. Photo: The Everett Collection.

18. Clara Bow.

[*One of the most famous film stars of the 1920s, Bow was known as the "It" girl, a reference to her appearance in a film emphasizing her sex appeal. Born to poor parents in a tenement, she dropped out of school after seventh grade to work. Like many young working women, she escaped from her dreary life by going to the movies frequently and reading magazines about movie stars. At 16, she won a contest sponsored by a movie magazine; the prize was a screen test and a part in a film. Bow then moved to Hollywood, got a contract with a major studio, had many public love affairs, and partied constantly. To many people, she was the embodiment of the "flapper." In 1926, after one of her lovers staged a dramatic, but unsuccessful, suicide attempt because Bow had rejected him, she told a reporter from the Los Angeles* Examiner:]

"Mr. Savage is just an episode in my young life," she declared. "He says he triedta commit suicide 'cause I turned him down—'gave him the gate,' he calls it.

"Well, lemme tell ya this," said Clara with sudden, scornful authority on the subject, "when a man attempts suicide over a woman, he don't cut his wrists with a safety razor blade, then drape himself over a couch with a cigarette between his lips. No, they don't do it that way. They use *pistols*."

[In another interview, when asked if she really lived the carefree, happy life of one of the young women she portrayed in a film, Bow replied:]

"I wish I were," sighed Clara. "She's much happier than I am. . . ."

"All the time the flapper is laughin' and dancin', there's a feelin' of tragedy underneath. . . . She's unhappy and disillusioned, and that's what people sense. That's what makes her different."

First written passage in Source 19 from Margaret Mead, *Blackberry Winter* (New York: Simon and Schuster [Touchstone], 1972), p. 145. Second through fourth written passages from Margaret Mead, *Coming of Age in Samoa* (New York: Harper Collins [Perennial Classics], 1928 [2001]), pp. 139, 160, 170. Photo: The Everett Collection.

19. Margaret Mead.

[Brought up in an extended, academic family, Mead studied psychology and anthropology in college. After beginning her graduate work in 1926, she sailed alone to Pago Pago (Samoa) where she lived in villages and studied how people in this preindustrial culture raised their children. Mead was particularly interested in girls and the socialization process by which they became women. The result of her field studies was the classic cross-cultural study, Coming of Age in Samoa, *first published in 1928. Mead's work raised important questions about gender roles at a time when women's behavior*

◆ CHAPTER 6

The "New" Woman:
Social Science
Experts and the
Redefinition of
Women's Roles
in the 1920s

seemed to be changing rapidly. Married three times, Mead continued to do field work and publish the results for the rest of her life. Mead's first husband was a fellow graduate student and Episcopal minister who studied in Europe while she was in Samoa. In her autobiography, she writes about preparing for her trip.]

When I set out for Samoa I had half a dozen cotton dresses (including two very pretty ones) for I had been told that silk rotted in the tropics. But when I arrived, I found that the Navy wives dressed in silk. I had a small strongbox in which to keep my money and papers, a small Kodak, and a portable type-writer. Although I had been married for two years, I had never stayed alone in a hotel and I had made only short journeys by train as far as the Middle West. . . . I had never been to sea.

[*To Mead, anthropology was a way of answering the questions about American society in which she was interested.*]

In all of these comparisons between Samoan and American culture, many points are useful only in throwing a spotlight upon our own solutions, while in others it is possible to find suggestions for change. Whether or not we envy other peoples one of their solutions, our attitude towards our own solutions must be greatly broadened and deepened by a consideration of the way in which other peoples have met the same problems. Realising that our own ways are not humanly inevitable nor God-ordained, but are the fruit of a long and turbulent history, we may well examine in turn all of our institutions, thrown into strong relief against the history of other civilisations, and weighing them in the balance, be not afraid to find them wanting.

[*Some of the most striking differences Mead found in Samoa had to do with attitudes toward sex and sexuality.*]

Similarly, our children are faced with half a dozen standards of morality: a double sex standard for men and women, a single standard for men and women, and groups which advocate that the single standard should be freedom while others argue that the single standard should be absolute monogamy. . . .

The Samoan child faces no such dilemma. Sex is a natural, pleasurable thing; the freedom with which it may be indulged in is limited by just one consideration, social status. Chiefs' daughters and chiefs' wives should indulge in no extra-marital experiments.

[*Mead clearly stated the ramifications of her cross-cultural study in her concluding chapters.*]

At the present time we live in a period of transition. We have many standards but we still believe that only one standard can be the right one. . . . But it is unthinkable that a final recognition of the great number of ways in which man, during the course of history and at the present time, is solving the problems of life, should not bring with it in turn the downfall of our belief in a single standard. And when no one group claims ethical sanction for its customs, and each group welcomes to its midst only those who are temperamentally fitted for membership, then we shall have realised the high point of individual choice and universal toleration which a heterogeneous culture and a heterogeneous culture alone can attain. Samoa knows but one way of life and teaches it to her children. Will we, who have the knowledge of many ways, leave our children free to choose among them?

Questions to Consider

The Evidence is grouped into three broad categories—*sex and sexuality, women's work inside and outside the home,* and *marriage and the family*—and then presents material on three "new" women. There is some unavoidable overlap among the first three categories. In the section on sex and sexuality, a variety of social scientists comment on the changing standards. W. I. Thomas (Source 1) was one of the pioneers of social psychology and the sociological case study. Alyse Gregory (Source 2) was a feminist, a statistical researcher for the Carnegie Educational Foundation, and a "new" woman herself. Ernest Groves (Source 3), deeply affected by Freudian psychology, was a professor of social science and the author of numerous college textbooks on child and family studies. Psychologist John Watson (Source 4), in contrast, was the founder of American behaviorism, a school of thought that maintained that human behavior was conditioned by the environment and training of the individual. What is the *message* of each piece of evidence? What *assumptions* does each author reveal? How were *attitudes* about women's sexuality changing? What *difficulties* were involved in these changes?

The section on women's work inside and outside the home also includes an assortment of writings by social scientists in various fields. Dr. Gwendolyn Hughes (Source 5) was a social research fellow at Bryn Mawr College for Women when she prepared *Mothers in Industry,* a massive research project involving twelve thousand households of wage-earning women in Philadelphia. As participants in the scientific management movement of the early twentieth century, both Christine Frederick (Source 6), an educator, and Dr. Lillian M. Gilbreth (Source 7), a consulting engineer, sought to apply the standards of industrial efficiency to housekeeping. Alice Rogers Hager (Source 8) and Caroline Manning (Source 10) were re-

◆ CHAPTER 6

The "New" Woman:
Social Science
Experts and the
Redefinition of
Women's Roles
in the 1920s

searchers and writers for the Women's Bureau of the U.S. Department of Labor. Dr. Benjamin R. Andrews (Source 9) was a professor of economics at Columbia University. When looking for the *message, assumptions,* and *issues* in this section, be especially aware of which women—immigrants, native born, highly educated professionals, or ordinary homemakers—are the subjects of each piece of evidence. In what ways are the situations of all classes of women similar? In what ways are they different? What recommendations do the social scientists make? Do these apply to all classes of women? Why or why not? This section is especially useful for considering the *difficulties* involved in redefining modern women's roles.

The next section of the evidence focuses on women's roles in marriage and the family. W. I. Thomas (Source 11), John Watson (Source 12), and Ernest Groves (Source 13) are identified earlier. Although they are all psychologists, you should note the major differences in their ideas about married women's roles and happiness. Dr. Lorine Pruette (Source 14) was an economist whose dissertation, *Women and Leisure,* was published in 1924. Married and divorced twice, Pruette

became a freelance consultant in order to try to adapt to her husbands' academic career moves. The last two selections in this section are from books by sociology professors: Dr. Willystine Goodsell (Source 15) taught at Teachers College, Columbia University, and Dr. Ernest Mowrer (Source 16) taught at Northwestern University. Apply the same methodology to this section that you used for the other two sections.

New woman was a term that attempted to make sense of the changes that people observed around them with regard to women's roles. The section "Three New Women" (Sources 17 through 19) provides photographs, biographical information, and some of their own words for three famous women of the 1920s. It is easy to see the differences among these women, but be sure also to identify their similarities. What makes each of them a "new" woman compared with women of the previous generation?

Finally, try to pull all the material together to understand the degree to which women's roles (sexual, economic, and as wives and mothers) were—or were not—being redefined by social scientists in the 1920s.

◆

Epilogue

During the Great Depression in the 1930s, social scientists eagerly enlisted in New Deal experiments, such as efforts to help the unemployed, create model communities in rural areas, and devise programs for families in trouble.

African American sociologists began publishing studies of southern black family and community experiences during this era, although very little was done to alleviate the problems of black poverty. For all practical purposes, the stock market crash of 1929 and the deep depression that lasted throughout the 1930s ended the fascination with the "new woman" and replaced it with sympathy and concern for the "forgotten man." Women who worked, especially married women, were perceived as taking jobs away from unemployed men who desperately needed to support their families. In hard times, people clung to traditional male and female roles: Men should be the breadwinners, and women should stay home and take care of the family. Women's fashions changed just as dramatically. Clothing became more feminine, hemlines dropped, and hairstyles were no longer short and boyish.

Yet women, including married women, continued to move into paid employment throughout the 1930s, and with the United States' entry into World War II, millions of women who had never held paying jobs before went to work in factories and shipyards, motivated by patriotism and a desire to aid the war effort. By the 1950s, women workers, having been replaced by returning veterans, were once again being urged to stay at home and fulfill their destinies as wives and mothers. Women's educational achievements and age at marriage dropped; the white middle-class birthrate nearly doubled. Women were still entering the work force, but in feminized clerical and retail jobs and in professions such as elementary school teaching and nursing. Fashions changed from knee-length tailored suits and dresses and "Rosie the Riveter" slacks to puff-sleeved, tiny-waisted, full-skirted, ankle-length dresses.

The discomfort about changes in women's roles, so prominent in the 1920s, was also present in the 1960s and 1970s. Unisex fashions, the development and widespread use of the birth control pill, the availability of legal abortions, the rise of women's athletics, and the influx of young women into graduate and professional programs all seemed to threaten both women's traditional roles in marriage and the family and men's traditional role as breadwinners. In this era, there was also a new awareness about the importance of socioeconomic class, race, and ethnicity—as well as about their impact on women's options. Old assumptions about heterosexuality and homosexuality were questioned and, in many cases, rejected. A new, broader-based women's movement led to the formation of new feminist organizations, and a revised version of the ERA was passed but not ratified by the states. By the 1980s, a conservative backlash against these changes was well under way. Today the roles of women and girls continue to change and are still being redefined.

7

Documenting the Depression: The FSA Photographers and Rural Poverty

The Problem

On a cold, rainy afternoon in the spring of 1936, Dorothea Lange was driving home from a month-long field trip to central California. One of several young photographers hired by the Historical Section of the Farm Security Administration (FSA), Lange had been talking with migrant laborers and taking photographs of the migrants' camps.

After passing a hand-lettered road sign that read PEA PICKERS CAMP, Lange drove on another twenty miles. Then she stopped, turned around, and went back to the migrant camp. The pea crop had frozen, and there was no work for the pickers, but several families were still camped there. Lange approached a woman and her daughters, talked with them briefly, asked to take a few pictures, and left ten minutes later. The result was one of the most famous images of the Great Depression, *Migrant Mother* (see Source 8).

On the opening day in 1938, over seven thousand visitors attended the first International Exposition of Pho-

tography in New York City. The FSA's exhibit was a very small part of the three thousand photographs displayed, yet it drew shocked comments from many viewers. "Wake up, smug America," read one response card. "It makes you think of tomorrow and what it will bring," another viewer reflected after seeing the powerful images of rural poverty, dislocation, and suffering. "It brings home to me some of the things in our country that we need to do something about," a third viewer wrote.[1] These photographs moved Americans deeply and helped create support for New Deal legislation and programs to aid migrant workers, sharecroppers, tenant farmers, and small-scale farmers.

In this chapter, you will analyze documentary photographs from the FSA to determine how and why they were so effective in creating support for New Deal legislation to aid rural Americans.

1. James Curtis, *Mind's Eye, Mind's Truth: FSA Photography Reconsidered* (Philadelphia: Temple University Press, 1990), pp. 5–6.

Background

In 1930, President Herbert Hoover was at first bewildered and then defensive about the rapid downward spiral of the nation's economy. Hoover, like many other Americans, believed in the basic soundness of capitalism, advocated the values of individualism, and maintained that the role of the federal government should be limited. Nevertheless, Hoover was a compassionate man. As private relief sources dried up, he authorized public works projects and some institutional loans, at the same time vetoing other relief bills and trying to convince the nation that prosperity would return soon. The media, especially newspapers and middle-class magazines, followed Hoover's lead.

Americans turned out at the polls in record numbers for the election of 1932—and voted for the Democratic candidate, Franklin D. Roosevelt, in equally record numbers. As unemployment increased dramatically along with bank and business failures, Congress reacted by rapidly passing an assortment of programs collectively known as the New Deal. Calling together a group of experts (mainly professors and lawyers) to form a "brain trust," the newly elected president acted quickly to try to restore the nation's confidence. In his fireside radio chats, as well as in his other speeches, Roosevelt consistently reassured the American public that the country's economic institutions were sound.

Like her husband, First Lady Eleanor Roosevelt was tireless in her efforts to mitigate the effects of the depression. With boundless energy, she traveled throughout the country, observing conditions firsthand and reporting back to her husband. One of the few New Dealers deeply committed to civil rights for African Americans, she championed both individuals and the civil rights movement whenever she could. Although she was criticized and ridiculed for her nontraditional behavior as first lady, to millions of Americans, Eleanor Roosevelt was the heart of the New Deal. In fact, during the depression, more than 15 million Americans wrote directly to the president and first lady about their personal troubles and economic difficulties.

In an emergency session early in 1933, Congress began the complicated process of providing immediate relief for the needy and legislation for longer-term recovery and reform. Banking, business, the stock market, unemployed workers, farmers, and young people were targets of this early New Deal legislation.

The New Deal administration soon realized that the problems of farmers were going to be especially difficult to alleviate. To meet the unusual European demand for farm products during World War I, many American farmers had overexpanded. They had mortgaged their farms and borrowed money to buy expensive new farm equipment, but most had not shared in the profits of the so-called prosperous decade of the 1920s.

Unfortunately, the New Deal's Agricultural Adjustment Act benefited only relatively large, prosperous farmers. Intended to reduce farm production

◆ CHAPTER 7

Documenting the
Depression:
The FSA
Photographers
and Rural Poverty

and thus improve the prices farmers received for their goods, the act unintentionally encouraged large farmers to accept payment for reducing their crops, use the money to buy machinery, and evict the sharecroppers and tenants who had been farming part of their land. Explaining to Dorothea Lange why his family was traveling to California, one farmer simply said they had been "tractored out." With no land of their own to farm, sharecroppers and tenants packed their few belongings and families into old trucks and cars and took to the road looking for seasonal agricultural work in planting, tending, or picking produce.

In so doing, they joined thousands of other American farm families who lived in the Dust Bowl—the plains and prairie states where unwise agricultural practices and a long drought had combined to create terrifying dust storms that blotted out the sun, blew away the topsoil, and actually buried some farms in dust. These Dust Bowl refugees, along with former tenants and sharecroppers, joined Mexican Americans already working as migrant laborers in California. For those left behind, especially in the poverty-stricken areas of the rural Midwest and South, conditions were almost as terrible as in the migrant camps.

It was to aid these displaced farmers that President Roosevelt created the Resettlement Administration (RA), which two years later became the Farm Security Administration. The RA was headed by Rexford Tugwell, an economics professor from Columbia University. A former Progressive, Tugwell was an optimist who believed that if the public was educated about social and economic problems, Americans would support legislation to correct whatever was wrong. To accomplish this task, Tugwell hired his former graduate student, Roy Stryker, to direct the Historical Section of the agency.

Stryker in turn hired a small group of photographers to travel around the country and take photos illustrating the difficulties faced by small farmers, tenants, and sharecroppers, and to a lesser extent, the FSA projects intended to ameliorate these problems.

Although not a photographer himself, Stryker had definite ideas about what the photographers who worked for him should be doing. When he discovered that Carl Mydans, who had been assigned to the Cotton Belt of the South, knew nothing about the subject, Stryker postponed Mydans's departure until he had lectured the photographer about the geography, history, and issues surrounding cotton cultivation. To Dorothea Lange, an experienced reformer and photographer, Stryker wrote:

We need to vary the diet in some of our exhibits here by showing some western poverty instead of all south and east. . . . When you get to Los Angeles, I think it might be worthwhile to see if you can pick up some good slum pictures there also. Do not forget that we need some of the rural slum type of thing as well as the urban.

Some photographers, such as the well-known Walker Evans, ignored Stryker's instructions much of the time. "After all, the Resettlement Administration is putting out to you each month a pretty nice sum of money,"

Stryker wrote to Evans in 1936, "and they have a right to expect certain returns." When Evans asked for a leave of absence to work on a *Fortune* magazine assignment with writer James Agee, Stryker readily agreed.[2]

Hoping to mobilize public opinion in support of FSA-funded projects such as model migrant camps, rural cooperatives, health clinics, and federal relief for the poorest families, Stryker made the photographs widely available to national middle-class magazines and local newspapers. The Historical Section also organized traveling exhibits and encouraged authors to use the photographs in their books.

These photographic images were intended to elicit emotional responses from viewers. What kinds of subjects did the photographs portray? In what ways did the impact of the depression, as visualized in the photographs, seem to endanger traditional American values and deeply held beliefs? In other words, why were these images so effective in creating support for New Deal legislation to help rural Americans?

The Method

By the end of the nineteenth century, technological advances had made using cameras and developing photographs easier, but both the equipment and the developing methods were still cumbersome and primitive by today's standards. Nevertheless, people were fascinated by photography, and many talented amateurs, such as E. Alice Austen, spent hours taking pictures of their families, friends, and homes. Indeed, these photographs are an important source of evidence for social historians trying to reconstruct how Americans lived in the past.

Documentary photography, however, has a different purpose: reform. During the Progressive era of the late nineteenth and early twentieth centuries, middle-class Americans increasingly became concerned about the growing number of poor families who depended on the labor of their children to supplement their meager standard of living. First Jacob Riis, the author of *How the Other Half Lives* (1890), and then Lewis Hine, in his work for the National Child Labor Committee, photographed the living and working conditions of young children and documented the ill effects of child labor. These photographs were used to persuade the public to support the strict regulation or abolition of child labor.

Roy Stryker was impressed by the power of such photographs and had used many of Hine's images to illustrate Rexford Tugwell's reform-oriented economics textbook in the 1920s. The dozen or so talented photographers whom Stryker hired to work for the Historical Section of the FSA were relatively young (most were in their twenties or thirties) and came from a variety of backgrounds. Most of

2. F. Jack Hurley, *Portrait of a Decade: Roy Stryker and the Development of Documentary Photography in the Thirties* (Baton Rouge: Louisiana State University Press, 1972), pp. 57–58, 70, 64.

◆ CHAPTER 7

Documenting the
Depression:
The FSA
Photographers
and Rural Poverty

the photographers, including Dorothea Lange, Walker Evans, Jack Delano, Carl Mydans, John Collier, Marion Post Wolcott, and Theodor Jung, were either established professionals or serious amateurs. Others took their first professional photographs for the Historical Section: Ben Shahn and Russell Lee had been painters, and Arthur Rothstein and John Vachon were unemployed college students. All the photographers were white, except Gordon Parks, a twenty-nine-year-old African American fashion photographer who joined the Historical Section in 1941. Parks never photographed farmers while at the FSA; instead, he sensitively documented the lives of African Americans and racial discrimination in Washington, D.C.

The documentary tradition in American photography was never based on neutrality or objectivity—in fact, complete objectivity would be impossible even if it were desirable. As soon as a photographer frames a picture in the camera's viewfinder, poses subjects, or rearranges things in any way, elements of manipulation and interpretation enter the image-making process. Further personal interpretation may be introduced in the cropping and printing of a photograph as well as in the selection of one image over another of the same subject. In order to encourage child labor reforms, Progressive-era photographers such as Lewis Hine often posed their subjects in ways that emphasized their dirtiness and poverty. Similarly, in an effort to educate viewers about depression conditions in rural America, the FSA photographers sought to document the suffering and poverty of their subjects—farmers and

sharecroppers—in images that also portrayed the dignity and will to survive of these rural Americans.

To create an effective photograph, for example, Arthur Rothstein moved the steer skull (shown in Source 3) from parched soil in South Dakota to a location where he could photograph it against a background of overgrazed scrub vegetation (thereby creating a variation on Source 3). For the photograph in Source 4, an image of a man and his children running from an approaching dust storm, Rothstein darkened the sky to re-create what it looked like during the dust storm (since he obviously could not photograph the actual storm). Dorothea Lange, who had been a successful portrait photographer before she joined the FSA, took six photos of a migrant mother and the four of her seven children who were present at the time. Lange posed the woman and her children and kept moving in closer and closer until she captured the image that she thought best portrayed both the plight of the migrants and the nobility of the mother. The resulting image (Source 8) came to be considered an archetypal work of art and is now in the Museum of Modern Art.

Perhaps the most extreme manipulation of photographic images is seen in the work of Walker Evans, who worked briefly for the FSA. When he and James Agee were in Alabama photographing tenant farmers for their book *Let Us Now Praise Famous Men* (1941), Evans rearranged furniture, posed and reposed people, and cleaned up what he thought was clutter. Working with a huge eight-by-ten view camera, Evans considered himself an artist who saw the potential for beauty in the poverty and hard lives of the tenant farmers. Evans may also have thought middle-class viewers would react more sympathetically to his somewhat romantic vision of the rural poor than to the actual realities of their poverty.

Stryker himself was an able administrator who planned the field trips, developed background reading lists for the photographers, and wrote "shooting scripts" to guide them once they were in the field. "As you are driving through the agricultural areas . . . ," Stryker wrote to Dorothea Lange in California, "would you take a few shots of various types of farm activities such as your picture showing the lettuce workers?" But beyond these kinds of general suggestions, Stryker gave his photographers remarkable freedom, concentrating himself on coordinating their activities, selecting images for the files, promoting the wide use of their photos, and defending the Historical Section against congressional criticism and budget cuts.

When analyzing these pictures, then, you must remember that documentary photographs are not intended to present a balanced or an unbiased view. Instead, these photographs are intended to appeal to viewers' emotions and motivate viewers to work for and support change. As a student looking at these photographs, you will need to be specific about *what* is portrayed, *what* you feel, and *why* the photograph makes you feel that way. Finally, try to make some connections between the photographs and the federal programs to aid the rural poor.

♦ CHAPTER 7

Documenting the
Depression:
The FSA
Photographers
and Rural Poverty

♦

The Evidence

Sources 1 through 17 from United States Farm Security Administration, Historical Division, Library of Congress, Washington, D.C.

1. Abandoned Farm Home, Ward County, North Dakota, 1940 (John Vachon).

2. "Tractored-out" Farm, Hall County, Texas, 1938 (Dorothea Lange).

3. Skull, South Dakota Badlands, 1936 (Arthur Rothstein).

✦ CHAPTER 7

Documenting the
Depression:
The FSA
Photographers
and Rural Poverty

4. Farmer and Sons in Dust Storm, Cimarron County, Oklahoma, 1936 (Arthur Rothstein).

5. Family Moving to Krebs, Oklahoma, from Idabel, Oklahoma, 1939 (Dorothea Lange).

6. Migrant Family Living in a Shack Built on an Abandoned Truck Bed, Highway 70, Tennessee, 1936 (Carl Mydans).

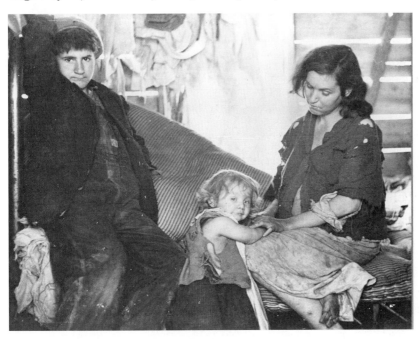

7. Migrants from Oklahoma, Blyth, California, 1936 (Dorothea Lange).

◆ CHAPTER 7

Documenting the
Depression:
The FSA
Photographers
and Rural Poverty

8. Migrant Mother, Nipomo, California, 1936 (Dorothea Lange).

9. Mexican Migrant Worker's Home, Imperial Valley, California, 1937 (Dorothea Lange).

10. Living Quarters of Fruit-Packing-House Workers, Berrien, Michigan, 1940 (John Vachon).

11. Plantation Owner and Field Hands, Clarksdale, Mississippi, 1936 (Dorothea Lange).

✦ CHAPTER 7

Documenting the
Depression:
The FSA
Photographers
and Rural Poverty

12. Cotton Pickers, Pulaski County, Arkansas, 1935 (Ben Shahn).

13. Owner of the General Store, Bank, and Cotton Gin, Wendell, North Carolina, 1939 (Marion Post Wolcott).

14. FSA Client and His Family, Beaufort, South Carolina, 1936 (Carl Mydans).

15. Mule Dealer, Creedmoor, North Carolina, 1940 (Arthur Rothstein).

✦ CHAPTER 7

Documenting the
Depression:
The FSA
Photographers
and Rural Poverty

16. Bud Fields and His Family, Tenant Farmers, Hale County, Alabama, 1936 (Walker Evans).

17. Christmas Dinner, Tenant Farmer's Home, Southeastern Iowa, 1936 (Russell Lee).

Questions to Consider

The photographs in Sources 1 through 4 illustrate what happened to the once-fertile farmlands of the plains and prairies. How would you describe these pictures to someone who could not see them? What happened to the land? What was the impact on people who lived there?

Sources 5 through 8 show photographs of farm families who were on the road. They had left or been evicted from the farms where they had lived and were looking for jobs as migrant workers. How would middle-class Americans have felt when they saw these pictures? Which photograph do you think is the most effective? Why?

Sources 9, 10, 12, 14, 16, and 17 show the living and working conditions at migrant camps and for the tenant and sharecropper families who did not leave their homes. What do you notice most when you look at these photographs? What do these images reveal about women? children? family? In contrast, the images in Sources 11, 13, and 15 are of men who were relatively well off during the depression. How are they portrayed? What characteristics do they seem to have? What is your reaction to these images?

During an interview conducted many years after his work in Georgia as an FSA photographer, Jack Delano remarked that "you couldn't work down there very long without becoming acutely aware of the race problem. . . ."[3] Reexamine Sources 11 through 15. What do these images tell you about the living conditions of rural blacks in the South? About the economic and social relationships between blacks and property-owning whites? Compare the images of black and white tenant farmers depicted in Sources 14 and 16.

Finally, think about the photographs as a whole. What messages did they send to the middle-class Americans who saw them in newspapers, magazines, books, or traveling exhibits? What major problems did the photographs portray, and what kinds of programs did the FSA propose to try to aid poor farmers? Why do you think these documentary photographs were so effective in creating sympathy and support for aid to these farmers?

Epilogue

The images taken by photographers for the FSA brought shocking views of rural poverty throughout the South and West to the attention of all Americans. Most of the photographers had never been in southern states and were surprised by the appalling conditions of rural African Americans and the harsh effects of the Jim Crow laws. Stryker

3. Louis Schmeir and Denise Montgomery, "The Other Depression: The Black Experience in Georgia Through an FSA Photographer's Lens," *Georgia Historical Quarterly* 78 (1994): 135.

◆ CHAPTER 7

Documenting the
Depression:
The FSA
Photographers
and Rural Poverty

was aware of the political dangers in displaying too much sympathy for blacks, however, and he carefully chose the images that would be exhibited. Many middle-class white Americans had been unaware of the living and working conditions for white families caught in the sharecropping or tenant farmer system. The impact of the depression on women and children, as portrayed by the photographers, was especially distressing. Homeless families living in cars or camping out and families on the road looking for work were especially powerful images for middle-class Americans, who believed that home and family provided stability for the nation.

By 1941, the FSA photographs were well known to millions of Americans, and the Historical Section had justified its existence. That year also saw the publication of the classic book *Let Us Now Praise Famous Men: Three Tenant Families,* written by James Agee and illustrated with photos by FSA photographer Walker Evans. After the Japanese attack on Pearl Harbor in December 1941 and the United States' subsequent entry into World War II, the direction of the Historical Section changed. The buildup of defense industries and the effects of the war on everyday Americans dominated the photographers' assignments. Eventually, the Historical Section was moved to the Office of War Information, and in 1943, after transferring more than 130,000 FSA photographs to the Library of Congress, Roy Stryker resigned from government service.

America's participation in World War II finally brought an end to the Great Depression—and an end to the New Deal as well. Stryker spent the next decade working for Standard Oil of New Jersey, and most of the former FSA photographers did freelance work, taught courses, or found permanent jobs in photojournalism with magazines such as *Life* and *Look*. Ben Shahn went back to his first love, painting, and became a well-known artist. Marion Post Wolcott got married and raised a family, returning to photography only when she was in her sixties. The plight of the rural poor was once again forgotten, and middle-class materialism and conformity dominated the cold war years of the 1950s.

Yet a whole new generation was soon to rediscover the work of the FSA photographers. In 1962, Edward Steichen, head of the photography department at the New York Museum of Modern Art and a photographer himself, mounted a major exhibition of the FSA images called "The Bitter Years, 1935–1941." By the end of the 1960s, young Americans also had rediscovered some of the same problems the New Deal photographers had captured in their pictures: rural poverty, racial discrimination, and social injustice. Once again, Americans demanded reform, especially during the presidencies of John F. Kennedy and Lyndon Johnson.

8

Going to War with Japan: A Problem in Diplomacy and Causation

The Problem

On Sunday afternoon, December 7, 1941, a record crowd of over 55,000 people packed the Polo Grounds in New York City to watch the National Football League game between the New York Giants and the Brooklyn Dodgers.[1] Unbeknownst to the players, the fans, or the many people listening to the game over WOR radio in New York, at almost the same time as the opening kickoff Japanese war planes were beginning their attack on Pearl Harbor in Hawaii, the home of the United States Navy's Pacific Fleet.[2] In an assault that lasted only ninety minutes, over 2,400 Americans were killed, 8 battleships were sunk or badly crippled, and 188 U.S. fighter planes were destroyed. Although WOR interrupted its broadcast of the football game at 2:26 P.M. Eastern Time to report the attack, at the Polo Grounds the contest continued. Sometime during the second half, the public address announcer advised all Navy personnel to report to their posts immediately and all Army men to report to their stations on Monday morning.

The next day, President Franklin Roosevelt went before a joint session of Congress to request a declaration of war against Japan. In a six and one-half minute address, the president referred to December 7 as "a date which will live in infamy" and vowed, even on that dark day, that "we will gain the inevitable triumph—so help us God."[3]

1. The Brooklyn Dodgers were an NFL team from 1930 until 1943. December 7, 1941, was designated as "Tuffy" Leemans Day to honor the Giants' star running back. Alphonse "Tuffy" Leemans (1912–1979) played for the Giants from 1936 to 1943 and was inducted into the NFL Hall of Fame in 1978.
2. The Pacific Fleet had been stationed in San Francisco but was moved to Pearl Harbor in 1940 as a warning to Japanese expansionists.

3. Samuel I. Rosenman, comp., *The Public Papers and Addresses of Franklin D. Roosevelt* (New York: Harper & Bros., 1950), Vol. 10, pp. 514–516. The Senate approved the war declaration 82–0 (with 14 not voting) and the House by 388–1.

✦ CHAPTER 8

Going to War
with Japan:
A Problem in
Diplomacy and
Causation

Later that day, Congress declared war on the Imperial Government of Japan.

Over four decades after Pearl Harbor, both Japanese and American historians have begun to re-examine the causes of the attack on Pearl Harbor. Most American historians have come to agree with Jonathan Utley and Michael Barnhart that Pearl Harbor began "a war that neither nation desired, but one that neither could avoid."[4] In other words, the causes of the December 7 attack can be found only by examining the years and even decades of Japanese-American relations prior to Pearl Harbor. Why did Japan choose to attack Pearl Harbor? How can we re-examine Japanese-American relations to find the causes of that event?

Your task in this chapter is to answer those two questions. One of the most difficult things historians must do is analyze the *causes* of particular events (the American Revolution, the Cherokee removal, the abolitionist movement, and so forth). And yet, although it is difficult, establishing causation is a task historians are uniquely trained to do—to sift through the evidence to understand why one person or group or even nation behaved the way that he/she/it did. Many people believe that such examinations and analyses may help contemporary people avoid the pitfalls of the past. If that is so, then historians can study the past in order to serve the present.

✦

Background

When U.S. Commodore Matthew Perry sailed into Edo (now Tokyo) Bay with a force of two steam-powered frigates and two sloops-of-war, it was the first time that a foreigner had set foot in Japan in over two hundred years. Fearing the loss of economic control and the increasing number of converts to Christianity, the Japanese had gradually expelled European traders and outlawed, persecuted, and even murdered Christian missionaries and converts. Yet in 1854, Perry was able to force Japan to

open diplomatic and commercial relations with the United States, and in the following years other Western nations were able to extract similar privileges from the Japanese government.

Popular Japanese reaction against treaties that favored Western international traders was one cause of the fall of the government and the 1867 rise of the new, young, dynamic emperor Mutsuhito, a period referred to as the Meiji Restoration.[5] And yet, instead of returning to strict seclusion and wholesale persecution and expulsion of foreigners, Mutsuhito adopted the policy of modernizing Japan by bringing in Western technicians and advisers in in-

4. Jonathan G. Utley, *Going to War with Japan, 1937–1941* (Knoxville: University of Tennessee Press, 1985), p. xii; Michael A. Barnhart, *Japan Prepares for Total War: The Search for Economic Security, 1919–1941*, (Ithaca, N.Y.: Cornell University Press, 1987), p. 21.

5. Meiji: enlightened government.

dustry, trade, finance, military science, and government. Prince Iwakura Tomomi spoke for many in the new Japanese leadership when he counseled that "We should not despise them [the West] as barbarians but treat them as courteously as we would friends."[6] Under Iwakura's leadership, Japanese students began to study abroad and foreign instructors were invited to Japan. In 1872, Japan opened its first railway line and in that same year inaugurated a national education system. In 1889, a written constitution was adopted, the first written constitution outside of the West.

Japan's modernization was nothing short of astounding. From the 1870s until 1914, the gross national product grew at an average rate of 3 percent per year, as high or higher than the growth rates of any European nation. In 1905, Japan built its first battleship from home-produced steel, and by 1914, the nation was self-sufficient in iron, steel, engineering, and chemicals. By 1915, Japan was able to export 22 percent of its gross national product, which could be traded for natural resources and helped sustain a fairly high level of prosperity. In truth, Japan had become the sole success story of industrial capitalism in the non-Western world.[7]

Japan's remarkably rapid industrial modernization, however, brought several problems to the ambitious nation. To begin with, rapid economic growth coupled with general prosperity touched off a demographic revolution in which Japan's population grew by around one million persons per year, making it increasingly difficult to produce enough food to feed its mushrooming population. In addition, approximately 250,000 people were entering the job market each year, and jobs would have to be found or created to maintain the nation's prosperity and political stability. But Japan's need to import food and create jobs meant that it was necessary for industry to continue to grow so as to increase exports. Industrial growth, however, was limited by the nation's paucity of raw materials, especially iron and oil. Thus the need to import even more raw materials put even more pressure on industries to increase production, an upward spiral that became even more frantic by the advent of the Great War (World War I) in 1914.[8]

Japan's industrial surge took place at the same time that Western nations were engaged in imperialist ventures—in the late nineteenth and early twentieth centuries. As a result, Japan saw Western expansion in the Pacific, especially that of Great Britain and the United States, as a national threat. As Prime Minister Yamagata Aritoma put it in 1890, "[T]he heritages and re-

6. Akira Iriye, *Japan and the Wider World, from the Mid-Nineteenth Century to the Present* (London: Longman, 1997), p. 1.

7. Rondo Cameron, *A Concise Economic History of the World* (New York: Oxford University Press, 1993), pp. 273–274. For the first battleship, see Haruo Tohmatsu and H. P. Willmott, *A Gathering Darkness: The Coming of War to the Far East and the Pacific, 1921–1942* (Lanham, Md.: Rowman and Littlefield, 2004), p. 2.

8. On demography, see Herbert Feis, *The Road to Pearl Harbor: The Coming of the War Between the United States and Japan* (Princeton: Princeton University Press, 1950), p. 3. By 1941, Japan was importing 20 percent of its rice and wheat, 67 percent of its soybeans, and almost all of its sugar. Tohmatsu and Willmott, *A Gathering Darkness*, p. 87.

✦ CHAPTER 8

Going to War
with Japan:
A Problem in
Diplomacy and
Causation

sources of the East are like so many pieces of meat about to be devoured by tigers." Equally serious, Japan was dependent on the United States to buy Japanese exports and to furnish Japan with desperately needed raw materials. If that commerce was interrupted, Japan's industry would collapse and its people would suffer. As a result, in the 1880s, as the nation became increasingly obsessed with national economic security, Japan began a major buildup of its military.[9]

Western nations were shocked by what appeared to be Japan's almost-overnight military prowess. Fearing that political instability in Korea would be an invitation to Western imperialists, in 1894 Japan declared war on China, demolished the Chinese fleet in five hours, and made Korea in essence a dependency of Japan, and Taiwan, the Pescadores Islands, and the Liaodong peninsula possessions of Japan. Then, in 1904–1905, Japan humiliated Imperial Russia in a war that was ended by negotiations led by U.S. President Theodore Roosevelt, principally because he did not want either nation to become the principal power in the Pacific.

After the conclusion of the Great War in 1918, the major powers sought to limit the armaments race that some believed had been one of the causes of that conflict. In 1921–1922 in Washington, D.C., Japan agreed to limit its battleship strength to 60 percent of that of the United States and Great Britain. Although Japan signed the document (along with an agreement that recognized the territorial integrity of China), Japan was humiliated by doing so, feeling that the document showed a lack of respect for the Asian nation. Moreover, Japan was outraged by the United States' increasingly restrictive immigration laws, especially the 1924 immigration act that permanently excluded Japanese as "aliens ineligible to citizenship." On July 1, 1924, a national "Humiliation Day" was celebrated in Tokyo, marked by "Hate America" mass meetings. A few years later, in a roundtable discussion at a Tokyo elementary school, the students were asked whether they thought there would be a war between Japan and the United States. "Yes," said one discussant, "I think so. Americans are so arrogant. I'd like to show them a thing or two."[10]

Japan's demographic and economic difficulties, coupled with its rising anti-Western xenophobia,[11] enhanced the power and popularity of the nation's

9. For Yamagata Aritoma, see Akira Iriye, *Japan and the Wider World*, p. 13. In 1929, 43 percent of Japanese exports went to the United States. See Alfred E. Eckes, Jr., *The United States and the Global Struggle for Minerals* (Austin, Tex.: University of Texas Press, 1979), p. 69.

10. On the Washington Naval Conference, see Tohmatsu and Willmott, *A Gathering Darkness*, pp. 7–8. For the text of the Nine Power Treaty (1922), see Henry L. Stimson, *The Far Eastern Crisis: Recollections and Observations* (New York: Harper and Row, 1936), Appendix 2, pp. 267–270. For earlier U.S. immigration and other restrictions on the Japanese, see Murakami Hyoe, *Japan: the Years of Trial, 1919–1952* (Tokyo: Japan Culture Institute, 1982), p. 18–19. See also Eleanor Tupper and George E. McReynolds, *Japan in American Public Opinion* (New York: Macmillan, 1937), p. 202. For the elementary school, see Saburo Ienaga, *The Pacific War: World War II and the Japanese, 1931–1945* (New York: Pantheon Books, 1978), p. 29.

11. Xenophobia: the extreme fear or dislike of strangers or foreigners, from the Greek word *xenos*, meaning "stranger."

military establishment, the only government institution that did not report to the nation's parliament (the Diet) but only to the emperor. Since 1925, military training had become a curricular requirement for all boys in middle schools and above. Thus, young men had come to believe that most of Japan's problems had military solutions. And if those "solutions" were bloody, the gains would more than offset the sacrifices. As one popular Japanese song put it, "As always our troops are victorious, victorious."[12]

In the worldwide economic depression of the late 1920s and 1930s, most industrialized nations threw up tariff barriers to keep foreign imports from competing with their own struggling industries. Between 1929 and 1931 alone, Japanese exports dropped 50 percent, making it extremely difficult to purchase needed food as well as to import raw materials. Soon the situation was desperate.[13]

On September 18, 1931, Japan began its conquest of Manchuria, a 585,000-square-mile region in northernmost China. Southern Manchuria fell to Japanese troops within 48 hours, and the remainder of the area was subdued weeks afterward. Soon the Japanese military established the puppet government of Manchukuo (their new name for Manchuria) and began relocating approximately 500,000 people (includ-

ing 25,000 farmers and 50,000 teenagers) from Japan to the new Japanese province. Ultimately, the plan called for the resettlement of one million Japanese households (five million people), which would relieve population pressures in Japan as well as provide for the growth of food and the extraction of natural resources in Manchukuo. Other nations were outraged, and the League of Nations protested vigorously. But the League was toothless, and Japan responded by withdrawing from the League of Nations. The United States, not a member of the League, also protested, but mired in its own depression with up to 25 percent of the work force unemployed and with isolationist feeling running high, the nation similarly did nothing.[14]

Then, on July 7, 1937, a minor incident at the Marco Polo Bridge a few miles south of Beijing ignited a full-scale war between Japan and China. Japanese military planners confidently boasted that China would be subdued in three months, but when the conflict rapidly ground down into a bloody stalemate, Japanese planes began indiscriminantly bombing Chinese military forces and civilians, a tactic that endangered the lives of several Western businessmen, merchants, government and military personnel, and missionaries. For his part, U.S. President Franklin Roosevelt urged all American nationals to leave China, warning that all

12. For military training and the popular song, see Saburo Ienaga, *The Pacific War,* pp. 6, 28.
13. Tohmatsu and Willmott, *A Gathering Darkness,* p. 15; Eckes, *Global Struggle for Minerals,* p. 70. At the time, the United States and Great Britain controlled roughly 75 percent of the world's known mineral resources. *Ibid.,* p. 62.

14. On the conquest of Manchuria, see Stimson, *The Far Eastern Crisis,* pp 33–46. On the resettlement plans, see Akira Iriye, *Power and Culture: The Japanese-American War, 1941–1945* (Cambridge: Harvard University Press, 1981), p. 3.

♦ CHAPTER 8

Going to War
with Japan:
A Problem in
Diplomacy and
Causation

who remained did so "at their own risk."[15]

Clearly, the United States and Japan appeared to be on a collision course, heading full steam toward what historian Michael Barnhart called "a war that neither nation desired, but one that neither could avoid." And yet September 2, 1937 (the day President Roosevelt urged all Americans to leave China) was still years from December 7, 1941. Both nations were presided over by intelligent and experienced leaders. Why were they unable to steer their respective ships away from a collision with one another? Both nations sought to achieve their national goals without going to war with one another. Why were they unable to do so? How can we re-examine Japanese-American relations to find the causes of that war? Why did the Japanese attack Pearl Harbor?

As you begin to think about these questions, you quickly will appreciate the fact that by the early twentieth century the world's demographic, economic, and political bands were drawing much tighter. A stock market crash in New York in 1929 could have worldwide effects, as could a revolution in Russia in 1917, a change of government in Germany in 1933, or a minor incident at the Marco Polo Bridge in 1937. Thus the outbreak of war in Europe in 1939 could have profound effects on Japanese-American relations, as could Hitler's invasion of the Soviet Union in 1941. We will help you make these connections (see the Evidence section of this chapter), but for more assistance consult your instructor.

The Japanese attack on Pearl Harbor on December 7, 1941 (December 8 in Japan), is one of the most important events in American—and world—twentieth-century history. Every living American who was an adult in 1941 can tell you exactly where he or she was and precisely what he or she was doing when that individual heard the news . . . for instance, over WOR radio in New York, although not at the Polo Grounds. Why did the Japanese attack Pearl Harbor?

♦

The Method

As with other historians, those historians specializing in international relations (sometimes referred to as "diplomatic historians") deal with separate but related questions:

1. What is *actually* occurring or taking place? (reality)

2. What does a particular person, government, or nation *believe* is occurring or taking place? (perceptions)

---

15. Tohmatsu and Willmott, *A Gathering Darkness,* pp. 57–59; Utley, *Going to War with Japan,* pp. 5–13; Barnhart, *Japan Prepares for*

Total War, p. 91. Tohmatsu and Willmott claim that Japanese naval officer Nakajima Chikuhei was the first to advocate the bombing of civilians to terrorize them to surrender. European historians give that dubious distinction to Italian General Giulio Douhet. See Tohmatsu and Willmott, *A Gathering Darkness,* p. 75.

3. What causes a particular person, government, or nation to choose a certain course of action? (motivation) In virtually all problems in international relations, both past and present, these three interrelated questions must be asked and answered.

In this problem in international relations, you will be dealing with *two* nations: Japan and the United States. In the Problem section of this chapter, we agreed with historians Michael Barnhart and Jonathan Utley that World War II was (to use Barnhart's words) "a war that neither nation desired, but one that neither could avoid."[16] To fully understand the meaning of that assertion, however, you must examine the reality, perceptions (of both nations), and motivations (also of both nations). Answering those questions will bring you to a deeper understanding of the causes of the Japanese attack on Pearl Harbor.

Begin your analysis with Japan. As you work through the evidence, keep in mind the following questions:

1. What were the demographic, economic, political, and international situations in Japan? (reality)
2. How did Japan view the world? itself? its goals and obstacles? (perceptions)
3. What strategies were available that would allow Japan to achieve its goals? Why did they choose the particular strategy they did? (motivation)

As you deal with the questions of Japan's world view and the possible obstacles that threatened to block Japan from achieving its goals, you will see that the United States in particular and Western powers in general might play a large role (reality? perception?). Here you must judge how *accurate* or *inaccurate* (reality) those perceptions were. Immediately, you will see how the questions are interrelated.

Then repeat the process for the United States, this time assessing Japan's role in helping or hindering the United States from achieving its goals (again, reality? perception?).

Because there is a great deal of evidence and because you will have to examine it twice (once for Japan and once for the United States), it will be important that you take careful notes as you go along. It might be particularly helpful to take notes in the form of a chart, with headings for reality, perceptions, motives, and strategies. Your biggest problem, of course, is determining the extent to which a particular perception is *real* or *not real*. For example, Japan clearly believed that the United States was doing everything it could to thwart Japan's demographic and economic goals. How true or false was this perception?

Because the international situation was extremely fluid and volatile in the late 1930s, we have inserted some important events in the Evidence section to assist you.

16. Barnhart, *Japan Prepares for Total War,* p. 21.

✦ CHAPTER 8
Going to War
with Japan:
A Problem in
Diplomacy and
Causation

✦

The Evidence

Source 1 from *Peace and War: United States Foreign Policy, 1931–1941* (Washington, D.C.: Government Printing Office, 1943), pp. 319–320.

1. Memorandum by Secretary of State Cordell Hull Regarding Conversation with Japanese Ambassador Yoshida, June 13, 1936.

Mr. Yoshida, Japanese Ambassador to England, came in and stated that he was very desirous of promoting better relations and better understanding between our two countries. He said that the one big fact which he wanted the American people to recognize was the immense and rapidly growing population of Japan and the absolute necessity for more territory for their existence in anything like a satisfactory way. He referred to the fact that there was misunderstanding and misapprehension on the part of our people in this respect as it related to Japanese movements in and about China; that this also was probably true as to the British; that the Japanese armaments were not intended for war against any particular country, especially us. . . .

In reply, I told Mr. Yoshida that I would speak frankly but in the friendliest possible spirit and say that the impression among many persons in this country was that Japan sought absolute economic domination, first of eastern Asia, and then, of other portions as she might see fit; that this would mean political as well as military domination in the end; that the upshot of the entire movement would be to exclude countries like the United States from trading with all of those portions of China thus brought under the domination or controlling influence so-called of Japan. . . .

I continued with the statement that there was no reason, in my judgment, why countries like Japan, the United States, and England could not in the most amicable spirit, and with perfect justice and fairness to each, agree to assert and abide by the worldwide principle of equality in all commercial and industrial affairs, and each country solemnly agree that it would not resort to force in connection with the operation of this rule of equality, and why Governments like the three mentioned could not sit down together and in a spirit of fair dealing and fair play confer and collaborate and not cease until they had found a way for amicable and reasonable adjustments or settlements.

[*On July 7, 1937, a small number of Chinese and Japanese soldiers clashed on the Marco Polo Bridge near Beijing. Although the Japanese government was willing to allow the incident to pass without further conflict, the Japanese army initiated a full-scale invasion of China, leading to a major protracted war between the two nations. Japan shocked many throughout the world by its indiscriminate bombing of civilians.*]

Source 2 from George H. Gallup, *The Gallup Poll: Public Opinion, 1935–1971* (New York: Random House, 1972), p. 70.

2. Public Opinion Poll, September 19, 1937.

Q: Should U.S. banks lend money to Japan and China during the present war?

Yes: 5%

No: 95%

Source 3 from Samuel I. Rosenman, ed., *The Public Papers and Addresses of Franklin D. Roosevelt* (New York: Harper and Brothers, 1950), Vol. 6, pp. 407–408, 410–411.

3. Speech by President Franklin Roosevelt in Chicago, October 5, 1937.

The political situation in the world, which of late has been growing progressively worse, is such as to cause grave concern and anxiety to all the peoples and nations who wish to live in peace and amity with their neighbors. . . .

Without a declaration of war and without warning or justification of any kind, civilians, including vast numbers of women and children, are being ruthlessly murdered with bombs from the air. In times of so-called peace, ships are being attacked and sunk by submarines without cause or notice. Nations are fomenting and taking sides in civil warfare in nations that have never done them any harm. Nations claiming freedom for themselves deny it to others.

Innocent peoples, innocent nations, are being cruelly sacrificed to a greed for power and supremacy which is devoid of all sense of justice and humane considerations. . . .

If those things come to pass in other parts of the world, let no one imagine that America will escape, that America may expect mercy, that this Western Hemisphere will not be attacked and that it will continue tranquilly and peacefully to carry on the ethics and the arts of civilization. . . .

It seems to be unfortunately true that the epidemic of world lawlessness is spreading.

When an epidemic of physical disease starts to spread, the community approves and joins in a quarantine of the patients in order to protect the health of the community against the spread of the disease. . . .

War is a contagion, whether it be declared or undeclared. It can engulf

◆ CHAPTER 8

Going to War
with Japan:
A Problem in
Diplomacy and
Causation

states and peoples remote from the original scene of hostilities. We are determined to keep out of war, yet we cannot insure ourselves against the disastrous effects of war and the dangers of involvement. We are adopting such measures as will minimize our risk of involvement, but we cannot have complete protection in a world of disorder in which confidence and security have broken down.

If civilization is to survive the principles of the Prince of Peace must be restored. Trust between nations must be revived.

Most important of all, the will for peace on the part of peace-loving nations must express itself to the end that nations that may be tempted to violate their agreements and the rights of others will desist from such a course. There must be positive endeavors to preserve peace.

[*Roosevelt's speech was met with a wave of harsh criticism from Americans who thought his remarks smacked of warmongering.*]

Source 4 from Ryusaka Tsunoda, et. al., comp., *Sources of Japanese Tradition* (New York: Columbia University Press, 1958), Vol. 2, pp. 289–290.

4. Hashimoto Kingoro, "Address to Young Men," late 1930s.

We have already said that there are only three ways left to Japan to escape from the pressure of surplus population. We are like a great crowd of people packed into a small and narrow room, and there are only three doors through which we might escape, namely emigration, advance into world markets, and expansion of territory. The first door, emigration, has been barred to us by the anti-Japanese immigration policies of other countries. The second door, advance into world markets, is being pushed shut by tariff barriers and the abrogation of commercial treaties. What should Japan do when two of the three doors have been closed against her?

It is quite natural that Japan should rush upon the last remaining door. . . .

[*The address then dealt with the Western powers' condemnation of Japan's 1931 invasion of Manchuria.*]

And if it is still protested that our actions in Manchuria were excessively violent, we may wish to ask the white race just which country it was that sent warships and troops to India, South Africa, and Australia and slaughtered innocent natives, bound their hands and feet with iron chains, lashed their backs with iron whips, proclaimed these territories as their own, and still continues to hold them to this very day?

Source 5 from John Toland, *The Rising Sun: The Decline and Fall of the Japanese Empire, 1936–1945* (New York: Random House, 1970), p. 48.

5. Japanese Diplomat Yosuke Matsuoka, October 1937.

Japan is expanding. And what country in its expansion era has ever failed to be trying to its neighbors? Ask the American Indian or the Mexican how excruciatingly trying the young United States used to be once upon a time.

[*On December 12, 1937, Japanese military airplanes attacked and bombed the United States gunboat* Panay, *20 miles upriver from Nanking, China. The gunboat was there to protect three Standard Oil Company tankers and to evacuate American citizens from Nanking in the wake of the Japanese advance. Three Americans were killed, along with one Italian journalist, and several were wounded.*]

Source 6 from *Peace and War,* pp. 395–396.

6. Hull to U.S. Ambassador to Japan Joseph Grew, December 13, 1937.

Please communicate promptly to Hirota a note as follows:

The Government and people of the United States have been deeply shocked by the facts of the bombardment and sinking of the U. S. S. *Panay* and the sinking or burning of the American steamers *Meiping, Meian* and *Meisian* [Meihsia] by Japanese aircraft. . . .

[*At first the Japanese claimed that the planes did not know the* Panay *and the three tankers were American ships, an assertion easily refuted because the* Panay *both flew the U.S. flag and had the flag painted on the ship. Also, it later was learned that Japanese aircraft had bombed and strafed the* Panay's *lifeboats.*]

Since the beginning of the present unfortunate hostilities between Japan and China, the Japanese Government and various Japanese authorities at various points have repeatedly assured the Government and authorities of the United States that it is the intention and purpose of the Japanese Government and the Japanese armed forces to respect fully the rights and interests of other powers. On several occasions, however, acts of Japanese armed forces have violated the rights of the United States, have seriously endangered the lives of American nationals, and have destroyed American property. In several instances, the Japanese Government has admitted the facts, has expressed regrets, and has given assurances that every precaution will be taken against recurrence of such incidents. In the present case, acts of Japanese armed forces have taken place in complete disregard of American rights, have

◆ CHAPTER 8

Going to War
with Japan:
A Problem in
Diplomacy and
Causation

taken American life, and have destroyed American property both public and private.

In these circumstances, the Government of the United States requests and expects of the Japanese Government a formally recorded expression of regret, an undertaking to make complete and comprehensive indemnifications, and an assurance that definite and specific steps have been taken which will ensure that hereafter American nationals, interests and property in China will not be subjected to attack by Japanese armed forces or unlawful interference by any Japanese authorities or forces whatsoever.

[*The Japanese government apologized and paid an indemnity of around $2 million.*]

Source 7 from Joseph C. Grew, *Turbulent Era: A Diplomatic Record of Forty Years, 1904–1945*, Walter Johnson, ed. (Boston: Houghton Mifflin, 1952), Vol. 2, p. 1205.

7. Grew (U.S. Ambassador to Japan) to Admiral H. E. Yarnell (Commander, U.S. Asiatic Fleet), January 10, 1938.

If it were not for the irresponsibility of these younger Japanese officers I would have felt that the *Panay* incident might be a blessing in disguise because it certainly jolted the Government into a realization of the dangers into which Japan was running with regard to the United States. Our action in accepting their apologies, offer of indemnification and assurances for the future must have been a very great relief to them. As for the civilian population, I have been really touched by the depth and genuineness of their feeling of shame which has been expressed to me in countless visits and letters from people in all walks of life. The donations for the survivors and the families of the dead already amount to more than fifteen thousand yen, but this sum will be turned over to some Japanese individual or organization to devote to some constructive purpose in the interests of Japanese-American friendship as our Government does not wish it to go to any American nationals. Nevertheless I cannot for a moment look into the future with any feeling of confidence.

Source 8 from Gallup, *The Gallup Poll,* p. 85.

8. Gallup Poll, January 16, 1938.

Q: Regarding American military personnel in China, should we withdraw or stay?

Withdraw 70%

Stay 30%

Source 9 from *Peace and War,* p. 422.

9. Joseph C. Green (Chief of U.S. State Department's Office of Arms and Munitions Control) to 148 Companies Manufacturing Airplane Parts, July 1, 1938.

As some misunderstanding appears to have arisen as to the purport of the statement made by the Secretary of State in his press conference on June 11 in regard to bombing civilian populations from the air, I am addressing this letter in regard to the matter to all persons and companies registered as man-ufacturers or exporters of airplanes or aeronautical equipment.

In view of the fact that the Secretary's statement definitely condemned bombing of civilian populations from the air, it should be clear to all con-cerned that the Government of the United States is strongly opposed to the sale of airplanes or aeronautical equipment which would materially aid or en-courage that practice in any countries in any part of the world. Therefore, in view of this policy, the Department would with great regret issue any licenses authorizing exportation, direct or indirect, of any aircraft, aircraft armament, aircraft engines, aircraft parts, aircraft accessories, aerial bombs or torpedoes to countries the armed forces of which are making use of airplanes for attack upon civilian populations.

[*Green was a fifth-level State Department officer. When Hull learned of Green's deci-sion, he quickly reversed it. (Utley,* Going to War with Japan, *p. 120.)*]

✦ CHAPTER 8

Going to War
with Japan:
A Problem in
Diplomacy and
Causation

Source 10 from *Papers Relating to the Foreign Relations of the United States: Japan, 1931–1941* (Washington, D.C.: Government Printing Office, 1943), Vol. I, p. 478.

10. Statement by the Japanese Government, November 3, 1938.

What Japan seeks is the establishment of a new order which will insure the permanent stability of East Asia. In this lies the ultimate purpose of our present military campaign.

This new order has for its foundation a tripartite relationship of mutual aid and co-ordination between Japan, Manchoukuo and China in political, economic, cultural and other fields. Its object is to secure international justice, to perfect the joint defence against Communism, and to create a new culture and realize a close economic cohesion throughout East Asia. This indeed is the way to contribute toward the stabilization of East Asia and the progress of the world.

What Japan desires of China is that that country will share in the task of bringing about this new order in East Asia. She confidently expects that the people of China will fully comprehend her true intentions and that they will respond to the call of Japan for their co-operation. Even the participation of the Kuomintang Government would not be rejected, if, repudiating the policy which has guided it in the past and remolding its personnel, so as to translate its re-birth into fact, it were to come forward to join in the establishment of the new order.

Japan is confident that other Powers will on their part correctly appreciate her aims and policy and adapt their attitude to the new conditions prevailing in East Asia. For the cordiality hitherto manifested by the nations which are in sympathy with us, Japan wishes to express her profound gratitude.

The establishment of a new order in East Asia is in complete conformity with the very spirit in which the Empire was founded; to achieve such a task is the exalted responsibility with which our present generation is entrusted. It is, therefore, imperative to carry out all necessary internal reforms, and with a full development of the aggregate national strength, material as well as moral, fulfil at all costs this duty incumbent upon our nation.

Such the Government declare to be the immutable policy and determination of Japan.

Source 11 from Grew, *Turbulent Era*, Vol. 2, p. 1207.

11. Grew Memoirs, December 1938.

On December 1, I had a long and important talk with an influential colleague anent these subjects. He feels that there is little time to be lost if assistance to Chiang Kai-shek[17] is to be effective, and he also feels that unless Anglo-American measures are taken against Japan, preferably supported by France, the discrimination against foreign interests in China will be progressive. He also believes that economic sanctions, or merely the definite threat of them, would rapidly force Japan to come to terms. With that thesis I disagree.

[*On September 1, 1939, Germany invaded Poland. England and France declared war on Germany two days later.*]

Source 12 from *Foreign Relations: Japan*, Vol. 2, pp. 19–29.

12. Grew's Address to the American-Japan Society at Tokyo, October 19, 1939.

I turn now to some of the thoughts of the American Government and of the American people with regard to the situation in East Asia in general and to our relations with Japan in particular. It is trite to say—but all too often the fact is overlooked—that in our democratic system the policies and measures of our Government reflect, and inevitably must reflect, public opinion. If therefore in any given case or situation we search for the underlying causation of American policy, or of any specific measure or series of measures taken by our Government, we must first try to analyze the state of public opinion in the United States and the developments which have induced that state of public opinion, factors which in turn have given rise to some specific policy or some specific measure or measures of our Government. . . .

I suppose that there is not a person here who does not know that American public opinion strongly resents some of the things that Japan's armed forces are doing in China today, including actions against American rights and legitimate interests in China. On that subject public opinion in the United States is unanimous. And, mind you, I know whereof I speak, from personal talks

17. Chiang Kai-shek (also Jiang Jieshi): key political and military leader in China from 1925 to 1949, when the Communists overthrew his government and he was forced to retreat to Taiwan. He died there in 1975.

◆ CHAPTER 8

Going to War
with Japan:
A Problem in
Diplomacy and
Causation

with a very large number of people in diverse walks of life throughout our country, constituting a reliable cross-section of the American public. . . .

There's the story. It is probable that many of you are not aware of the increasing extent to which the people of the United States resent the methods which the Japanese armed forces are employing in China today and what appear to be their objectives. In saying this, I do not wish for one moment to imply that the American people have forgotten the long-time friendship which has existed between the people of my country and the people of Japan. But the American people have been profoundly shocked over the widespread use of bombing in China, not only on grounds of humanity but also on grounds of the direct menace to American lives and property accompanied by the loss of American life and the crippling of American citizens; they regard with growing seriousness the violation of and interference with American rights by the Japanese armed forces in China in disregard of treaties and agreements entered into by the United States and Japan and treaties and agreements entered into by several nations, including Japan.

Sources 13 through 16 from *Peace and War*, pp. 202–207.

13. White House Press Release, December 2, 1939.

The President, after consultation with the Secretary of State this morning, released the following statement:

"The American Government and the American people have for some time pursued a policy of wholeheartedly condemning the unprovoked bombing and machine-gunning of civilian populations from the air.

"This Government hopes, to the end that such unprovoked bombing shall not be given material encouragement in the light of recent recurrence of such acts, that American manufacturers and exporters of airplanes, aeronautical equipment and materials essential to airplane manufacture, will bear this fact in mind before negotiating contracts for the exportation of these articles to nations obviously guilty of such unprovoked bombing."

14. State Department Press Release, December 20, 1939.

The Department, after consultation with the War and Navy Departments, has decided that the national interest suggests that for the time being there should be no further delivery to certain countries of plans, plants, manufacturing rights, or technical information required for the production of high quality aviation gasoline.

This decision has been reached with a view to conserving in this country certain technical information of strategic importance and as an extension of the announced policy of this Government in regard to the sale of airplanes, aeronautical equipment, and materials essential to airplane manufacture to countries the armed forces of which are engaged in unprovoked bombing or machine-gunning of civilian populations from the air.

The interested American oil companies have been informed of the Government's decision in this matter.

15. Memorandum by Hull, January 6, 1940.

The Japanese Ambassador called and handed me the attached notes, which are self-explanatory. I inquired whether he desired a written reply to the note in regard to moral sanctions, including an alleged contract between a Japanese company and American citizens concerning technical processes and manufacturing rights for the production of certain petroleum products. He said that the Japanese Government would like to have a written reply. I then remarked that he no doubt was aware of the fact that the so-called moral embargo on all phases of the airplane situation found its origin in and was based on the bombing of civilian populations from the air in China by the Japanese, and that I would probably list a great number of these bombings as reported to this Government and allow them to be published together with the balance of the contents of the note. The Ambassador appeared very startled at this idea, and repeated the request of his Government for a written reply.

With regard to technical processes for high-test gasoline, I stated that this Government, concerned as it is with the increase of war and the use or threat of force in so many parts of the world, feels constrained to conserve a number of the more vital interests it has in defense commodities or materials, and that this, together with our abhorrence of the bombings of civilian populations, is the basis for the conservation of the gasoline manufacturing processes to which the Ambassador referred.

✦ CHAPTER 8

Going to War
with Japan:
A Problem in
Diplomacy and
Causation

16. Japanese Ambassador Kensuke Horinouchi to Hull, January 6, 1940.

Sɪʀ: I have the honor to state that, as the result of a communication through a circular letter of July 1, 1938, addressed by the Department of State to manufacturers and exporters of aircraft and aircraft parts, in which it was mentioned that "the Department of State would with great regret issue any licenses authorizing exportation, direct or indirect, of any aircraft, aircraft armament, aircraft engines, aircraft parts, aircraft accessories, aerial bombs or torpedoes to countries the armed forces of which are making use of airplanes for attack upon civilian populations," it has virtually become impossible for Japanese firms to import any airplanes and airplane parts of American make.

As repeatedly stated by my Government, military operations of the Japanese air forces in China have been directed solely against warlike organizations and establishments of the Chinese. No bombing or machine-gunning has been resorted to against civilian populations as such. The Japanese Government, therefore, cannot but take exception to any treatment of Japan as a country "the armed forces of which are making use of airplanes for attack upon civilian populations." . . .

[Here Horinouchi claimed that the United States' actions were in violation of the 1911 commercial treaty between the United States and Japan.]

While my Government was keenly alive to the unfortunate consequences of the said communication to American exporters, it did not relinquish the hope that the United States Government, in harmony with its fair and just trade policy, would before long retract it.

Source 17 from *New York Times,* January 25, 1940.

17. "Japanese Abandon Last-Minute Talks on U.S. Pact Lapse."[18]

TOKYO, Thursday, Jan. 25—Newspapers today accused Washington of a concerted effort to wreck Japan's program for creation of a "New Order in East Asia." Among officials and business leaders alike, resentment against the United States, because of Washington's refusal to accept Japan's plea for a

18. The U.S.-Japanese commercial treaty was due to expire.

working agreement to replace the expiring Japanese-American treaty, was keen.

Officials said bluntly, in private conversation, that President Roosevelt's action in abrogating the commercial treaty, effective tomorrow, was a political move involving the most serious potential consequences and that the President was using the trade treaty as "a club to wreck the New Order in East Asia."

It was understood that a move for last-minute conversations here between Foreign Minister Hachiro Arita and United States Ambassador Joseph C. Grew, in a final effort to find some working agreement to replace the treaty, was abandoned after Ambassador Kensuke Horinouchi had been told by the State Department in Washington that no "stop-gap" arrangement was desired by the United States.

Source 18 from Gallup, *The Gallup Poll*, p. 208.

18. Gallup Poll, February 14, 1940.

Q: Should the U.S. government forbid the sale of arms, airplanes, gasoline, and other war materials to Japan?

Yes: 75%

No: 25%

Source 19 from *Foreign Relations: Japan*, Vol. 2, p. 55.

19. Grew to Hull, February 29, 1940.

Replying to an interpellation in a committee meeting of the Lower House yesterday afternoon, the Foreign Minister made a statement with regard to Japanese-American relations of which the following is reported to be the substance:

"Even though the United States does not understand the object of Japan's Holy War with China, opposes the establishment of a new order in East Asia on all fronts, and even though the United States should insist upon carrying through its demands, the Japanese Government is not afraid of the future.

◆ CHAPTER 8

Going to War
with Japan:
A Problem in
Diplomacy and
Causation

The situation has not reached that stage, however. With respect to the problem of opening the Yangtze to navigation, the Japanese Government, as I have repeatedly stated, does not entertain for a moment the idea that a new commercial treaty can be had in return for the opening of the Yangtze River. The question of the opening of the Yangtze and other problems pending between the United States and Japan which are capable of settlement will be dealt with appropriately, that is to say, they will be handled in accordance with Japan's 'independent' policy which is, after all, what we mean by 'Imperial way' diplomacy. To leave unsettled those problems which are capable of being settled and to employ them to obtain advantages in dealing with other problems is a policy contrary to the spirit of the Imperial way. We do not know precisely what the American Government has under consideration, but if it is determined to ignore completely the object of Japan's Holy War and to refuse to lift a finger, Japan should display an attitude of resolution. The purpose of Japan's Holy War is clear: it is the establishment of a new order in East Asia. From whatever angle this may be viewed it is open and aboveboard.

[*In April 1940, German troops invaded Denmark and Norway. One month later, combined air and land assaults overran Belgium and the Netherlands. In June, France surrendered to Germany.*]

Source 20 from *Foreign Relations: Japan,* Vol. 2, p. 281.

20. Japanese Press Release, April 15, 1940.

On being questioned by newspapermen concerning Japan's position with regard to possible involvement of the Netherlands in the European war and its repercussions in the Netherlands East Indies, Foreign Minister Arita replied as follows:

"With the South Seas regions, especially the Netherlands East Indies, Japan is economically bound by an intimate relationship of mutuality in ministering to one another's needs. Similarly, other countries of East Asia maintain close economic relations with these regions. That is to say, Japan, these countries and these regions together are contributing to the prosperity of East Asia through mutual aid and interdependence.

"Should hostilities in Europe be extended to the Netherlands and produce repercussions, as you say, in the Netherlands East Indies, it would not only interfere with the maintenance and furtherance of the above-mentioned relations of economic interdependence and of co-existence and co-prosperity, but would also give rise to an undesirable situation from the standpoint of the peace and stability of East Asia. In view of these considerations, the Japanese Government can not but be deeply concerned over any development accompanying an aggravation of the war in Europe that may affect the *status quo* of the Netherlands East Indies."

Source 21 from *Peace and War*, pp. 515–516.

21. Statement by Hull, April 17, 1940.

I have noted with interest the statement by the Japanese Minister for Foreign Affairs expressing concern on the part of the Japanese Government for the maintenance of the *status quo* of the Netherlands Indies.

Any change in the status of the Netherlands Indies would directly affect the interests of many countries.

The Netherlands Indies are very important in the international relationships of the whole Pacific Ocean. The islands themselves extend for a distance of approximately 3,200 miles east and west astride of the Equator, from the Indian Ocean on the west far into the Pacific Ocean on the east. They are also an important factor in the commerce of the whole world. They produce considerable portions of the world's supplies of important essential commodities such as rubber, tin, quinine, copra, et cetera. Many countries, including the United States, depend substantially upon them for some of these commodities.

Intervention in the domestic affairs of the Netherlands Indies or any alteration of their *status quo* by other than peaceful processes would be prejudicial to the cause of stability, peace, and security not only in the region of the Netherlands Indies but in the entire Pacific area.

Source 22 from *From the Morgenthau Diaries: Years of Urgency, 1938–1941*, edited by John Morton Blum. Copyright © 1964 by John M. Blum and the Estate of Henry Morgenthau, Jr. Reprinted by permission of Houghton Mifflin Company. All rights reserved.

22. U.S. Secretary of the Treasury Henry Morgenthau, Recollections of July 1940.

[*On July 18, 1940, Morgenthau dined with British Ambassador Lord Lothian, Ambassador Carey of Australia, U.S. Secretary of War Henry Stimson, and U.S. Secretary of the Navy Frank Knox. The conversation turned to Japanese expansion in the Pacific.*]

♦ CHAPTER 8
Going to War
with Japan:
A Problem in
Diplomacy and
Causation

"Nobody," Morgenthau broke in, "has asked me or even suggested to me that we stop shipping aviation gasoline." Stimson said that in speeches during the last year he had been making precisely that point.

"If you will stop shipping aviation gasoline to Japan," Lothian suggested, "we will blow up the oil wells in the Dutch East Indies so that the Japanese can't come down and get that . . . we have felt that if we put too much pressure on Japan they would go down and take those oil wells." At the same time the Royal Air Force could concentrate its bombing attacks on German plants producing synthetic gasoline.

His "breath . . . taken away," Morgenthau said he would propose the idea "at once." Stimson encouraged him, remarking incidentally that so long as Japan was tied down in China she was unlikely to make excursions farther south.

On his way home from the dinner Morgenthau decided to proceed through Harold Ickes,[19] who, during the last Cabinet meeting, had advocated a total embargo on oil in order to conserve declining American fuel reserves. If Ickes could now carry that case with the President, Morgenthau felt that it "would keep the State Department from opposing the idea . . . and then it would be up to us to find out and make certain that there is enough oil flowing from Venezuela and Colombia which the British could get to take care of themselves." If then the British "would blow up the wells, it would simply electrify the world and really put some belief in England." Destruction of the wells, Morgenthau surmised, would eliminate Japanese ambitions for the Dutch East Indies and thus encourage the Australians, who were "shaking like aspen leaves." Lothian's plan would entirely alter the situation in the Pacific, whereas "if we don't do something and do it fast, Japan is just going to gobble up one thing after another."

Morgenthau elaborated his thoughts in a memorandum of July 19, 1940, for Roosevelt and Ickes. That day at the White House the Secretary "told the President that this thing might give us peace in three to six months and he read the thing very carefully. . . . The President was tremendously interested. He said this is very much along the idea he had a couple of months ago whereby he was talking about blockading all of Europe and just leaving a small channel open directly to England through which all ships would have to pass. . . . He then went on down and talked about the wells in Iraq, and so on. After he had been going on about half an hour, they came in and said Stimson and Knox were outside and he said, 'What do you think of having them in?' I said, 'By all means,' they were great guys."

19. Harold Ickes: U.S. Secretary of the Interior and a strong opponent of Japanese expansion.

Sumner Welles—Hull was away at the Havana Conference of American Republics[20]—also joined them, and there followed what Stimson described as a "very important conference on the general situation in the world." At an opportune moment, Roosevelt presented the proposal which he had just received, without attributing it to Morgenthau, but Welles maintained that it would cause the Japanese to make war on Great Britain. Morgenthau and Stimson "argued very hard . . . and Stimson gave his usual argument, that the only way to treat Japan is not to retreat. And then Welles talked about . . . making peace for China and Japan, that is what we want." . . .

[The meeting ended without a decision. Morgenthau then recalled a Cabinet meeting on July 25, 1940. Earlier that day, President Roosevelt placed scrap metal, oil, and oil products on the list of vital materials that should not be exported. The State Department, "terribly upset" according to Morgenthau, took it upon itself to redraft Roosevelt's order by backing away from a total embargo of oil.]

That afternoon Morgenthau took to the Cabinet meeting a letter of protest against the proposed change in the President's orders. That change, the letter read, "would be a most serious mistake, since crude oil and various other petroleum products can be converted into aviation gasoline and this restriction would not apply to diesel oil, used by submarines and tanks. . . . I understand that the State Department's objection is that the sweeping petroleum and scrap embargo could not be administered effectively. May I most respectfully suggest that if the Division of Controls of the State Department and the Administrator of Export Controls cannot administer this proclamation effectively the Treasury Department can. As a practical matter the enforcement of the embargo . . . is a comparatively easy problem. In the case of Foreign Exchange Control, which is a much more complex problem . . . the Treasury has not found the task impossible of achievement, nor has the effort expended been unjustified by the results achieved. The objections raised to the oil and scrap metal control reinforce a growing impression on my part that there is something very seriously wrong with the personnel or system in effect for administering the export controls."

The Cabinet meeting, as Stimson reported it, was frantic. Welles and Morgenthau struck out at each other as soon as it began, and "the President raised his hands in the air, refused to participate in it and said that those two men must go off in a corner and settle their issue. Accordingly, after the Cabinet meeting . . . Morgenthau and Welles got together and thrashed it out. I

20. Sumner Welles, Undersecretary of State, who attended the Cabinet meeting because Hull was in Havana. Welles and Hull opposed a "hard line" against Japan, fearing it would drive that nation into war.

✦ CHAPTER 8

Going to War
with Japan:
A Problem in
Diplomacy and
Causation

myself was very glad to find that my own views as to aviation oil had been apparently now accepted by the State Department, and also scrap iron. Morgenthau had apparently won his victory in substance."

Source 23 accessed from http://www.worldfuturefund.org/wffmaster/Reading/Japan/Japan-1940.htm.

23. Official Statement of the Japanese Government on the Greater East Asia Co-Prosperity Sphere, August 1, 1940.

The world stands at a great historic turning point, and it is about to witness the creation of new forms of government, economy, and culture, based upon the growth and development of sundry groups of states. Japan, too, is confronted by a great trial such as she has never experienced in history. In order to carry out fully at this juncture our national policy in accordance with the lofty spirit in which the country was founded, it is an important task of urgent necessity to us that we should grasp the inevitable trends in the developments of world history, effect speedily fundamental renovations along all lines of government, and strive for the perfection of a state structure for national defense. Accordingly, the general lines of the country's fundamental national policies have been formulated as follows. . . .

The basic aim of Japan's national policy lies in the firm establishment of world peace in accordance with the lofty spirit of Hakko Ichiu,[21] in which the country was founded, and in the construction, as the first step, of a new order in Greater East Asia, having for its foundation the solidarity of Japan, Manchoukou and China.

Japan will, therefore, devote the total strength of the nation to the fulfillment of the above policy by setting up swiftly an unshakable national structure of her own adapted to meet the requirements of new developments both at home and abroad. . . .

The Government will strive for the repletion of armaments adequate for the execution of the national policies, by taking into consideration the new developments both at home and abroad, and constructing a state structure for national defense, capable of bringing into full play the total strength of the nation.

Japan's foreign policy, which aims ultimately at the construction of a new order in Greater East Asia, will be directed, first of all, toward a complete set-

21. Hakko Ichiu: "Eight corners of the world under one roof," signifying cultural dominance of Asia by Japan.

tlement of the China Affair, and the advancement of the national fortune by taking a far-sighted view of the drastic changes in the international situation and formulating both constructive and flexible measures.

Source 24 from Nobutaka Ike, trans. and ed., *Japan's Decision for War: Records of the 1941 Policy Conferences*, pp. 5, 7, 8, 12. Copyright © 1967 by the Board of Trustees of the Leland Stanford Junior University, renewed 1995 by the author. All rights reserved.

24. High-Level Japanese Government Meeting, September 19, 1940.

[*Those at the meeting discussed the ramifications of an alliance with Germany and Italy, which was announced the following week, on September 27, 1940.*]

FUSHIMI: I foresee that as a result of this alliance our trade with Great Britain and the United States will undergo a change; and that if worst comes to worst, it will become increasingly difficult to import vital materials. Moreover, it is quite likely that a Japanese-American war will be a protracted one. What are the prospects for maintaining our national strength in view of the present situation, which finds our national resources depleted because of the China Incident? And what measures are contemplated?

PRIME MINISTER KONOYE: We can anticipate that trade relations with Britain and the United States will deteriorate even more. If worst comes to worst, it may become impossible to obtain any imported goods. At the present time our country depends to a large extent on Britain and the United States for her principal war materials. Accordingly, we cannot help but experience considerable difficulties. . . .

[*A discussion ensued on Japanese steel production and oil stockpiles and on Japan's access to oil and scrap metal in the event of war with the United States.*]

HOSHINO: The oil situation is as I have already explained. If there should be a fairly prolonged war, it will be necessary to get oil from northern Sakhalin and the Netherlands East Indies. Also it will be necessary to get additional supplies from the Soviet Union and Europe through the good offices of Germany. In short, it will be essential to acquire a large amount of oil any way we can. The Netherlands East Indies and northern Sakhalin are the places one thinks of first; once we have made up our minds, we will have to get oil from these places. . . .

FUSHIMI: May I interpret this to mean that there is, in general, no assurance that additional oil can be obtained? I will add that we cannot count on sup-

✦ CHAPTER 8

Going to War
with Japan:
A Problem in
Diplomacy and
Causation

plies from the Soviet Union. In the end, we will need to get oil from the Netherlands East Indies. There are two ways of getting it—by peaceful means, and by the use of force. The Navy very much prefers peaceful means.

MATSUOKA: In negotiating the Pact, we paid most attention to the question of procuring oil. Even though British and American capital is involved, since it is under Dutch control we asked Ott[22] and Stahmer[23] what Germany, which controls the Netherlands, could do to help us obtain oil from the Netherlands East Indies, and develop Japanese enterprises there in the future. They said that Germany could do a good deal. . . .

HARA: It is necessary now to get Germany and Italy to acknowledge Japan's freedom of action in the Netherlands East Indies. I want to refer to the Foreign Minister's statement on the interpretation of a covert attack. I would like to ask if, supposing that the United States should lease bases in New Zealand, Australia, etc. and encircle Japan, we have decided whether such an act should be interpreted as an American attack on Japan.

MATSUOKA: The object of this Pact[24] is to prevent the United States from encircling us in that way. The only thing that can prevent an American encirclement policy is a firm stand on our part at this time. As to whether an encirclement—should such a thing take place—is to be regarded as an attack, no doubt the Supreme Command and the War and Navy Ministers have views on the subject. I am inclined to think that it should be decided on the basis of the situation at that time.

TOJO: One can only decide on the basis of the situation at that time.

HARA: The United States is a self-confident nation. Accordingly, I wonder if our taking a firm stand might not have a result quite contrary to the one we expect.

MATSUOKA: I see your point; but Japan is not Spain. We are a great power with a strong navy in Far Eastern waters. To be sure, the United States may adopt a stern attitude for a while; but I think that she will dispassionately take her interests into consideration and arrive at a reasonable attitude. As to whether she will stiffen her attitude and bring about a critical situation, or will levelheadedly reconsider, I would say that the odds are fifty-fifty.

22. Ott: Eugen Ott, German Ambassador to Japan.
23. Stahmer: Heinrich Stahmer, German minister to Japan, under Ott.
24. Pact: The Tripartite Pact, between Germany, Italy, and Japan.

Source 25 from *Peace and War,* pp. 612–613.

25. Hull's Statement Before the House of Representatives Committee on Foreign Affairs, January 15, 1941.

It has been clear throughout that Japan has been actuated from the start by broad and ambitious plans for establishing herself in a dominant position in the entire region of the Western Pacific. Her leaders have openly declared their determination to achieve and maintain that position by force of arms and thus to make themselves masters of an area containing almost one half of the entire population of the world. As a consequence, they would have arbitrary control of the sea and trade routes in that region.

Previous experience and current developments indicate that the proposed "new order" in the Pacific area means, politically, domination by one country. It means, economically, employment of the resources of the area concerned for the benefit of that country and to the ultimate impoverishment of other parts of the area and exclusion of the interests of other countries. It means, socially, the destruction of personal liberties and the reduction of the conquered peoples to the role of inferiors.

It should be manifest to every person that such a program for the subjugation and ruthless exploitation by one country of nearly one half of the population of the world is a matter of immense significance, importance, and concern to every other nation wherever located.

Notwithstanding the course which Japan has followed during recent years, this Government has made repeated efforts to persuade the Japanese Government that her best interests lie in the development of friendly relations with the United States and with other countries which believe in orderly and peaceful processes among nations. We have at no time made any threats.

Sources 26, 30, and 35 from Cordell Hull, *The Memoirs of Cordell Hull* (New York: Macmillan, 1948), Vol. 2, pp. 983–984. Reprinted by permission of the Estate of Cordell Hull.

26. Hull's Memoirs, January 1941.

Japan knew that our economic pressure was growing. By the beginning of 1941, shipments to her from the United States of iron, steel, most other important metals, high-octane gasoline, and plants for producing it had virtu-

✦ CHAPTER 8

Going to War
with Japan:
A Problem in
Diplomacy and
Causation

ally ceased. We still permitted shipments of petroleum lest Japan use such an embargo as an excuse for taking over the oil production of the Netherlands East Indies. She also knew that our aid to China was growing. Beginning in January, the American Volunteer Group of airmen with American-made planes began to give the Chinese aerial support. And she also knew that the major portion of our fleet was still in the Pacific.

What Japan did not know was whether and in what circumstances we would use force. Isolationist sentiment in the United States was still strong, as the Lend-Lease debate in Congress showed. But she also saw that the Administration was acting with determination, and that an increasing number of Americans were coming to realize the dangers threatening us in both the Atlantic and the Pacific.

Members of the Japanese Government were giving vent to ever more bellicose statements, with Foreign Minister Matsuoka as their bellwether. Perhaps they hoped they could cow the United States, already preoccupied with Europe, into agreeing to a Japanese East Asia so as to avoid war. A Japanese East Asia meant Nipponese predominance in China, Malaya, French Indo-China, the Dutch East Indies, and the Philippines. Matsuoka said to the Japanese Diet on January 21 that he wanted the United States to realize the vital concern to Japan of the establishment of an East Asia "co-prosperity sphere," to agree to her supremacy in the Western Pacific, and to cease our economic restrictions against her. He aimed his speech at the statement I had made to the House Foreign Affairs Committee six days before.

In reply I issued a press statement on the following day, saying: "We have threatened no one, invaded no one, and surrounded no one. We have freely offered and now freely offer cooperation in peaceful life to all who wish it. This devotion to peaceful and friendly processes naturally warrants no implication of a desire to extend frontiers or assume hegemony. Our strategic line must depend primarily on the policies and courses of other nations."

[*In January 1941, the Japanese military began to plan for a secret attack on the U.S. naval base at Pearl Harbor. The head of the planning group was Admiral Yamamoto Isoruku.*]

Source 27 from *Peace and War,* pp. 618–619.

27. Telegram from Grew to Hull, January 27, 1941.

A member of the Embassy was told by my colleague that from many quarters, including a Japanese one, he had heard that a surprise mass attack on Pearl Harbor was planned by the Japanese military forces, in case of "trouble" between Japan and the United States; that the attack would involve the use of all the Japanese military facilities. My colleague said that he was prompted to pass this on because it had come to him from many sources, although the plan seemed fantastic.

[*Hull alerted Naval Intelligence, which reported that "based on known data regarding the present disposition of Japanese Naval and Army forces, no move against Pearl Harbor appears imminent or planned for the foreseeable future." Toland,* The Rising Sun, *p. 151.*]

Source 28 from Gallup, *The Gallup Poll,* p. 266.

28. Gallup Poll Taken February 24, 1941.

Q: Should the United States keep Japan from seizing the Dutch East Indies and Singapore?

Yes: 56%

No: 24%

Undecided: 20%

Source 29 from *Peace and War,* pp. 656–657.

29. Confidential Memorandum, Draft of a Proposal, Japanese Ambassador Nomura to Hull, May 12, 1941.

The Governments of the United States and of Japan accept joint responsibility for the initiation and conclusion of a general agreement disposing the resumption of our traditional friendly relations.

Without reference to specific causes of recent estrangement, it is the sincere desire of both Governments that the incidents which led to the deteriora-

✦ CHAPTER 8

Going to War
with Japan:
A Problem in
Diplomacy and
Causation

tion of amicable sentiment among our peoples should be prevented from recurrence and corrected in their unforeseen and unfortunate consequences.

It is our present hope that, by a joint effort, our nations may establish a just peace in the Pacific; and by the rapid consummation of an entente cordiale [*amicable understanding*], arrest, if not dispel, the tragic confusion that now threatens to engulf civilization.

For such decisive action, protracted negotiations would seem ill suited and weakening. Both Governments, therefore, desire that adequate instrumentalities should be developed for the realization of a general agreement which would bind, meanwhile, both Governments in honor and in act.

It is our belief that such an understanding should comprise only the pivotal issues of urgency and not the accessory concerns which could be deliberated at a conference and appropriately confirmed by our respective Governments.

[*Japan demanded that the United States recognize Japan's "relationship of neighborly friendship with China," request that Chang Kai-shek negotiate peace with Japan, resume normal trade relations with Japan, agree that Japan's "expansion in the direction of the Southwestern Pacific area is declared to be of a peaceful nature, and assist Japan's procurement of natural resources such as oil, rubber, tin, and nickel. . . . The present understanding shall be kept as a confidential memorandum between the Governments of the United States and of Japan." Hull called the draft "totally unacceptable."*]

Source 30 from Hull, *Memoirs*, Vol. 2, pp. 1012–1014.

30. Hull on Japanese Expansion.

We had, in fact, very definite knowledge of what Japan was planning. On the surface, an Imperial Conference was held in Tokyo on July 2, following which military steps of an alarming nature began to be taken. Between one and two million men were called to the armed forces, Japanese merchant vessels were suddenly recalled from the Atlantic, travel restrictions and strict censorship of mails and communications were imposed in Japan. The various steps taken were indicative of preparations for a major war. . . .

[*Hull reported that the United States had intercepted messages from the Japanese government in which Japan informed Germany of its plans to advance into French Indochina and Thailand. The messages made clear that the Japanese government wanted to keep the United States from stopping Japanese expansion but was prepared to meet American force with Japanese force.*]

Shortly thereafter Japanese troops on July 21 occupied the southern portions of Indo-China and were now in possession of the whole of France's strategic province, pointing like a pudgy thumb toward the Philippines, Malaya, and the Dutch East Indies.

Welles telephoned me at White Sulphur Springs on July 23 to talk over with me what he should say to Nomura who had requested an interview with him. We knew that the topic Nomura had in mind was the invasion of Indo-China.

Nomura had come to see me at White Sulphur Springs ten days before, on July 13. He arrived without making an appointment, and I refused to see him. I was not well, and I knew Nomura had nothing new to offer. Furthermore, my associates and I thought it a good idea psychologically not to be too eager to see Nomura each time he requested an interview. Too much evidence on our part that we were anxious to reach a settlement with Japan induced the Japanese to narrow their concessions and enlarge their demands.

When Welles telephoned me, I said to him that the invasion of Southern Indo-China looked like Japan's last step before jumping off for a full-scale attack in the Southwest Pacific. Since it came in the midst of the conversations we were holding with Japan, I said I could see no basis for pursuing the conversations further.

Source 31 from Herbert Feis, *Road to Pearl Harbor: The Coming of the War Between the United States and Japan* (Princeton: Princeton University Press, 1950), pp. 215–216.

31. Outline of Decisions Reached at the Japanese Imperial Conference, July 2, 1941.

1. The Imperial Government is determined to follow a policy which will result in the establishment of the Greater East Asia Co-Prosperity Sphere and world peace, no matter what international developments take place.
2. The Imperial Government will continue its effort to effect a settlement of the China Incident and seek to establish a solid basis for the security and preservation of the nation. This will involve an advance into the Southern Regions and, depending on future developments, a settlement of the Soviet Question as well.
3. The Imperial Government will carry out the above program no matter what obstacles may be encountered. . . .

In carrying out the plans outlined in the foregoing article, we will not be deterred by the possibility of being involved in a war with England and America.

✦ CHAPTER 8

Going to War
with Japan:
A Problem in
Diplomacy and
Causation

[*At this conference it was decided that Japan would move troops into southern French Indochina.*]

Sources 32 and 33 from *Foreign Relations: Japan*, pp. 264–267.

32. Excerpt from President Roosevelt's Radio Address, July 25, 1941.

All right. Now the answer is a very simple one. There is a world war going on, and has been for some time—nearly two years. One of our efforts, from the very beginning, was to prevent the spread of that world war in certain areas where it hadn't started. One of those areas is a place called the Pacific Ocean—one of the largest areas of the earth. There happened to be a place in the South Pacific where we had to get a lot of things—rubber—tin—and so forth and so on—down in the Dutch Indies, the Straits Settlements, and Indochina. And we had to help get the Australian surplus of meat and wheat, and corn, for England.

It was very essential from our own selfish point of view of defense to prevent a war from starting in the South Pacific. So our foreign policy was—trying to stop a war from breaking out down there. At the same time, from the point of view of even France at that time—of course France still had her head above water—we wanted to keep that line of supplies from Australia and New Zealand going to the Near East—all their troops, all their supplies that they have maintained in Syria, North Africa and Palestine. So it was essential for Great Britain that we try to keep the peace down there in the South Pacific.

All right. And now here is a nation called Japan. Whether they had at that time aggressive purposes to enlarge their empire southward, they didn't have any oil of their own up in the north. Now, if we cut the oil off, they probably would have gone down to the Dutch East Indies a year ago, and you would have had war.

Therefore, there was—you might call—a method in letting this oil go to Japan, with the hope—and it has worked for two years—of keeping war out of the South Pacific for our own good, for the good of the defense of Great Britain, and the freedom of the seas.

33. White House Press Release, July 25, 1941.

In view of the unlimited national emergency declared by the President, he has today issued an Executive Order freezing Japanese assets in the United States in the same manner in which assets of various European countries were frozen on June 14, 1941. This measure, in effect, brings all financial and import and export trade transactions in which Japanese interests are involved under the control of the Government, and imposes criminal penalties for violation of the Order.

[*Japan occupied southern Indochina without incident on July 27–28, 1941.*]

Source 34 from Gallup, *The Gallup Poll*, p. 311.

34. Gallup Pool Taken November 14, 1941.

Q: Should the United States take steps now to prevent the Japanese from becoming more powerful, even if this means risking a war with Japan?

Yes: 64%

No: 25%

Source 35 from Hull, *Memoirs*, Vol. 2, p. 1069.

35. Hull's Memoirs, November 20, 1941.

JAPAN'S LAST-WORD PROPOSAL, handed me by Ambassadors Nomura and Kurusu on November 20, in the nature of a temporary agreement or modus vivendi, was clearly unacceptable. In six points the Tokyo Government put conditions that would have assured Japan domination of the Pacific, placing us in serious danger for decades to come.

These were:

Japan and the United States to make no armed advance into any region in Southeast Asia and the Southwest Pacific area;

Japan to withdraw her troops from Indo-China when peace was restored between Japan and China or an equitable peace was established in the Pacific area;

✦ CHAPTER 8

Going to War
with Japan:
A Problem in
Diplomacy and
Causation

Japan meantime to remove her troops from southern to northern Indo-China upon conclusion of the present agreement which would later be embodied in the final agreement;

Japan and the United States to cooperate toward acquiring goods and commodities that the two countries needed in the Netherlands East Indies.

Japan and the United States to restore their commercial relations to those prevailing prior to the freezing of assets, and the United States to supply Japan a required quantity of oil;

The United States to refrain from such measures and actions as would prejudice endeavors for the restoration of peace between Japan and China.

My associates and I subjected these points and their implications to minute study, but it required very little scrutiny to see that they were utterly unacceptable.

The commitments we should have to make were virtually a surrender.

✦

Questions to Consider

Before you begin to consider the worldviews, self-perceptions, and strategic options of the United States and Japan, it would be helpful for you to begin by understanding the world situation in the 1930s and early 1940s, especially as they applied to the Pacific Ocean area. What were the demographic, economic, and political situations in the United States and in Japan? Use the Background section of this chapter, your text, and your instructor as good resources.

Now consider Japan. How did that nation perceive its demographic, economic, political, and international situations? How did it view the world around it (a friendly place? a hostile and dangerous place?)? See especially Sources 4, 10, 15, 16, and 23. How did Japan perceive its opportunities and challenges? See especially Sources 1, 4, 5, 10, 15, 19, 20, and 23. What strate-

gies were available to Japan? See Sources 10, 19, 20, 23, 24, 29, 31, and 35.

Next repeat the process for the United States. How did that nation perceive itself? the world? its challenges (Japan?)? its strategies?

Public opinion is an important factor in shaping foreign policy in many nations. How can the Gallup polls (Sources 2, 8, 18, 28, 34) be used to examine the effects public opinion have on policymaking?

The evidence for the United States shows clearly that there were sharp disagreements *within* the government over the conduct of American relations with Japan (see especially Sources 9 and 22). Does this suggest that people in the American federal government had different—and opposing—worldviews, perceptions of challenges, and suggested strategies? This also was the case in the Japanese government (especially in the clashes between the civilian government and the military (see the Background section of this chapter), but evidence of that has not been included.

Once you have examined the worldviews and self-perceptions of the United States and Japan, make a list of the ways each nation viewed the other. Then make a list of the strategies available to each government. Finally, determine why each government chose the strategy it ultimately adopted.

Keep the central questions in mind: Why did Japan attack Pearl Harbor? What were the causes of that event?

Epilogue

U.S. Secretary of State Cordell Hull was infuriated by the Japanese attack on Pearl Harbor, especially since high-level diplomatic negotiations were still going on between the two nations and the Japanese negotiators did not meet with Hull to break off talks until after the attack on Pearl Harbor already had taken place. Nearly apoplectic with rage, the American secretary verbally lashed the Japanese diplomats, calling them "scoundrels and piss-ants."[25]

The United States' declaration of war against Japan brought that nation's Tripartite Pact partners Germany and Italy into the war against the United States as well. On December 11, Hitler asked the *Reichstag* to declare war against the "half Judaized and the other half Negrified" American nation. Italy joined in soon thereafter.

Fortunately for the United States, the Pacific Fleet's aircraft carriers were at sea on December 7, 1941. Although the United States and Great Britain

agreed that Germany must be defeated before the Allies could turn their attention to Japan, the U.S. Navy was ordered to block Japanese expansion until more forces could come to its aid. At the Battle of the Coral Sea (May 7–11, 1942), the Japanese threat to Australia was blunted. Then, on June 4–5, 1942, the two carrier fleets clashed at the Battle of Midway. American planes sank four Japanese carriers and destroyed hundreds of planes. Although the war continued for three bloody years, the Japanese offensive had been broken. Near the end, the desperate Japanese military sent waves of *kamikaze* ("divine wind") fighter planes against American warships while at the same time American aircraft firebombed Tokyo. Finally in August 1945, United States B-29 bombers dropped two atomic bombs, on Hiroshima and Nagasaki. On August 14, 1945, Japan surrendered.

After the war, the United States occupied Japan. And yet, instead of a harsh and vindictive occupation, the period was one of reform and rebuilding. The Japanese Diet adopted a new

25. For Hull's verbal attack, see Dean Acheson, *Present at the Creation: My Years in the State Department* (New York: W. W. Norton, 1969), p. 35

◆ CHAPTER 8

Going to War
with Japan:
A Problem in
Diplomacy and
Causation

constitution (written by U.S. General Douglas MacArthur's staff) that placed sovereignty with the people, gave women the right to vote, and incorporated some of the American Bill of Rights. At the same time, the United States helped rebuild the Japanese economy, which ultimately became the most powerful economy in Asia and one of the most dynamic in the world. By 2000, the Japanese economy was larger than that of France and Germany combined and was, next to that of the United States, the largest in the world.

Unquestionably, the United States hoped that a reconstructed and economically vibrant Japan would serve as a bulwark against the spread of Communism in Asia. Not so anticipated, however, was the Japanese people's enthusiastic adoption of some aspects of American culture (baseball, rock and roll music, American films, American fast food, and so on) and the extent to which Japan became the United States' main competitor in such sectors of the world economy as automobiles, computers and other electronics, and steel.

Of course, one of Japan's principal economic problems remained: the lack of raw materials. A revived industrial sector was even more in need of massive amounts of energy than had previously been the case. Since the 1960s, the nation has sought to decrease its dependency on imported oil, and to a certain extent it has done so. In 1965, imported oil supplied 60 percent of Japan's energy needs; by 2000, it had fallen to 43 percent. At the same time, nuclear energy output has soared and now provides around 18 percent of that nation's total energy needs.[26]

In his thoughtful book *Going to War with Japan: 1937–1941,* historian Jonathan Utley asserts that nations "do not choose to go to war; . . . they choose to follow a course of action that *results* in war, which is an entirely different thing."[27] Now that you have analyzed the evidence in this chapter, do you think Utley's statement accurately depicts U.S.-Japanese relations from the 1930s to December 7, 1941? How would you prove such a hypothesis? If you do *not* think Utley's assertion accurately describes U.S.-Japanese relations, what alternative explanation would you offer? How would you use the evidence to prove such a hypothesis?

Why did Japan attack Pearl Harbor? What were the causes of that event?

As for Tuffy Leemans and the New York Giants, on December 7 they lost to the Brooklyn Dodgers 21–7. On December 21, the Chicago Bears defeated the Giants 37–9 to win the NFL championship.

26. Exxon, *World Energy Outlook* (December 1980), p. 35.
27. Utley, *Going to War with Japan,* p. xii.

Separate but Equal? African American Educational Opportunities and the *Brown* Decision

◆

The Problem

In the mid-1890s, Homer Plessy took his seat in a passenger coach on a Louisiana train. Plessy's racial heritage was seven-eighths European American and one-eighth African American, and the railroad compartment in which he was sitting was reserved for whites. Asked to vacate his seat and move to the compartment reserved for blacks, Plessy refused and was arrested. He had violated an 1890 Louisiana law that required separate railroad accommodations for African Americans and for whites. People who broke the law by sitting in the wrong compartment or coach were fined twenty-five dollars or, if they could not pay, had to serve twenty days in jail. Plessy's action was actually part of a strategy planned by a group of Creole men in New Orleans to test the new race-based law.

After his arrest, Plessy sued, and the case eventually reached the U.S. Supreme Court on appeal. The majority opinion in *Plessy v. Ferguson* was that the Louisiana law was constitutional.[1] Because it provided for "separate but equal" accommodations, the law had not violated any rights guaranteed by the Fourteenth Amendment. In other words, states could legally segregate blacks and whites as long as they provided "separate but equal" facilities for African Americans. In an impassioned dissent, Justice John Marshall Harlan disagreed. "Our Constitution is color-blind," he argued, "and neither knows nor tolerates classes among citizens." But Harlan's opinion was not supported by other judges or by the general public.

In fact, for almost sixty years *Plessy v. Ferguson* provided a powerful basis for other judicial decisions upholding segregation laws. Finally, in *Brown v. Board of Education of Topeka* (1954),

1. Seven justices agreed with the majority opinion, one abstained, and one (Harlan) dissented.

✦ CHAPTER 9

Separate but Equal?
African American
Educational
Opportunities and
the *Brown* Decision

the Supreme Court unanimously declared that separate but equal schools
were unconstitutional. Why did the
Court reverse itself after so many

years? In this chapter, you will be asked
to identify some of the major arguments that finally caused the Supreme
Court to change its thinking.

✦

Background

In the aftermath of the Civil War, much
of the South was in economic and political chaos. Struggles between President Andrew Johnson and the Radical
Republicans over who should control
Reconstruction meant delay and confusion in readmitting the former Confederate states to the Union and providing
economic relief where it was most
needed. After nearly removing President Johnson from office, however, the
Radicals were able to implement their
plans in Congress.

Perhaps no other question of the Reconstruction era was more trouble-
some and divisive than that of the role
of the newly freed slaves. Three
amendments to the United States Constitution were intended to settle the legal questions: the Thirteenth Amendment, which freed the slaves; the
Fourteenth Amendment, which defined
citizenship and extended the protection of the Bill of Rights to citizens
of the separate states; and the Fifteenth Amendment, which gave African American men the vote. Would the
freed slaves have full political rights?
Should they be given land to farm?
Could they be protected against discrimination and violence? Although African Americans briefly enjoyed some
political rights and protection, by the
late nineteenth century all these questions had been answered negatively.

The South had returned to white political control; the Ku Klux Klan and other
vigilante groups had limited African
American opportunities; and the sharecropping, tenant farming, and crop lien
systems had impoverished poor whites
and blacks alike. Furthermore, the
Union army had withdrawn, and the
federal Civil Rights Act of 1875 had
been declared unconstitutional. As the
majority of people in the North and
West turned their attention to their
own problems, African Americans in
the South were left to fend for themselves.

In 1900, approximately seven million
of the nation's ten million African
Americans lived in the rural South, although more and more younger African Americans were leaving the grinding poverty of the farms and moving to
nearby cities and towns seeking better
opportunities. The black codes of the
Redemption era had evolved into Jim
Crow laws that segregated everything
from schools and parks to hospitals and
cemeteries, while lynching took the
lives of seventy-five to one hundred African American men each year. The
trickle of African Americans moving
North was accelerated by World War I;
almost half a million southern blacks
moved to northern cities such as Chicago, Cleveland, and Philadelphia to
obtain jobs during the war.

By 1920, there were a million and a half African Americans in northern cities. Although rarely segregated by law and permitted to vote, nevertheless they usually faced pervasive discrimination in their search for housing and jobs. Membership in the National Association for the Advancement of Colored People (NAACP) grew steadily as a new black middle class increasingly identified with the civil rights program of W. E. B. Du Bois rather than the accommodationist message of Booker T. Washington.

In the 1920s, a section of New York City called Harlem became the center for a ferment of African American cultural creativity, the Harlem Renaissance. Poets, novelists, artists, actors, dancers, and musicians all explored ways to express their African American experience. Well-to-do whites often supported such efforts and patronized Harlem night spots such as the Cotton Club. Harlem was also badly overcrowded, with decaying housing, epidemic disease, widespread unemployment, and a rising crime rate. The Harlem Renaissance had little meaning for many poor blacks who had recently emigrated from the South. For these newcomers, Jamaican-born Marcus Garvey and his Universal Negro Improvement Association seemed to offer a more practical alternative. Glorifying black cultural roots and sponsoring cooperative business ventures, Garvey also called on African Americans to return to Africa to found a new nation.

Garvey was convicted of fraud, imprisoned, and finally deported in the late 1920s, and the Harlem Renaissance was submerged by the stock market crash of 1929 and the ensuing depression. Both urban and rural blacks suffered extreme hardships during the Great Depression. New Deal urban relief programs were administered locally, and generally African Americans were among the last to receive aid. In the rural South, the New Deal agricultural policies had the unintended result of causing the eviction of sharecroppers and tenant farmers. Violence against African Americans also increased during the depression.

Not until the 1940s did the situation of African Americans begin to improve. In many ways, World War II was a turning point. From the beginning, black leaders declared a "Double V" campaign: a fight against fascism abroad and a fight against racism at home. The NAACP, with half a million members by the end of the war, was joined by the newly formed Congress of Racial Equality (CORE). While the NAACP pursued a strategy of boycotts and legal challenges, CORE began to experiment with nonviolent protests against racial discrimination during the 1940s. Full war production opened up new economic opportunities, nearly a million more African Americans continued the exodus from the South to northern cities, and almost a million blacks served in the armed forces. In spite of some serious race riots during 1943, African Americans entered the postwar era with rising expectations of equality.

Nowhere were these demands for equality more insistent or pressing than in education. For more than a decade, NAACP lawyers had been involved in cases testing the validity of state segregation laws. By the early 1950s, the

◆ CHAPTER 9

Separate but Equal?
African American
Educational
Opportunities and
the *Brown* Decision

Supreme Court had begun strictly scrutinizing separate but equal education to determine whether it really was equal. In 1938, the Court heard a case where a young African American college graduate and Missourian, Lloyd Gaines, had been denied entry into the University of Missouri Law School because he was black.[2] There was no black law school in Missouri, so the state had offered to pay his tuition to any law school in a neighboring state that would accept him. Gaines had been denied equal protection of the laws, the Supreme Court ruled, because Missouri had not provided the same opportunities to black students as it had to white students. Ten years later, a similar case, involving a young woman, Ada Sipuel, who was refused admission to the law school of the University of Oklahoma because of her race, was decided the same way.[3]

In two cases decided in 1950, the Supreme Court expanded the understanding of separate but equal. A black graduate student, George McLaurin, had been admitted to the University of Oklahoma, but was forced to sit at special tables in the cafeteria and in the library and to sit in a separate row in his classes. This was *not* equal treatment, the Court declared.[4] In the second case, *Sweatt v. Painter,* a black student was denied admission to the University of Texas Law School.[5] The state then built two new law schools for African

Americans. When the Supreme Court justices compared the faculties, curricula, and libraries of the black and white schools, however, they found substantial inequalities. The opinion went even further, noting that intangible factors such as alumni networks, traditions, and prestige were also superior at the University of Texas Law School. Finally, the Court noted that no student could really learn to practice law at a school that was isolated from 85 percent of the population of the state.

All of these cases involved graduate or professional training and were decided on the question of the *equality* of the facilities. The plaintiffs won these cases because their educational facilities or opportunities were unequal to those provided for whites. In each case, then, *Plessy v. Ferguson* and the doctrine of separate but equal still formed the basis for the decision. Furthermore, the Supreme Court had clearly stated its reluctance to decide any broad constitutional issues, preferring instead to focus on specific questions raised by specific cases. "We have frequently reiterated that this Court will decide constitutional questions only when necessary to the disposition of the case at hand," wrote Chief Justice Fred Vinson in *Sweatt v. Painter* (1950), "and that such decisions will be drawn as narrowly as possible."

In spite of the cautious stance of the Supreme Court, significant trends and events during the late 1940s and early 1950s were creating a climate more supportive of African American civil rights. The Nazi Holocaust that killed six million Jews and the cold war confrontations with the Soviet Union made Americans more aware of the

2. *Missouri ex rel. Gaines v. Canada,* 305 U.S. 337 (1938).
3. *Sipuel v. Board of Regents of the University of Oklahoma,* 332 U.S. 631 (1948).
4. *McLaurin v. Oklahoma State Regents,* 339 U.S. 637 (1950).
5. *Sweatt v. Painter,* 339 U.S. 629 (1950).

democratic ideals of the United States. In his widely read book, *The American Dilemma,* sociologist Gunnar Myrdal had pointed out America's shortcomings with regard to race relations, and many whites began to feel guilty about the typical treatment of African Americans in the United States.

An outpouring of social science literature also focused on inequality and its effects. Popularized through paperback books, middle-class magazines, and television, much of this research seems relatively unsophisticated by our standards today, although it was pioneering in its time period. For example, Professor Kenneth Clark of City College of New York did research to determine the effects of racial segregation on young African American children. After giving the children identical pink dolls or brown dolls (or pictures of the two sets of dolls), Clark asked the children which dolls were "nice," which dolls were "bad," and which doll the child would rather play with. The majority of the African American children preferred the white doll, identifying the white doll as "nice" and the brown doll as "bad." Such research not only was widely publicized but was also used in court cases by the NAACP to demonstrate the negative psychological effects of segregated schooling on African American children.

Finally, the personnel of the Supreme Court itself had begun to change. Five justices were still serving who had been appointed by President Franklin D. Roosevelt between 1937 and 1941, and President Truman had appointed four new justices between 1945 and 1949. After the Court had started to consider the *Brown* case, the relatively conservative chief justice, Fred Vinson, died suddenly from a heart attack at age sixty-three, and President Eisenhower appointed the more liberal Earl Warren, a former governor of California, to replace Vinson as chief justice.

In 1951, Topeka, Kansas, was a pleasant city of approximately 100,000 residents, 7,500 of whom were African American. The state capital, Topeka, had a city college, a good public library, several city parks, a major psychiatric research institute, and more than one hundred churches. It was also segregated. Jim Crow laws and local customs prevented blacks from using white hotels, restaurants, movies, or the municipal swimming pool, and the elementary schools were segregated.

Oliver Brown was a thirty-two-year-old World War II veteran, union member, welder, and assistant pastor of his church. Not a militant, he was not even a member of the NAACP. The Browns lived in a racially mixed neighborhood near a railroad yard, and their oldest daughter, Linda, had to walk about six blocks through the tracks to get to her school bus stop. A white elementary school was located only seven blocks in the other direction from her house, but it refused to accept her because she was an African American. Brown reported this to the local NAACP and became the first plaintiff in the suit against the Board of Education of Topeka.

In spite of assistance from the national NAACP and the presentation of nationally known social science experts who testified about the negative effects of segregated education, Brown and the other plaintiffs lost the case. The school facilities and other measurable

♦ CHAPTER 9

Separate but Equal?
African American
Educational
Opportunities and
the *Brown* Decision

educational factors at the white and black elementary schools were roughly equal, the Kansas court said, referring to the precedent set by the *Plessy* case in 1896. Thus, the segregated schools were legal. However, the Kansas District Court also attached several "findings of fact" to its opinion, including one that directly reflected the impact of the social science evidence the NAACP had introduced. "Segregation . . . has a detrimental effect upon the colored children," wrote the judge, and he concluded that legal segregation created a sense of inferiority that tended "to retard the educational and mental development of Negro children and to deprive them of some of the benefits they would receive in a racially integrated school system."

By the fall of 1952, five cases challenging the constitutionality of racially segregated schools had been appealed to the U.S. Supreme Court. In addition to Kansas, South Carolina, Virginia, Delaware, and District of Columbia plaintiffs all argued that although the educational facilities for whites and African Americans were equal (or were in the process of being equalized), racial segregation itself was unconstitutional because it violated the equal protection clause of the Fourteenth Amendment.[6] The five cases were argued together late in 1952, and the next spring, the Court asked for a reargument in the fall term of 1953. The first part of the decision was not announced until May 1954. *Brown I,* as it came to be called, declared that racially segregated education was indeed unconstitutional. The Court then called for another reargument, this time to determine how the desegregation decision should be implemented. In May 1955, after unusually long oral arguments, the Court announced in *Brown II* that there would be a flexible timetable for desegregation, which would be overseen by the federal district courts.

What persuaded the U.S. Supreme Court to reverse its thinking after upholding the constitutionality of segregation since *Plessy v. Ferguson* in 1896? What were some of the major arguments that changed the justices' opinions?

♦

The Method

Whenever possible, courts make decisions based on *precedents:* similar cases that other courts have already decided that lay out a direction for new decisions to follow. As we have seen, *Plessy v. Ferguson* (1896), the case that upheld racial segregation if separate but equal facilities were provided, was just such a precedent. For the next sixty years, the courts had simply decided whether the racially segregated facilities were equal and never considered the effects of segregation itself. But in *Brown v. the Board of Education of Topeka, Kansas,* and the four other cases argued at the same time, everyone agreed that the facilities were basically

6. Because Washington, D.C., is not a state, this case was argued on the basis of the Fifth Amendment.

equal or were being equalized. The question now was whether segregation itself violated the Constitution.

Cases are argued before the U.S. Supreme Court in two stages. First, lawyers for both sides submit written arguments called *briefs*. These briefs discuss the factual background of the case and, more important, develop a legal, constitutional argument supporting the decision that they believe the Court should make. In *Brown* and the other cases, the defendants basically argued that segregated education was not unconstitutional because equal facilities had been provided, and the plaintiffs insisted, based on social science research, that racial segregation itself caused inequality in education.

With permission, organizations and individuals who are not directly involved in the case may also file briefs explaining their interest and stating their opinions about the case. Seven of these *amicus curiae* (friend of the court) briefs were filed in the initial phase of the *Brown* school segregation cases, *Brown I,* and they reflect important changes in public opinion about African Americans and equality. Eventually some two dozen *amicus* briefs were filed, including those that the U.S. Supreme Court invited for *Brown II* from the attorneys general of all the southern states that permitted or required segregated educational facilities.

In the second stage, oral argument, lawyers speak for a limited time to clarify points in their briefs and to answer any questions the justices might have. At the time of the *Brown* case, Robert Carter and Thurgood Marshall were lawyers for the NAACP's Legal Defense and Educational Fund. Carter later became general counsel for the NAACP, and Thurgood Marshall served as a U.S. circuit court judge and then as solicitor general of the United States. He was appointed to the U.S. Supreme Court in 1967. The defense attorneys were either hired by the school system being sued or provided by the attorney general's office of that particular state. In both cases, they were paid by taxpayers' money. John W. Davis represented the defendants in the South Carolina case, *Briggs v. Elliot,* which the U.S. Supreme Court considered along with *Brown* and the three other school cases. Widely admired by other attorneys, Davis had served as a U.S. congressman, U.S. solicitor general, ambassador to Great Britain, and president of the American Bar Association. In 1922, he had declined a nomination to the U.S. Supreme Court and, in 1924, he had run unsuccessfully for president of the United States.

Finally, after considerable discussion among themselves, the justices reached a decision. Because a Supreme Court decision affects so many people's lives either directly or indirectly, it usually contains a carefully worded explanation of the Court's reasoning. Justices who do not agree with the decision may write a dissent, but the decision in the *Brown* case was unanimous. In this chapter, you will read the relevant section of the Fourteenth Amendment, identify the arguments used in the early *amicus curiae* briefs and the oral exchanges between the lawyers and the Court, and study excerpts from the *Brown I* decision to explain why the Supreme Court decided that racially segregated education was unconstitutional.

✦ CHAPTER 9
Separate but Equal?
African American
Educational
Opportunities and
the *Brown* Decision

✦

The Evidence

Source 1 from United States Constitution, Fourteenth Amendment.

1. First Section of the Fourteenth Amendment to the Constitution.

All persons born or naturalized in the United States, and subject to the jurisdiction thereof, are citizens of the United States and of the State wherein they reside. No State shall make or enforce any law which shall abridge the privileges or immunities of citizens of the United States; nor shall any State deprive any person of life, liberty, or property, without due process of law; nor deny to any person within its jurisdiction the equal protection of the laws.

Source 2 from Justice Henry Brown, writing for the majority, *Plessy v. Ferguson,* 163 U.S. 537 (1896).

2. Excerpts from *Plessy v. Ferguson*, 1896.

[*The opinion begins by reviewing the facts of the case and denying one of Plessy's arguments based on the Thirteenth Amendment, which abolished slavery and involuntary servitude.*]

The object of the [14th] amendment was undoubtedly to enforce the absolute equality of the two races before the law, but in the nature of things it could not have been intended to abolish distinctions based upon color, or to enforce social, as distinguished from political, equality, or a commingling of the two races upon terms unsatisfactory to either. Laws permitting, and even requiring their separation in places where they are liable to be brought into contact do not necessarily imply the inferiority of either race to the other, and have been generally, if not universally, recognized as within the competency of the state legislatures in the exercise of their policy power. . . .

[*Justice Brown then states that "colored" men were assigned to "colored" railway cars and "whites" to "white" cars, thus neither was being deprived of any property.*]

So far, then, as a conflict with the 14th Amendment is concerned, the case reduces itself to the question of whether the statute of Louisiana is a reasonable regulation, and with respect to this there must necessarily be a large discretion on the part of the legislature. In determining the question of reasonableness it is at liberty to act with reference to the established usages, customs, and traditions of the people, and with a view to the promotion of their comfort, and the preservation of the public peace and good order. . . .

We consider the underlying fallacy of the plaintiff's argument to consist in the assumption that the enforced separation of the two races stamps the colored race with a badge of inferiority. If this be so, it is not by reason of anything found in the act, but solely because the colored race chooses to put that construction upon it. . . .

Legislation is powerless to eradicate racial instincts or to abolish distinctions based upon physical differences, and the attempt to do so can only result in accentuating the difficulties of the present situation. If the civil and political right of both races be equal, one cannot be inferior to the other civilly or politically. If one race be inferior to the other socially, the Constitution of the United States cannot put them upon the same plane.

✦ CHAPTER 9

Separate but Equal?
African American
Educational
Opportunities and
the *Brown* Decision

Source 3 from the Library of Congress.

3. Photograph of Kenneth Clark Observing a Child Choosing Between Dolls.

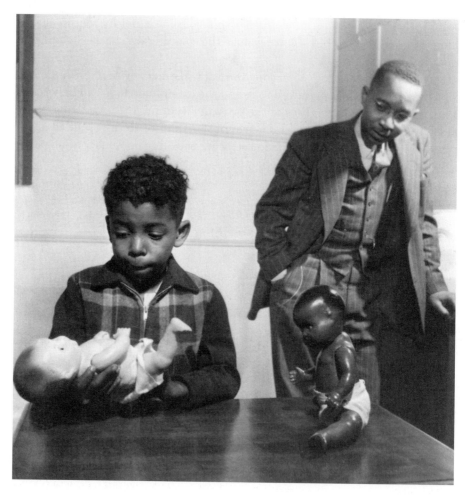

Source 4: Clark excerpt from *Records and Briefs of the U.S. Supreme Court 349 U.S. 294, Part 2.* Found in Mark Whitman, ed., *Removing a Badge of Slavery: The Record of Brown v. Board of Education* (Princeton and New York: Markus Wiener Publishers, Inc., 1993), pp. 49–50; Holt excerpt from *Records and Briefs of the U.S. Supreme Court 349 U.S. 294, Part 1.* Found in *Removing a Badge of Slavery,* pp. 60–61; Speer excerpt from *Records and Briefs of the U.S. Supreme Court 349 U.S. 294, Part 1.* Found in *Removing a Badge of Slavery,* pp. 70–71.

4. Excerpts from the Social Science Testimony.

KENNETH CLARK—*BRIGGS* TRIAL

[Clark is asked to describe the questions that he asked while testing the children.]

I presented these dolls to them and I asked them the following questions in the following order: "Show me the doll that you like best or that you'd like to play with," "Show me the doll that is the 'nice' doll," "Show me the doll that looks 'bad'," and then the following questions also: "Give me the doll that looks like a white child," "Give me the doll that looks like a colored child," and "Give me the doll that looks like you."

[Clark then discusses the results of his test.]

I found that of the children between the ages of six and nine whom I tested, which were a total of sixteen in number, that ten of those children chose the white doll as their preference; the doll which they liked best. Ten of them also considered the white doll a "nice" doll. And, I think you have to keep in mind that these two dolls are absolutely identical in every respect except skin color. Eleven of these sixteen children chose the brown doll as the doll which looked "bad." This is consistent with previous results which we have obtained testing over three hundred children, and we interpret it to mean that the Negro child accepts as early as six, seven, or eight the negative stereotypes about his own group. . . . Every single child, when asked to pick the doll that looked like the white child, made the correct choice. . . . Every single child, when asked to pick the doll that was like the colored child; every one of them picked the brown doll.

✦ CHAPTER 9

Separate but Equal?
African American
Educational
Opportunities and
the *Brown* Decision

LOUISA HOLT—*BROWN* TRIAL

[Holt is asked whether legally enforced segregation has any adverse effects on African American children and their learning experiences.]

The fact that it is enforced, that it is legal, I think, has more importance than the mere fact of segregation by itself does because this gives legal and official sanction to a policy which inevitably is interpreted both by white people and by negroes as denoting the inferiority of the negro group. Were it not for the sense that one group is inferior to the other, there would be no basis, and I am not granting that this is a rational basis, for such segregation. . . .

A sense of inferiority must always affect one's motivation for learning since it affects the feeling one has of one's self as a person, as a personality or a self or an ego identity. . . . That sense of ego identity is built up on the basis of attitudes that are expressed toward a person by others who are important.

[Topeka schools were segregated only through sixth grade. Holt is asked whether black students could overcome the effects of grade-school segregation when they attended integrated junior and senior high schools.]

There is evidence emerging from a study now going on at Harvard University that the later achievement of individuals in their adult occupational careers can be predicted at the first grade. If that is true, it means that the important effects of schooling in relation to later achievement are set down at that early age, and I therefore don't think that simply removing segregation at a somewhat later grade could possibly [undo] those effects.

HUGH W. SPEER—*BROWN* TRIAL

[Speer is asked to explain what the word curriculum *means to educators and how it applies to this case.]*

By "curriculum" we mean something more than the course of study. As commonly defined and accepted now, "curriculum" means the total school experience of the child. Now, when it comes to the mere prescription of the course of study, we found no significant difference. But, when it comes to the total school experience of the child, there are some differences. In other words, we consider that education is more than just remembering something. It is concerned with a child's total development, his personality, his personal and social adjustment. Therefore it becomes the obligation of the school to provide the kind of an environment in which the child can learn knowledge and skills such as the three "R's" and also social skills and social attitudes and appreciations and interests, and these considerations are all now part of the curriculum. . . .

And we might add the more heterogeneous the group in which the children participate, the better [they] can function in our multi-cultural and multi-group society. For example, if the colored children are denied the experience in school of associating with white children, who represent 90% of our national society in which these colored children must live, then the colored child's curriculum is being greatly curtailed. The Topeka curriculum or any school curriculum cannot be equal under segregation.

Source 5 from the *amicus curiae* briefs for *Brown v. Board of Education of Topeka, Kansas,* 347 U.S. 483 (1954).

5. Excerpts from the *Amicus Curiae* Briefs, *Brown v. Board of Education,* 1952.

AMERICAN VETERANS COMMITTEE, INC. (AVC)

The American Veterans Committee (AVC) is a nationwide organization of veterans who served honorably in the Armed Forces of the United States during World Wars I and II, and the Korean conflict. We are associated to promote the democratic principles for which we fought, including the elimination of racial discrimination. Most of us served overseas. There was no "community pattern" of racial discrimination and segregation when the chips were down and there was only the mud, the foxholes, and the dangers of the ocean and of mortal battle in the fight to preserve our Nation's democratic ideals. We believe that the segregation here involved is of the same cloth as the racism against which we fought in World War II, and that its continuance is detrimental to our national welfare, both at home and abroad.

AMERICAN JEWISH CONGRESS

The American Jewish Congress is an organization committed to the principle that the destinies of all Americans are indissolubly linked and that any act which unjustly injures one group necessarily injures all. . . .

Believing as we do that Jewish interests are inseparable from the interests of justice, the American Jewish Congress cannot remain impassive or disinterested when persecution, discrimination or humiliation is inflicted upon

✦ CHAPTER 9

Separate but Equal?
African American
Educational
Opportunities and
the *Brown* Decision

any human being because of his race, religion, color, national origin or ancestry. Through the thousands of years of our tragic history we have learned one lesson well: the persecution at any time of any minority portends the shape and intensity of persecution of all minorities.

CONGRESS OF INDUSTRIAL ORGANIZATIONS (CIO)

The CIO is an organization dedicated to the maintenance and extension of our democratic rights and civil liberties and therefore has a deep interest in the elimination of segregation and discrimination from every phase of American life.

The CIO's interest is also direct and personal. The CIO . . . is endeavoring to practice non-segregation and non-discrimination in the everyday functioning of union affairs. Repeatedly in the past this endeavor has been obstructed by statutes, ordinances, and regulations which require segregation in public dining places, public meeting halls, toilet facilities, etc. These laws attempt to require CIO unions to maintain "equal but separate" facilities in their own semi-public buildings, despite the avowed desire of the membership to avoid segregation in any form.

AMERICAN FEDERATION OF TEACHERS

In a broad sense, the consequence [of segregation] is a denial of the highest ends of education, both to the dominant and minority groups. In an atmosphere of inequality, it is no more feasible to teach the principles of our American way to the white children than to the Negroes. The apparent insincerity of such teaching is as destructive to the moral sense of the majority as to the sense of justice of the minority. . . .

For if justice is relative and depends on race or color how can we teach that ours is a government of laws and not of men? And if justice is relative and considers race and color then a different flag waves over a colored school and the pledge to the flag must mean different things. The one nation is really not one nation but at least two, it is found to be divisible, and liberty, like justice, has two meanings.

FEDERATION OF CITIZENS' ASSOCIATIONS OF [WASHINGTON,] D.C.

The undersigned submit this brief because our organizations represent groups of Americans in the Washington community and throughout the nation of many creeds and many races who are deeply committed to the preservation and extension of the democratic way of life and who reject as inimical to the welfare and progress of our country artificial barriers to the free and natural association of peoples, based on racial or creedal differences. We believe this to be of especial importance in the Nation's capital. We are united in the belief that every step taken to make such differences irrelevant in law, as they are in fact, will tend to cure one of our democracy's conspicuous failures to practice the ideals we proclaim to the world, and to bring us closer to that peace and harmony with other peoples throughout the world for which we all strive.

ATTORNEY GENERAL OF THE UNITED STATES

This contention [about the unconstitutionality of segregation] raises questions of the first importance in our society. For racial discriminations imposed by law, or having the sanction or support of government, inevitably tend to undermine the foundations of a society dedicated to freedom, justice, and equality. The proposition that all men are created equal is not mere rhetoric. It implies a rule of law—an indispensable condition to a civilized society—under which all men stand equal and alike in the rights and opportunities secured to them by their government. . . . The color of a man's skin—like his religious beliefs, or his political attachments, or the country from which he or his ancestors came to the United States—does not diminish or alter his legal status or constitutional rights. . . .

It is in the context of the present world struggle between freedom and tyranny that the problem of racial discrimination must be viewed. The United States is trying to prove to the people of the world, of every nationality, race, and color, that a free democracy is the most civilized and most secure form of government yet devised by man. We must set an example for others by showing firm determination to remove existing flaws in our democracy.

◆ CHAPTER 9

Separate but Equal?
African American
Educational
Opportunities and
the *Brown* Decision

Source 6 from *Oral Arguments of the Supreme Court of the United States* (Frederick, Md.: University Publications, 1984).

6. Excerpts from the Oral Arguments, U.S. Supreme Court.

BROWN, 1952

MR. CARTER. We have one fundamental contention which we will seek to develop in the course of this argument, and that contention is that no state has any authority under the equal protection clause of the Fourteenth Amendment to use race as a factor in affording educational opportunities among its citizens. . . .

JUSTICE MINTON. Mr. Carter, I do not know whether I have followed you on all the facts on this. Was there a finding that the only basis of classification was race or color?

MR. CARTER. It was admitted—the appellees admitted in their answer—that the only reason that they would not permit Negro children to attend the eighteen white schools was because they were Negroes.

JUSTICE MINTON. Then we accept on this record that the only showing is that the classification here was solely on race and color?

MR. CARTER. Yes, sir. I think the state itself concedes this is so in its brief.

BRIGGS v. ELLIOTT, 1952

MR. MARSHALL. I want to point out that our position is not that we are denied equality in these cases [because of inferior physical facilities]. . . . We are saying that there is a denial of equal protection of the laws. . . .

So pursuing that line, we produced expert witnesses. . . .

Witnesses testified that segregation deterred the development of the personalities of these children. Two witnesses testified that it deprives them of equal status in the school community, that it destroys their self-respect. Two other witnesses testified that it denies them full opportunity for democratic social development. Another witness said that it stamps him with a badge of inferiority.

The summation of that testimony is that the Negro children have road blocks put up in their minds as a result of this segregation, so that the amount of education that they take in is much less than other students take in. . . .

MR. DAVIS. If the Court please, when the Court arose on yesterday, I was reciting the progress that had been made in the public school system in South

Carolina, and with particular reference to the improvement of the facilities, equipment [curriculum], and opportunities accorded to the colored students. . . .

Now what are we told here that has made all that body of activity and learning [all the state legislatures that passed segregation laws and all the court decisions upholding segregation] of no consequence? Says counsel for the plaintiffs . . . we have the uncontradicted testimony of expert witnesses that segregation is hurtful, and in their opinion hurtful to the children of both races, both colored and white. These witnesses severally described themselves as professors, associate professors, assistant professors, and one describes herself as a lecturer and advisor on [curriculum]. I am not sure exactly what that means.

I did not impugn the sincerity of these learned gentlemen and lady. I am quite sure that they believe that they are expressing valid opinions on their subject. But there are two things notable about them. Not a one of them is under any official duty in the premises whatever; not a one of them has had to consider the welfare of the people for whom they are legislating or whose rights they were called on to adjudicate. And only one of them professes to have the slightest knowledge of conditions in the states where separate schools are now being maintained. Only one of them professes any knowledge of the conditions within the seventeen segregating states.

Rebuttal

MR. MARSHALL. May it please the Court, so far as the appellants are concerned in this case, at this point it seems to me that the significant factor running through all these arguments up to this point is that for some reason, which is still unexplained, Negroes are taken out of the mainstream of American life in these states.

There is nothing involved in this case other than race and color, and I do not need to go into the background of the statutes or anything else. I just read the statutes, and they say, "White and colored."

While we are talking about the feeling of the people in South Carolina, I think we must once again emphasize that under our form of government, these individual rights of minority people are not to be left to even the most mature judgement of the majority of the people, and that the only testing ground as to whether or not individual rights are concerned is in this Court.

◆ CHAPTER 9

Separate but Equal?
African American
Educational
Opportunities and
the *Brown* Decision

BRIGGS v. ELLIOTT REARGUMENT, 1953

MR. DAVIS. Let me say this for the State of South Carolina. It does not come here as Thad Stevens[7] would have wished in sack cloth and ashes. It believes that its legislation is not offensive to the Constitution of the United States.

It is confident of its good faith and intention to produce equality for all of its children of whatever race or color. It is convinced that the happiness, the progress and the welfare of these children is best promoted in segregated schools. . . .

I am reminded—and I hope it won't be treated as a reflection on anybody—of Aesop's fable of the dog and the meat: The dog, with a fine piece of meat in his mouth, crossed a bridge and saw the shadow in the stream and plunged for it and lost both substance and shadow.

Here is equal education, not promised, not prophesied, but present. Shall it be thrown away on some fancied question of racial prestige?

MR. MARSHALL. It gets me . . . to one of the points that runs throughout the argument . . . on the other side, and that is that they deny that there is any race prejudice involved in these cases. They deny that there is any intention to discriminate.

But throughout the brief and throughout the argument they not only recognize that there is a race problem involved, but they emphasize that that is the whole problem. And for the life of me, you can't read the debates [about the passage of the Fourteenth Amendment], even the sections they rely on, without an understanding that the Fourteenth Amendment took away from the states the power to use race.

As I understand their position, their only justification for this [race] being a reasonable classification is, one, that they got together and decided that it is best for the races to be separated and, two, that it has existed for over a century. . . .

Those same kids in Virginia and South Carolina—and I have seen them do it—they play in the streets together, they play on their farms together, they go down the road together, they separate to go to school, they come out of school and play ball together. They have to be separated in school.

There is some magic to it. You can have them voting together, you can have them not restricted because of law in the houses they live in. You can have them going to the same state university and the same college,

---

7. Thaddeus Stevens (1792–1868) was a lifelong abolitionist and leader of the Radical Republicans.

but if they go to elementary and high school, the world will fall apart. And it is the same argument that has been made to this Court over and over again.

Source 7 from Chief Justice Earl Warren, *Brown v. Board of Education of Topeka, Kansas, et al.*

7. Excerpts from the *Brown I* Decision, 1954.

[Chief Justice Warren began by noting that all the cases had a common argument: that segregated public schools were not "equal," could not be made "equal," and thus denied African Americans the equal protection of the laws. He then briefly reviewed the inconclusive nature of information about the intent of the framers of the Fourteenth Amendment, the separate but equal doctrine established by the Plessy *case, and the subsequent cases involving racially segregated education that had been before the Supreme Court. He concluded that the Court must focus on "the effect of segregation itself on public education."]*

In approaching this problem, we cannot turn the clock back to 1868 when the Amendment was adopted, or even to 1896 when *Plessy v. Ferguson* was written. We must consider public education in the light of its full development and its present place in American life throughout the Nation. Only in this way can it be determined if segregation in public schools deprives these plaintiffs of the equal protection of the laws.

Today, education is perhaps the most important function of state and local governments. Compulsory school attendance laws and the great expenditures for education both demonstrate our recognition of the importance of education to our democratic society. It is required in the performance of our most basic public responsibilities, even service in the armed forces. It is the very foundation of good citizenship. Today it is a principal instrument in awakening the child to cultural values, in preparing him for later professional training, and in helping him to adjust normally to his environment. In these days, it is doubtful that any child may reasonably be expected to succeed in life if he is denied the opportunity of an education. Such an opportunity, where the state has undertaken to provide it, is a right which must be available to all on equal terms.

We come then to the question presented: Does segregation of children in public schools solely on the basis of race, even though the physical facilities and other "tangible" factors may be equal, deprive the children of the minority group of equal educational opportunities? We believe that it does.

◆ CHAPTER 9

Separate but Equal?
African American
Educational
Opportunities and
the *Brown* Decision

[Warren reviewed the findings of the Court and social science literature that segregation resulted in feelings of inferiority and hindered the development of African American children.]

We conclude that in the field of public education the doctrine of "separate but equal" has no place. Separate educational facilities are inherently unequal. . . .

[Noting the variety of local conditions and wide applicability of the desegregation decision, Warren asked the plaintiffs, their opponents, the attorney general of the United States, and the attorneys general of the states that would be affected to appear again before the Court in reargument, stating how they believed the Court's desegregation decision should be put into effect.]

◆

Questions to Consider

The Fourteenth Amendment was added to the Constitution after the Civil War. The first section (Source 1) was intended to protect the newly freed slaves against the actions of the states, in the same way that the Bill of Rights protects citizens against the actions of the central government. What are some of the "privileges and immunities" of the Bill of Rights? What do you think is meant by "due process of law"? By "equal protection of the laws"?

In many ways, the majority opinion in *Plessy* (Source 2) reflects the American public's attitude of the late nineteenth century. What did Justice Brown say was the intent of the Fourteenth Amendment? Why did the Supreme Court believe that the 1890 Louisiana law requiring separate railway cars for blacks and whites was "reasonable"? What was the Court's response to the argument that enforced segregation made blacks inferior to whites? Read the last two sentences of the *Plessy* excerpt carefully. What did the Supreme Court say about racial equality?

The social scientists who testified in the state trials that were combined with *Brown* included psychologists, sociologists, and educational specialists (see Source 4). The most controversial was Dr. Kenneth Clark, called the "Doll Man," who testified in all the trials except *Brown*. His cross-examination by T. Justin Moore, the lead attorney for the state of Virginia, was especially unpleasant. Moore persuaded the judge to allow him to pretend to be a stupid African American student and then forced Clark to pretend to interview him. In the *Briggs* trial, Clark described the actual reactions of the young African American children whom he had tested. What were the results of his tests? How did Clark explain why the children reacted the way they did?

Both Louisa Holt, a psychology professor, and Hugh Speer, a professor of Education, taught in Topeka, Kansas.

Both testified in the *Brown* trial. What did Holt believe was the major effect of segregation on young children? Did she think that the effects of childhood segregation could be overcome later? What is Speer's focus in his expert testimony? In what ways does he believe young children are harmed by segregation?

The 1952 *amicus curiae* briefs (Source 5) provide important clues to changing public opinion about racial discrimination. What were the specific, major arguments of the groups representing veterans, American Jews, labor unions of the CIO, unionized teachers, and Washington, D.C., citizens' organizations? Why did the attorney general argue against segregation?

The excerpts from the oral arguments (Source 6) are from the first hearing of *Brown* and the four other cases in 1952, and the reargument ordered by the Court in 1953. Remember that Robert Carter and Thurgood Marshall were the NAACP lawyers for the plaintiffs, and John W. Davis was the primary lawyer for the defense.

What was the fundamental argument Carter established in the *Brown* case? Why was it important? What was Marshall's major argument about the effects of racially segregated education? How did Davis respond? On what bases did Davis reject the findings of the NAACP's expert witnesses? What are the two major points of Marshall's rebuttal?

In the reargument, Davis used a story about a dog with some meat to make his point. What exactly *was* his point? How did Marshall summarize his opponents' defense of segregation? What was the point of his story about African American and white children?

Finally, analyze the arguments put forth by Chief Justice Earl Warren in *Brown I* (Source 7). What did he mean when he wrote, "We cannot turn the clock back"? Why did the Court hold that education is so important?

Now you are ready to summarize. What major arguments persuaded the Supreme Court to overturn the doctrine of separate but equal that had been established by *Plessy v. Ferguson*?

Epilogue

In less controversial cases, once the U.S. Supreme Court has announced a decision, all those affected by it comply voluntarily. Progress in desegregating the school systems, however, was slow and uneven. In some areas of the South that had practiced legal segregation, change came fairly easily and peacefully. In other areas, widespread public hostility escalated into mob violence.

Some systems, such as the Prince Edward County, Virginia, school district that was part of the original Supreme Court suits, simply abolished the public schools rather than desegregate. Ten years after the *Brown* decision, only about 10 percent of African American students in southern states were attending desegregated schools.

By the late 1960s, the federal govern-

✦ CHAPTER 9

Separate but Equal?
African American
Educational
Opportunities and
the *Brown* Decision

ment and U.S. court system had established new guidelines and timetables, backed by the threat of the possibility of losing federal funding, that accelerated desegregation in southern schools. Using the *Brown* decision as a precedent, the Supreme Court had also ordered the desegregation of public beaches, golf courses, and other recreational facilities throughout the South. By the 1970s, African American civil rights groups began to focus their attention on northern cities, where racially separate housing patterns had resulted in all-black and all-white neighborhood schools; but court-ordered busing of students to integrate education in these cities created hostility and often accelerated "white flight" to the suburbs. For example, by the early 1970s, after riots, real estate "block busting," and busing, Detroit, Michigan, had so few remaining white residents that *all* its public schools were predominantly African American.

Although the *Brown* decision did not bring about complete and immediate desegregation of all schools, its significance should not be underrated. The issues involved in the *Brown* case forced many whites to reconsider their ideas about race. Segregation laws based on race were struck down, and for the newly expanding African American middle class, *Brown* was a milestone, a case that established new ideals for public education. Looking back,

African American leaders have said that they were greatly encouraged in their struggle for further civil rights by the decision.

In 1955, Rosa Parks set off a year-long boycott by local African Americans after she refused to move from a seat reserved for whites on a Montgomery, Alabama, bus. Two years later, young black students were jeered at and abused when they tried to attend classes at Central High School in Little Rock, Arkansas; the national reaction caused a reluctant President Eisenhower to call out federal troops to escort these students to school.

Clearly, the *Brown* decision divided the nation and created opportunities for organizations based on racial hatred. Violent segregationists, often including law-enforcement personnel, opposed the African American freedom marches in places like Selma, Alabama, and the voter-registration drives in Mississippi during the 1960s. Yet the television and newspaper coverage of such racial confrontations also galvanized public opinion outside the South in support of such far-reaching civil rights legislation as the Civil Rights Act of 1964 and the Voting Rights Act of 1965. Today, in spite of the many accomplishments of the civil rights movement since the 1954 *Brown* decision, Americans are still striving to achieve equal educational opportunities for all.

10

A Generation in War and Turmoil: The Agony of Vietnam

◆

The Problem

When the middle-class readers of *Time* magazine went to their mailboxes in January 1967, they were eager to find out who the widely read newsmagazine had chosen as "Man of the Year." To their surprise, they discovered that the "inheritors"—the whole generation of young people under twenty-five years of age—had been selected as the major newsmakers of the previous year. *Time*'s publisher justified the selection of an entire generation by noting that, in contrast to the previous "silent generation," the young people of the late 1960s were dominating history with their distinctive lifestyles, music, and beliefs about the future of the United States.

Those who wrote to the editor about this issue ranged from a writer who thought the selection was a long-overdue honor to one who called it an "outrageous choice," from a correspondent who described contemporary young people as "one of our best generations" to one who believed the choice of a generation was "eloquent nonsense." Furthermore, many writers were frightened or worried about their children,

and some middle-aged correspondents insisted that they themselves belonged to the "put-upon" or "beaten" generation.

There is no doubt that there was a generation gap in the late 1960s, a kind of sharp break between the new generation of young people comprising nearly half the population and their parents. The first segment of the so-called baby-boom generation came to adulthood during the mid- to late 1960s,[1] a time marked by the high point of the civil rights movement, the rise of a spirit of rebellion on college campuses, and a serious division over the United States' participation in the Vietnam War. For most baby boomers, white and black alike, the war was the issue that concerned them most immediately, for this was the generation that would be called on to fight or to watch

1. Although the birthrate began to climb during World War II (from 19.4 births per 1,000 in 1940 to 24.5 per 1,000 in 1945), the term *baby boom* generally is used to describe the increase in the birthrate between 1946 and the early 1960s.

as friends, spouses, or lovers were called to military service.

Your tasks in this chapter include identifying and interviewing at least one member of the baby-boom generation (preferably born between 1946 and 1956)[2] about his or her experiences during the Vietnam War era. Then, using your interview, along with those of your classmates and those provided in the Evidence section of this chapter, determine the ways in which the baby-boom generation reacted to the Vietnam War. On what issues did baby boomers agree? On what issues did they disagree? Finally, how can a study of people of the same generation help historians understand a particular era in the past?

✦

Background

The year 1945 was the beginning of one of the longest sustained economic booms in American history. Interrupted only a few times by brief recessions, the boom lasted from 1945 to 1973. And although there were still pockets of severe poverty in America's deteriorating inner cities and in some rural areas such as Appalachia, most Americans had good cause to be optimistic about their economic situations.

The pent-up demand of the depression and war years broke like a tidal wave that swept nearly every economic indicator upward. Veterans returning from World War II rapidly made the transition to the civilian work force or used the GI Bill to become better educated and, as a result, secure better jobs than they had held before the war. Between 1950 and 1960, real wages increased by 20 percent, and disposable family income rose by a staggering 49 percent. The number of registered automobiles more than doubled between 1945 and 1955, and the American automobile industry was virtually unchallenged by foreign competition. At the same time, new home construction soared, as thirteen million new homes were built in the 1950s alone—85 percent of them in the new and mushrooming suburbs.[3]

New homes were financed by new types of long-term mortgage loans that required only a small down payment (5 to 10 percent) and low monthly payments (averaging $56 per month for a tract house in the suburbs). And these new homes required furniture and appliances, which led to sharp upturns in these industries. Between 1945 and 1950, the amount spent on household furnishings and appliances increased 240 percent, and most of these items were bought "on time" (that is, on installment plans).[4] Perhaps the most

2. A person born during the late 1950s to early 1960s would technically be considered a baby boomer but would probably have been too young to remember enough to make an interview useful.

3. There were 114,000 housing starts in 1944. In 1950, housing starts had climbed to nearly 1.7 million.

4. Between 1946 and 1956, short-term con-

coveted appliance was a television set, a product that had been almost nonexistent before the war. In 1950 alone, 7.4 million television sets were sold in the United States, and architects began designing homes with a "family room," a euphemism for a room where television was watched.

This new postwar lifestyle could best be seen in America's burgeoning suburbs. Populated to a large extent by new members of the nation's mushrooming middle class, suburbanites for the most part were better educated, wealthier, and more optimistic than their parents had been. Most men commuted by train, bus, or automobile back to the center city to work, while their wives remained in the suburbs, having children and raising them. It was in these suburbs that a large percentage of baby boomers were born.

Sociologist William H. Whyte called America's postwar suburbs the "new melting pot," a term that referred to the expectation that new middle-class suburbanites should leave their various class and ethnic characteristics behind in the cities they had abandoned and become homogeneous. Men were expected to work their way up the corporate ladder, tend their carefully manicured lawns, become accomplished barbecue chefs, and serve their suburban communities as Boy Scout leaders or Little League coaches. For their part, women were expected to make favorable impressions on their husband's bosses (to aid their husbands in their climb up the corporate ladder), provide transportation for the children to accepted after-school activities (scouts, athletics, music and dance lessons), and make a happy home for the family's breadwinner. Above all, the goal was to fit in with their suburban neighbors. Thus suburbanites would applaud the 1956 musical *My Fair Lady,* which was based on the premise that working-class flower seller Eliza Doolittle would be accepted by "polite society" as soon as she learned to speak properly.

The desire for homogeneity or conformity would have a less beneficial side as well. The cold war and the McCarthy era meant that the demand for homogeneity could be enforced by the threat of job loss and ostracism. In addition, many suburban women had met their husbands in college and hence had had at least some college education.[5] But the expectation that they be primarily wives and mothers often meant that they were discouraged from using their education in other ways. As a result, one survey of suburban women revealed that 11 percent of them felt that they experienced a "great deal of emotional disturbance." At the same time, men were expected to be good corporate citizens and good team players at work. It was rumored that IBM employees began each day by gathering together, facing the home office, and singing the praises of IBM

---

sumer credit rose from $8.4 billion to almost $45 billion, most of it to finance automobiles and home furnishings. The boom in credit card purchases ("plastic money") did not occur until the 1960s.

5. One midwestern women's college boasted that "a high proportion of our graduates marry successfully," as if that was the chief reason for women to go to college in the first place. Indeed, in many cases it was. See Elaine Tyler May, *Homeward Bound: American Families in the Cold War Era* (New York: Basic Books, 1988), p. 83.

and its executive vice president C. A. Kirk (to the tune of "Carry Me Back to Old Virginny"):

> Ever we praise our able leaders,
> And our progressive C. A. Kirk is one of them,
> He is endowed with the will to go forward,
> He'll always work in the cause of IBM.

Finally, homogeneity meant that suburbanites would have to purchase new cars, furniture, television sets, and so on to be like their neighbors (it was called "keeping up with the Joneses"), even though monthly payments already were stretching a family's income pretty thin.

There was an underside to the so-called affluent society. Indeed, many Americans did not share in its benefits at all. As middle-class whites fled to the suburbs, conditions in the cities deteriorated. Increasingly populated by the poor—African Americans, Latin American immigrants, the elderly, and unskilled white immigrants—urban areas struggled to finance essential city services such as police and fire protection. Poverty and its victims could also be found in rural areas, as Michael Harrington pointed out in his classic study *The Other America,* published in 1962. Small farmers, tenants, sharecroppers, and migrant workers not only were poor but often lacked any access to even basic educational opportunities and health care facilities.

Young people who lacked the money or who were not brought up with the expectation of earning a college degree tended to continue in more traditional life patterns. They completed their education with high school or before, al-though some attended a local vocationally oriented community college or trade school for a year or two. They often married younger than their college counterparts, sought stable jobs, and aspired to own their own homes. In other words, they rarely rejected the values of their parents' generation.

The baby boomers began leaving the suburbs for college in the early 1960s. Once away from home and in a college environment, many of these students began questioning their parents' values, especially those concerned with materialism, conformity, sexual mores and traditional sex roles, corporate structure and power, and the kind of patriotism that could support the growing conflict in Vietnam. In one sense, they were seeking the same thing that their parents had sought: fulfillment. Yet to the baby boomers, their parents had chased false gods and a false kind of fulfillment. Increasingly alienated by impersonal university policies and by the actions of authority figures such as college administrators, political leaders, and police officers, many students turned to new forms of religion, music, and dress and to the use of drugs to set themselves apart from the older generation. The term *generation gap* could be heard across the American landscape as bewildered, hurt, and angry parents confronted their children, who (in the parents' view) had "gotten everything." Nor could the children seem to communicate to their confused parents how bankrupt they believed their parents' lives and values actually were. In the midst of this generational crisis, the Vietnam War was becoming a major conflict.

The Japanese defeat of Western colonial powers, particularly Britain and France, in the early days of World War II had encouraged nationalist movements[6] in both Africa and Asia. The final surrender of Japan in 1945 left an almost total power vacuum in Southeast Asia. As Britain struggled with postwar economic dislocation and, within India, the independence movement, both the United States and the Soviet Union moved into this vacuum, hoping to influence the course of events in Asia.

Vietnam had long been a part of the French colonial empire in Southeast Asia and was known in the West as French Indochina. At the beginning of World War II, the Japanese had driven the French from the area. Under the leadership of Vietnamese nationalist and communist Ho Chi Minh, the Vietnamese had cooperated with American intelligence agents and fought a guerrilla-style war against the Japanese. When the Japanese were finally driven from Vietnam in 1945, Ho Chi Minh declared Vietnam independent.

The Western nations, however, did not recognize this declaration. At the end of World War II, France wanted to reestablish Vietnam as a French colony. But seriously weakened by war, France could not reassert itself in Vietnam without assistance. At this point, the United States, eager to gain France as a postwar ally and member of the North Atlantic Treaty Organization, and viewing European problems as being more immediate than problems in Asia, chose to help the French reenter

Vietnam as colonial masters. From 1945 to 1954, the United States gave more than $2 billion in financial aid to France so that it could regain its former colony. United States aid was contingent upon the eventual development of self-government in French Indochina.

Ho Chi Minh and other Vietnamese felt that they had been betrayed. They believed that, in return for fighting against the Japanese in World War II, they would earn their independence. Many Vietnamese viewed the reentry of France, with the United States' assistance, as a broken promise. Almost immediately, war broke out between the French and their westernized Vietnamese allies and the forces of Ho Chi Minh. In the cold war atmosphere of the late 1940s and early 1950s, the United States gave massive aid to the French, who, it was maintained, were fighting against monolithic communism.

The fall of Dien Bien Phu in 1954 spelled the end of French power in Vietnam. The U.S. secretary of state, John Foster Dulles, tried hard to convince Britain and other Western allies of the need for "united action" in Southeast Asia and to avoid any use of American ground troops (as President Truman had authorized earlier in Korea). The allies were not persuaded, however. Rather than let the area fall to the Communists, President Eisenhower and his secretary of state eventually allowed the temporary division of Vietnam into two sections: South Vietnam, ruled by westernized Vietnamese formerly loyal to the French, and North Vietnam, governed by the Communist Ho Chi Minh.

6. Those in nationalist movements seek independence for their countries.

Free and open elections to unify the country were to be held in 1956. However, the elections were never held because American policymakers feared that Ho Chi Minh would easily defeat the unpopular but pro–United States Ngo Dinh Diem, the United States' choice to lead South Vietnam. From 1955 to 1960, the United States supported Diem with more than $1 billion of aid as civil war between the South Vietnamese and the Northern Vietminh (later called the Vietcong) raged across the countryside and in the villages.

President Kennedy did little to improve the situation. Facing his own cold war problems, among them the building of the Berlin Wall and the Bay of Pigs invasion,[7] Kennedy simply poured more money and more "military advisers" (close to seventeen thousand by 1963) into the troubled country. Finally, in the face of tremendous Vietnamese pressure, the United States turned against Diem, and in 1963 South Vietnamese generals, encouraged by the Central Intelligence Agency, overthrew the corrupt and repressive Diem regime. Diem was assassinated in the fall of 1963, shortly before Kennedy's assassination.

Lyndon Johnson, the Texas Democrat who succeeded Kennedy in 1963 and won election as president in 1964, was an old New Dealer[8] who wished to extend social and economic programs to needy Americans. The "tragedy" of Lyndon Johnson, as the official White House historian, Eric Goldman, saw it, was that the president was increasingly drawn into the Vietnam War. Actually, President Johnson and millions of other Americans still perceived Vietnam as a major test of the United States' willingness to resist the spread of communism.

Under Johnson, the war escalated rapidly. In 1964, the Vietcong controlled almost half of South Vietnam, and Johnson obtained sweeping powers from Congress[9] to conduct the war as he wished. Bombing of North Vietnam and Laos was increased, refugees were moved to "pacification" camps, entire villages believed to be unfriendly were destroyed, chemical defoliants were sprayed on forests to eliminate Vietcong hiding places, and the number of troops increased until by 1968 about 500,000 American men and women were serving in Vietnam.

As the war effort increased, so did the doubts about it. In the mid-1960s, the chair of the Senate Foreign Relations Committee, J. William Fulbright, raised important questions about whether the Vietnam War was serving our national interest. Several members of the administration and foreign policy experts (including George Kennan, author of the original containment policy) maintained that escalation of the war could not be justified. Television news coverage of the de-

7. The Berlin Wall was a barricade created to separate East Berlin (Communist) from West Berlin. The Bay of Pigs invasion was a United States–sponsored invasion of Cuba in April 1961 that failed. The American role was widely criticized.
8. Johnson had served in Congress during the 1930s and was a strong supporter of New Deal programs.

9. The Tonkin Gulf Resolution gave Johnson the power to "take all necessary measures to repel any armed attack against the forces of the United States and to prevent further aggression."

struction and carnage, along with reports of atrocities such as the My Lai massacre,[10] disillusioned more and more Americans. Yet Johnson continued the bombing, called for more ground troops, and offered peace terms that were completely unacceptable to the North Vietnamese.

Not until the Tet offensive—a coordinated North Vietnamese strike across all of South Vietnam in January 1968, in which the Communists captured every provincial capital and even entered Saigon (the capital of South Vietnam)—did President Johnson change his mind. Two months later, Johnson appeared on national television and announced to a surprised nation that he had ordered an end to most of the bombing, asked North Vietnam to start real peace negotiations, and withdrawn his name from the 1968 presidential race. Although we now know that the Tet offensive was a setback for Ho Chi Minh, in the United States it was seen as a major defeat for the West, evidence that the optimistic press releases about our imminent victory simply were not true.

As the United States' role in the Vietnam War increased, the government turned increasingly to the conscription of men for military service (the draft). Early in the war, all college men up to age twenty-six could get automatic deferments, which allowed them to remain in school while noncollege men (disproportionately poor and black) were drafted and sent

to Vietnam. As the demand for men increased, however, deferments became somewhat more difficult to obtain. College students had to maintain good grades, graduate student deferments were ended, and draft boards increasingly were unsympathetic to pleas for conscientious objector status.[11] Even so, the vast majority of college students who did not want to go to Vietnam were able to avoid doing so, principally by using one of the countless loopholes in the system such as opting for ROTC (Reserve Officers' Training Corps) duty, purposely failing physical examinations, getting family members to pull strings, obtaining conscientious objector status, and so on. Only 12 percent of the college graduates between 1964 and 1973 served in Vietnam. Twenty-one percent of high school graduates and an even higher percentage of high school dropouts served.

As the arbitrary and unfair nature of the draft became increasingly evident, President Richard Nixon finally replaced General Lewis Hershey, who had headed the Selective Service System since 1948, and instituted a new system of conscription: a lottery. In this system, draft-age men were assigned numbers and were drafted in order from lowest to highest number until the draft quota was filled. With this action, the very real threat of the draft spread to those who had previously felt relatively safe. Already divided, an entire generation had to come face to face with the Vietnam War.

10. The My Lai massacre occurred in March 1968, when American soldiers destroyed a Vietnamese village and killed many of the inhabitants, including women and children.

11. Conscientious objectors are those whose religious beliefs are opposed to military service, such as the Society of Friends (Quakers).

✦

The Method

Historians often wish they could ask specific questions of the participants in a historical event—questions that are not answered in surviving diaries, letters, and other documents. Furthermore, many people, especially the poor, uneducated, and members of minority groups, did not leave written records and thus often are overlooked by historians.

When dealing with the comparatively recent past, however, historians do have an opportunity to ask questions by using a technique called *oral history*. Oral history—interviewing famous and not-so-famous people about their lives and the events they observed or participated in—can greatly enrich knowledge of the past. It can help capture the "spirit of an age" as seen through the eyes of average citizens, and it often bridges the gap between impersonal forces (wars, epidemics, depressions) and personal, individual responses to them. Furthermore, oral history allows the unique to emerge from the total picture: the conscientious objector who would not serve in the army, the woman who did not marry and devote herself to raising a family, and so forth.

Oral history is both fascinating and challenging. It seems easy to do, but it is really rather difficult to do well. There is always the danger that the student may "lead" the interview by imposing his or her ideas on the subject. It is equally possible that the student may be led away from the subject by the person being interviewed.

Still other problems sometimes arise.

The student may miss the subtleties in what is being said or may assume that an exceptional person is representative of many people. Some older people like to tell only the "smiling side" of their personal history—that is, they prefer to talk about the good things that happened to them, not the bad things. Others actually forget what happened or are influenced by reading or television. Some older people cannot resist sending a message to younger people by recounting how hard it was in the past, how few luxuries they had when they were young, how far they had to walk to school, and so forth. Yet oral history, when used carefully and judiciously along with other sources, is an invaluable tool that helps historians re-create a sense of our past.

Recently, much attention has been paid—and rightly so—to protecting the rights and privacy of human subjects. For this reason, the federal government requires that an interviewee consent to the interview and be fully aware of how the interview is to be used. The interviewer must explain the purpose of the interview, and the person being interviewed must sign a release form (for samples, see Sources 1 through 3). Although these requirements are intended to apply mostly to psychologists and sociologists, historians who use oral history are included as well.

When you identify and interview an individual of the baby-boom generation, you will be speaking with a member of a *birth cohort*. A birth cohort comprises those people born within a few years of one another who form a historical generation. Members of a birth cohort experience the same events—wars, depressions, assassinations, as well as personal experiences such as marriage and childbearing—at approximately the same age and often have similar reactions to them. Sociologist Glen Elder showed that a group of people who were relatively deprived as young children during the Great Depression grew up and later made remarkably similar decisions about marriage, children, and jobs. Others have used this kind of analysis to provide insights into British writers of the post–World War I era and to explain why the Nazi party appealed to a great many young Germans.

Yet even within a birth cohort, people may respond quite differently to the same event or experience. *Frame of reference* refers to an individual's personal background, which may influence that person's beliefs, responses, and actions. For example, interviews conducted with Americans who lived during the Great Depression of the 1930s reveal that men and women often coped differently with unemployment, that blacks and whites differed in their perceptions of how hard the times were, and that those living in rural areas had remarkably different experiences from city dwellers.

In this chapter, all the interviewees belong to the generation that came of age during the Vietnam War. Thus, as you analyze their frames of reference, age will not give you any clues. However, other factors, such as gender, race, socioeconomic class, family background, values, region, and experiences, may be quite important in determining the interviewees' frames of reference and understanding their responses to the Vietnam War. When a group of people share the same general frame of reference, they are a generational subset who tend to respond similarly to events. In other words, it may be possible to form tentative generalizations from the interviewees about how others with the same general frames of reference thought about and responded to the Vietnam War. To assist you in conducting your own interview of a member of the baby-boom generation (or birth cohort), we have included some instructions for interviewers and a suggested interview plan.

Instructions for Interviewers

1. Establish the date, time, and place of the interview well in advance. You may wish to call and remind the interviewee a few days before your appointment.
2. State clearly the purpose of the interview *at the beginning.* In other words, explain why the class is doing this project.
3. Prepare for the interview by carefully reading background information about the 1960s and by writing down and arranging the questions you will be asking to guide the interview.
4. Keep most of your major questions broad and general so that the interviewee will not simply answer with a word or two ("What was your job in the army?"). Specific questions such as "What did the people in your town think about

the war?" are useful for obtaining more details.

5. Avoid "loaded" questions such as "Everyone hated President Lyndon Johnson, didn't they?" Instead, keep your questions neutral: "What did you think about President Lyndon Johnson and his Vietnam strategy?"

6. Save any questions involving controversial matters for last. It is better to ask them toward the end of the interview, when the interviewee is more comfortable with you.

7. Be courteous, and be sure to give the person enough time to think, remember, and answer. Never argue, even if he or she says something with which you strongly disagree. Remember that the purpose of the interview is to find out what *that person* thinks, not what you think.

8. Take notes, even if you are tape-recording the interview (with permission). Notes will help clarify unclear portions of the tape and will be essential if the recorder malfunctions or the tape is accidentally erased.

9. Obtain a signed release form. Many who use the oral history method believe that the release forms should be signed at the beginning of the interview; others insist that this often inhibits the person who is to be interviewed and therefore should not be done until the end of the session. Although students who are using the material only for a class exercise are not always held strictly to the federal requirements, it is still better to obtain a signed release. Without such a release, the tape cannot be heard and used by anyone else (or deposited in an oral history collection), and the information the tape contains cannot be published or made known outside the classroom.

10. Write up the results of your interview as soon as possible after completing it. Even in rough form, these notes will help you capture the sense of what was said as well as the actual information that was presented.

A Suggested Interview Plan

Remember that your interviewee is a *person* with feelings, sensitivities, and emotions. If you intend to tape-record the interview, ask permission first. If you believe that a tape recorder will inhibit the person you have selected, leave it at home and rely on your ability to take notes.

The following suggestions may help you get started. People usually remember the personal aspects of their lives more vividly than they remember national or international events. That is a great advantage in this exercise because part of what you are attempting to find out is how this person lived during the 1960s. Begin by getting the following important data from the interviewee:

1. Name
2. Age in 1968
3. Race and sex
4. Where the person lived in the 1960s and what the area was like then

5. Family background (what the interviewee's parents did for a living; number of brothers and sisters; whether the interviewee considered himself or herself rich, middle class, or poor)
6. Educational background

Then move on to the aspects of the person's life that will flesh out your picture of the 1960s and early 1970s:

1. Was the person in college at any time? What was college life like during the period?
2. If the person was not in college, what did he or she do for a living? Did he or she live at home or away from home?
3. How did the person spend his or her leisure time? If unmarried, did the person go out on dates? What was dating like? Did he or she go to the movies (and if so, which ones)? Did he or she watch much television (and if so, which shows)?

These questions should give you a fairly good idea of how the person lived during the period. Now move on to connect the interviewee with the Vietnam War:

1. Did the person know anyone who volunteered or was drafted and sent to Vietnam? How did the inter-

viewee feel about that? Did the person lose any relatives or friends in Vietnam? What was his or her reaction to that?
2. *(Male):* Was the person himself eligible for the draft? Did he volunteer for service or was he drafted? Was he sent to Vietnam? If so, what were some memorable Vietnam experiences? What did the person's family think of his going to Vietnam? *(Female):* If you intend to interview a female who went to Vietnam as a nurse, alter the preceding questions as needed.
3. Was the person a Vietnam War protester? If so, what was that experience like? If not, did the person know any Vietnam War protesters? What did the person think of them?
4. Did the person know anyone who tried to avoid going to Vietnam? What did the person think of that?

Finally, review the national events and people of the Vietnam era and develop some questions to ask your interviewee about these events and people. As you can see in this plan, you want to guide the interview through three stages, from personal information and background to the interviewee's reactions to a widening sphere of experiences and events.

♦

The Evidence

Sources 1 and 2 from Collum Davis, Kathryn Back, and Kay MacLean, *Oral History: From Tape to Type* (Chicago: American Library Association, 1977), pp. 14, 15.

1. Sample Unconditional Release for an Oral Interview.

<u>Tri-County Historical Society</u>

For and in consideration of the participation by <u>Tri-County Historical Society</u> in any programs involving the dissemination of tape-recorded memories and oral history material for publication, copyright, and other uses, I hereby release all right, title, or interest in and to' all of my tape-recorded memoirs to <u>Tri-County Historical Society</u> and declare that they may be used without any restriction whatsoever and may be copyrighted and published by the said <u>Society,</u> which may also assign said copyright and publication rights to serious research scholars.

In addition to the rights and authority given to you under the preceding paragraph, I hereby authorize you to edit, publish, sell and/or license the use of my oral history memoir in any other manner which the <u>Society</u> considers to be desirable and I waive any claim to any payments which may be received as a consequence thereof by the <u>Society.</u>

PLACE   <u>Indianapolis,</u>

        <u>Indiana</u>

DATE   <u>July 14, 1975</u>

<u>Harold S. Johnson</u>
(Interviewee)

<u>Jane Rogers</u>
(for <u>Tri-County Historical Society</u>)

2. Sample Conditional Release for an Oral Interview.

<u>Tri-County Historical Society</u>

I hereby release all right, title, or interest in and to all or any part of my tape-recorded memoirs to <u>Tri-County Historical Society,</u> subject to the following stipulations:

That my memoirs are to be *closed* until five years following my death.

PLACE <u>Indianapolis,</u>
        <u>Indiana</u>
DATE <u>July 14, 1975</u>

<u>Harold S. Johnson</u>
(Interviewee)

<u>Jane Rogers</u>
(for <u>Tri-County Historical Society</u>)

Source 3 from the University of Tennessee.

3. Release Form Developed by a Large U.S. History Survey Class at the University of Tennessee, Knoxville, 1984.

This form is to state that I have been interviewed by _____ on
                                                     (Interviewer)
_____ on my recollections of the Vietnam War era. I understand that
(date)
this interview will be used in a class project at the University of Tennessee, and that the results will be saved for future historians.

_____
Signature

_____
Date

Sources 4 through 10 are from interviews conducted by the authors. Photographs were supplied by the interviewees.

4. Photograph of John and His Family (*left to right:* John's father, John, John's mother, and John's brother).

John

[*John was born in 1951. His father was a well-to-do and prominent physician, and John grew up in a midwestern town that had a major university. He graduated from high school in 1969 and enrolled in a four-year private college. John dropped out of college in 1971 and returned home to live with his parents. He found work in the community and associated with students at the nearby university.*]

My earliest memory of Vietnam must have been when I was in the seventh grade [1962–1963] and I saw things in print and in *Life* magazine. But I really don't remember much about Vietnam until my senior year in high school [1968–1969].

I came from a repressive private school to college. College was a fun place to hang out, a place where you went after high school. It was just expected of you to go.

At college there was a good deal of apprehension and fear about Vietnam—people were scared of the draft. To keep your college deferments, you had to keep your grades up. But coming from an admittedly well-to-do family, I somehow assumed I didn't have to worry about it too much. I suppose I was outraged to find out that it *could* happen to me.

No, I was outraged that it could happen to *anyone*. I knew who was going to get deferments and who weren't going to get them. And even today my feelings are still ambiguous. On one hand I felt, "You guys were so dumb to get caught in that machine." On the other, and more importantly, it was wrong that *anyone* had to go.

Why? Because Vietnam was a bad war. To me, we were protecting business interests. We were fighting on George III's side, on the wrong side of an anticolonial rebellion. The domino theory didn't impress me at all.[12]

I had decided that I would not go to Vietnam. But I wasn't really worried for myself until Nixon instituted the lottery. I was contemplating going to Canada when my older brother got a CO.[13] I tried the same thing, the old Methodist altar boy gambit, but I was turned down. I was really ticked when I was refused CO status. I thought, "Who are you to tell me who is a pacifist?"

My father was conservative and my mother liberal. Neither one intervened or tried to pressure me. I suppose they thought, "We've done the best we could." By this time I had long hair and a beard. My dad had a hard time.

The antiwar movement was an intellectual awakening of American youth. Young people were concentrated on college campuses, where their maturing intellects had sympathetic sounding boards. Vietnam was part of that awakening. So was drugs. It was part of the protest. You had to be a part of it. Young people were waking up as they got away from home and saw the world around them and were forced to think for themselves.

I remember an argument I had with my father. I told him Ho Chi Minh was a nationalist before he was a Communist, and that this war wasn't really against communism at all. It's true that the Russians were also the bad guys in Vietnam, what with their aid and support of the North Vietnamese, but they had no business there either. When people tried to compare Vietnam to World War II, I just said that no Vietnamese had ever bombed Pearl Harbor.

The draft lottery certainly put me potentially at risk. But I drew a high number, so I knew that it was unlikely that I'd ever be drafted. And yet, I wasn't concerned just for myself. For example, I was aware, at least intellec-

12. The domino theory, embraced by Presidents Eisenhower, Kennedy, and Johnson, held that if one nation fell to the Communists, the result would be a toppling of other nations, like dominoes.
13. A "CO" is a conscientious objector.

tually, that blacks and poor people were the cannon fodder in Vietnam. But I insisted that *no one,* rich or poor, had to go to fight this war.

Actually I didn't think much about the Vietnamese people themselves. The image was of a kid who could take candy from you one day and hand you a grenade the next. What in hell were we doing in that kind of situation?

Nor did I ever actually know anyone who went to Vietnam. I suppose that, to some extent, I bought the "damn baby napalmers" image. But I never had a confrontation with a veteran of Vietnam. What would I think of him? I don't know. What would he think of me?

Kent State[14] was a real shock to me. I was in college at the time, and I thought, "They were students, just like me." It seemed as if fascism was growing in America.

I was part of the protest movement. After Kent State, we shut down the campus, then marched to a downtown park where we held a rally. In another demonstration, later, I got a good whiff of tear gas. I was dating a girl who collapsed because of the gas. I recall a state policeman coming at us with a club. I yelled at him, telling him what had happened. Suddenly he said, "Here, hold this!" and gave me his club while he helped my date to her feet.

But there were other cops who weren't so nice. I went to the counter-inaugural in Washington in June 1973. You could see the rage on the cops' faces when we were yelling, "One, two, three, four, we don't want your f——ing war!" It was an awakening for me to see that much emotion on the subject coming from the other side. I know that I wasn't very open to other opinions. But the other side *really* was closed.

By '72 their whole machine was falling apart. A guy who gave us a ride to the counter-inaugural was a Vietnam vet. He was going there too, to protest against the war. In fact, he was hiding a friend of his who was AWOL,[15] who simply hid rather than go to Vietnam.

Then Watergate made it all worthwhile—we really had those f——ers scared. I think Watergate showed the rest of the country exactly what kind of "law and order" Nixon and his cronies were after!

I have no regrets about what I did. I condemn them all—Kennedy, Johnson, Nixon—for Vietnam. They all had a hand in it. And the war was wrong, in every way imaginable. While I feel some guilt that others went and were killed, and I didn't, in retrospect I feel much guiltier that I wasn't a helluva

---

14. Kent State: On May 4, 1970, in the midst of an antiwar rally on the campus of Kent State University in Ohio, panicked National Guard soldiers fired into a crowd of protesters. Four students, two of whom were on their way to class and were not demonstrators, were killed and eleven were wounded. The tragedy increased campus unrest throughout the nation.
15. "AWOL" is an acronym for absent without leave.

lot more active. Other than that, I wouldn't change a thing. I can still get angry about it.

How will I explain all that to my sons? I have no guilt in terms of "duty towards country." The *real* duty was to fight *against* the whole thing. I'll tell my sons that, and tell them that I did what I did so that no one has to go.

[*John chose not to return to college. He learned a craft, which he practices today. He married a woman who shared his views ("I wouldn't have known anyone on the other side, the way the country was divided"), had two children, and shared the responsibilities of child care. John and his wife are now divorced.*]

5. Photograph of Mike in Vietnam.

Mike

[Mike was born in 1948. His family owned a farm in western Tennessee, and Mike grew up in a rural environment. He graduated from high school in 1966 and enrolled in a community college not far from his home. After two quarters of poor grades, Mike left the community college and joined the United States Marine Corps in April 1967. He served two tours in Vietnam, the first in 1967 to 1969 and the second in 1970 to 1971.]

I flunked out of college my first year. I was away from home and found out a lot about wine, women, and song but not about much else. In 1967 the old system of the draft was still in effect, so I knew that eventually I'd be rotated up and drafted—it was only a matter of time before they got me.

My father served with Stilwell in Burma and my uncle was career military. I grew up on a diet of John Wayne flicks. I thought serving in the military was what was expected of me. The Marines had some good options—you could go in for two years and take your chances on the *possibility* of not going to Vietnam. I chose the two-year option. I thought what we were doing in Vietnam was a noble cause. My mother was against the war and we argued a lot about it. I told her that if the French hadn't helped us in the American Revolution, then we wouldn't have won. I sincerely believed that.

I took my six weeks of basic training at Parris Island [South Carolina]. It was sheer hell—I've never been treated like that in my life. Our bus arrived at Parris Island around midnight, and we were processed and sent to our barracks. We had just gotten to sleep when a drill instructor threw a thirty-two gallon garbage can down the center of the barracks and started overturning the metal bunks. We were all over the floor and he was screaming at us. It was that way for six weeks—no one ever talked to us, they shouted. And all our drill instructors geared our basic training to Vietnam. They were always screaming at us, "You're going to go to Vietnam and you're gonna f—— up and you're gonna die."

Most of the people in basic training with me were draftees. My recruiter apologized to me for having to go through boot camp with draftees. But most of the guys I was with were pretty much like me. Oh, there were a few s—— birds, but not many. We never talked about Vietnam—there was no opportunity.

There were a lot of blacks in the Corps and I went through basic training with some. But I don't remember any racial tension until later. There were only two colors in the Marine Corps: light green and dark green. My parents drove down to Parris Island to watch me graduate from basic training, and they brought a black woman with them. She was from Memphis and was the wife of one of the men who graduated with me.

After basic training I spent thirteen weeks in basic infantry training at Camp Lejeune [North Carolina]. Lejeune is the armpit of the world. And the harassment didn't let up—we were still called "scumbag" and "hairbag" and "whale——." I made PFC [private first class] at Lejeune. I was an 03-11 [infantry rifleman].

From Lejeune [after twenty days' home leave] I went to Camp Pendleton [California] for four-week staging. It was at Pendleton where we adjusted our training at Parris Island and Lejeune to the situation in Vietnam. I got to Vietnam right after Christmas 1967.

It was about this time that I became aware of antiwar protests. But as far as I was concerned they were a small minority of malcontents. They were the *protected,* were deferred or had a daddy on the draft board. I thought, "These people are disloyal—they're selling us down the drain."

We were not prepared to deal with the Vietnamese people at all. The only two things we were told was don't give kids cigarettes and don't pat 'em on the heads. We had no cultural training, knew nothing of the social structure or anything. For instance, we were never told that the Catholic minority controlled Vietnam and they got out of the whole thing—we did their fighting for them, while they stayed out or went to Paris or something. We had a Catholic chaplain who told us that it was our *duty* to go out and kill the Cong,[16] that they stood against Christianity. Then he probably went and drank sherry with the top cats in Vietnam. As for the majority of Vietnamese, they were as different from us as night and day. To be honest, I still hate the Vietnamese SOBs.

The South Vietnamese Army was a mixed bag. There were some good units and some bad ones. Most of them were bad. If we were fighting alongside South Vietnam units, we had orders that if we were overrun by Charley[17] that we should shoot the South Vietnamese first—otherwise we were told they'd turn on us.

I can't tell you when I began to change my mind about the war. Maybe it was a kind of maturation process—you can only see so much death and suffering until you begin to wonder what in hell is going on. You can only live like a nonhuman so long.

I came out of country[18] in January of 1969 and was discharged not too long after that. I came home and found the country split over the war. I thought, "Maybe there *was* something to this antiwar business after all." Maybe these guys protesting in the streets weren't wrong.

But when I got back home, I was a stranger to my friends. They didn't want to get close to me. I could feel it. It was strange, like the only friends I had were in the Marine Corps. So I re-upped[19] in the Marines and went back to Vietnam with a helicopter squadron.

Kent State happened when I was back in Vietnam. They covered it in *Stars and Stripes.*[20] I guess that was a big turning point for me. Some of the other Marines said, "Hooray! Maybe we should kill more of them!" That was it for me. Those people at Kent State were killed for exercising the same rights we

---

16. "Cong" is short for *Vietcong,* also known as "the VC."
17. "Charley" is a euphemism for *Vietcong.*
18. "Country" means Vietnam.
19. "Re-upped" means reenlisted.
20. *Stars and Stripes* is a newspaper written and published by the armed forces for service personnel.

were fighting for for the Vietnamese. But I was in the minority—most of the Marines I knew approved of the shootings at Kent State.

Meanwhile I was flying helicopters into Cambodia every day. I used pot to keep all that stuff out of my mind. Pot grew wild in Vietnam, as wild as the hair on your ass. The Army units would pick it and send it back. The first time I was in Vietnam nobody I knew was using. The second time there was lots of pot. It had a red tinge, so it was easy to spot.

But I couldn't keep the doubts out of my mind. I guess I was terribly angry. I felt betrayed. I would have voted for Lyndon Johnson—when he said we should be there, I believed him. The man could walk on water as far as I was concerned. I would've voted for Nixon in '68, the only time I ever voted Republican in my life. I believed him when he said we'd come home with honor. So I'd been betrayed twice, and Kent State and all that was rattling around in my head.

I couldn't work it out. I was an E5 [sergeant], but got busted for fighting and then again for telling off an officer. I was really angry.

It was worse when I got home. I came back into the Los Angeles airport and was spit on and called a baby killer and a mother raper. I really felt like I was torn between two worlds. I guess I was. I was smoking pot.

I went back to school. I hung around mostly with veterans. We spoke the same language, and there was no danger of being insulted or ridiculed. We'd been damn good, but nobody knew it. I voted for McGovern in '72—he said we'd get out no matter what. Some of us refused to stand up one time when the national anthem was played.

What should we have done? Either not gotten involved at all or go in with the whole machine. With a different attitude and tactics, we could have *won*. But really we were fighting for just a minority of the Vietnamese, the westernized Catholics who controlled the cities but never owned the backcountry. No, I take that back. There was no way in hell we could have won that damned war and won anything worth winning.

I went to Washington for the dedication of the Vietnam Veterans Memorial. We never got much of a welcome home or parades. The dedication was a homecoming for me. It was the first time I got the whole thing out of my system. I cried, and I'm not ashamed. And I wasn't alone.

I looked for the names of my friends. I couldn't look at a name without myself reflected back in it [the wall].

One of the reasons I went back to school was to understand that war and myself. I've read a lot about it and watched a lot of TV devoted to it. I was at Khe Sanh and nobody could tell about that who wasn't there. There were six thousand of us. Walter Cronkite said we were there for seventy-two days. I kept a diary—it was longer than that. I'm still reading and studying Vietnam, trying to figure it all out.

[*Mike returned to college, repeated the courses he had failed, and transferred to a four-year institution. By all accounts, he was a fine student. Mike is now employed as a park ranger. He is married, and he and his wife have a child. He is considered a valuable, respected, and popular member of his community. He rarely speaks of his time in the service.*]

6. Photograph of M.M., Boot Camp Graduation.

M.M.[21]

[*M.M. was born in 1947 and grew up in a midsize southern city. He graduated from high school in 1965. A standout in high school football, he could not get an athletic scholarship to college because of low grades. As a result, he joined the United States Army two months after graduating from high school to take advantage of the educational benefits he would get upon his discharge. He began his basic training in early September 1965.*]

I went into the service to be a soldier. I was really gung ho. I did my basic training at Fort Gordon [Georgia], my AIT [advanced infantry training] at Fort Ord [California], and ranger school and airborne at Fort Benning [Georgia].

21. Since M.M.'s first name is Mike, his initials are used here to avoid confusion with Mike in Source 5.

All of this was during the civil rights movement. I was told that, being black, I had a war to fight at home, not in Vietnam. That got me uptight, because that wasn't what I wanted to do—I'd done some of that in high school.[22] I had one mission accomplished, and was looking for another.

A lot of guys I went into the service with didn't want to go to Nam—they were afraid. Some went AWOL. One guy jumped off the ship between Honolulu and Nam and drowned. Another guy shot himself, trying to get a stateside wound. He accidentally hit an artery and died. Most of us thought they were cowards.

I arrived in Nam on January 12, 1966. I was three days shy of being eighteen years old. I was young, gung ho, and mean as a snake. I was with the Twenty-fifth Infantry as a machine gunner and rifleman. We went out on search and destroy missions.

I did two tours in Vietnam, at my own request. You could make rank[23] faster in Nam and the money was better. I won two silver stars and three bronze stars. For my first silver star, I knocked out two enemy machine guns that had two of our platoons pinned down. They were drawing heavy casualties. The event is still in my mind. Two of the bronze stars I put in my best friend's body bag. I told him I did it for him.

I had a friend who died in my arms, and I guess I freaked a little bit. I got busted[24] seven times. They [the army] didn't like the way I started taking enemy scalps and wearing them on my pistol belt. I kept remembering my friend.

I didn't notice much racial conflict in Nam. In combat, everybody seemed to be OK. I fought beside this [white] guy for eleven months; we drank out of the same canteen. When I got home, I called this guy's house. His mother said, "We don't allow our son to associate with niggers." In Vietnam, I didn't run into much of that.

The Vietnamese hated us. My first day in Vietnam, Westmoreland[25] told us that underneath every Vietnamese was an American. I thought, "What drug is he on?" But they hated us. When we weren't on the scene, the enemy would punish them for associating with us. They would call out to us, "G.I. Number Ten."[26] They were caught between a rock and a hard place.

We could have won the war several times. The Geneva Convention[27] wouldn't let us, and the enemy had the home court advantage. To win, it

22. M.M. participated in sit-ins to integrate the city's lunch counters and movie theaters.
23. "Make rank" means to earn promotions.
24. "Busted" means demoted.
25. General William Westmoreland was an American commander in Vietnam.
26. "Number Ten" means bad or no good.
27. "The Geneva Convention" refers to international agreements for the conduct of war and the treatment of prisoners. The agreements began to be drawn up in the 1860s.

would have taken hard soldiering, but we could have done it. America is a weak country because we want to be everybody's friend. We went in there as friends. We gave food and stuff to the Vietnamese and we found it in the hands of the enemy. We just weren't tough enough.

I got out of the Army in 1970. I was thinking about making the Army a career and was going to re-enlist. But when they wanted me to go back for a third tour in Vietnam, I got out. Hell, everybody told me I was crazy for doing two.

[*M.M. used his GI Bill benefits to obtain three years of higher education: two years at four-year colleges and one year at a business school. According to him, however, jobs were "few and far between." He described himself as "restless" and reported that automobile backfires still frightened him. He was married and divorced twice. In 1999, M.M. died at the age of fifty-two.*]

7. Photograph of Eugene *(second from right)* Marching.

Eugene

[*Eugene was born in 1948 in a large city on the West Coast. He graduated from high school in June 1967 and was drafted in August. Initially rejected because of a hernia, he had surgery to correct that problem and then enlisted in the Marine Corps.*]

It was pretty clear from basic training on, no ifs, ands, or buts, that we were going to Vietnam. The DIs[28] were all Vietnam vets, so we were told what to expect when we got there. They'd tell us what to do and all we had to do was do it.

I got to Vietnam in June of 1968. Over there, the majority of blacks stuck together because they had to. In the field was a different story, but in the rear you really caught it. Blacks would catch hell in the rear—fights and things like that. When we went to the movies with Navy guys, they put us in the worst seats. Sometimes they just wanted to start a fight. My whole time in Vietnam I knew only two black NCOs[29] and none above that.

We were overrun three times. You could tell when we were going to get hit when the Vietnamese in our camp (who cleaned up hooches) disappeared. Usually Charley had informants inside our base, and a lot of info slipped out. They were fully aware of our actions and weapons.

When we were in the rear, we cleaned our equipment, wrote letters home, went to movies, and thought a lot about what we'd do when we got out. I had

---

28. "DIs" are drill instructors.
29. "NCOs" are noncommissioned officers or sergeants.

training in high school as an auto mechanic, and I wanted to start my own business.

You had to watch out for the rookies until they got a feel for what was going on. We told one new LT,[30] "Don't polish your brass out here or you'll tip us off for sure." He paid us no mind and Charley knocked out him and our radio man one night.

You could get anything over there you wanted [drugs]. Marijuana grew wild in the bush. Vietnamese kids would come up to you with a plastic sandwich bag of twenty-five [marijuana] cigarettes for five dollars. It was dangerous, but we smoked in the bush as well as out. At the O.P.s,[31] everybody knew when the officer would come around and check. We'd pass the word: "Here comes the Man." That's why a lot of guys who came back were so strung out on drugs. And opium—the mamasans[32] had purple teeth because of it.

We could have won the war anytime we wanted to. We could have wiped that place off the map. There was a lot of talk that that's what we should have done. But we didn't because of American companies who had rubber and oil interests in Vietnam, and no telling what else. To them, Vietnam was a money-making thing. We were fighting over there to protect those businesses.

It was frustrating. The Army and Marines were ordered to take Hill 881 and we did, but it was costly. A couple of weeks later we just up and left and gave it back.

When I got out [in January 1970], I was an E5.[33] I couldn't find a job. So I talked to an Air Force recruiter. I got a release from the Marines[34] and joined the Air Force. I rigged parachutes and came out in 1975.

I stayed in LA[35] until 1977. Then I became a long-distance truck driver. I was doing pretty good when I got messed up in an accident. My truck jackknifed on ice in Pennsylvania and I hit the concrete barrier.

[*Eugene has not worked regularly since the accident and he sued the trucking company. He is divorced.*]

30. "LT" refers to a lieutenant.
31. "O.P.s" are outposts.
32. "Mamasans" refers to elderly Vietnamese women.
33. "E5" means sergeant.
34. Eugene had four years of reserve obligation.
35. Los Angeles, California.

8. Photograph of Helen *(left)* **at an Army Hospital in Phu Bai, South Vietnam.**

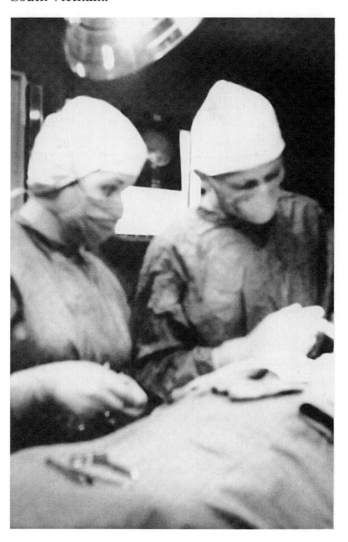

Helen

[*Helen was born in 1942 in Cleveland, Ohio, and grew up there. Since grade school, she had wanted to be a nurse. After graduation from high school, she spent three years in nurses' training to become a registered nurse. She worked for three years in the operating rooms of a major medical facility in Cleveland. In 1966, she joined the United States Navy.*]

I joined the Navy in 1966 and reported to Newport, Rhode Island, for basic training. Our classes consisted of military protocol, military history, and physical education. There was only a passing reference made to our medical assignments and what was expected of us.

I was assigned to the Great Lakes Naval Hospital [outside Chicago]. Although I had been trained and had experience as an operating room surgical nurse, at first I was assigned to the orthopedic wards. It was there that I got my first exposure to mass casualties [from Vietnam]. Depending on the extent of their injuries, we would see patients at Great Lakes about seven to ten days after them being wounded in Vietnam.

I became attached to some of the boys—they were young, scared and badly injured. I remember a Negro who in tears asked for his leg to be taken off—he couldn't stand the smell of it anymore and had been to surgery once too often for the removal of dead tissue. He was in constant pain.

On the wards, we always kept nightlights on. If someone darkened a ward by accident, it produced a sense of terror in the patients. Many were disoriented, and a lot had nightmares.

When I made the decision to go to Vietnam, I volunteered in 1968 and requested duty aboard a hospital ship. It was necessary to extend my time on active duty in order to go. I felt I had a skill that was needed and it was something I felt I personally had to do. I didn't necessarily agree with our policy on being there, but that wasn't the point.

The median age of our troops in Vietnam was nineteen years old. It was like treating our kid brothers. I would have done as much for my own brothers. I know this sounds idealistic, but that's the way I felt then.

The troops got six weeks of staging, preparing them for duty in Vietnam. Most of the nurses were given no preparation, no orientation as to what to expect when you go into a war zone. No one said, "These are the things you'll see," or "These are the things you'll be expected to do."

I was assigned to the U.S.S. *Sanctuary,* which was stationed outside of Da Nang harbor. The *Sanctuary* was a front-line treatment facility. Casualties were picked up in the field combat areas and then brought by Medevac choppers to the ship. During our heaviest months, we logged over seven hundred patient admissions per month. That was at the height of the Tet offensive in January through March, 1968. I had just gotten to Vietnam.

It was terribly intense. There was nothing to shelter you, no one to hold your hand when mass casualties came in. If you had time to think, you'd have thought, "My God, how am I to get through this?" We dealt with multiple amputations, head injuries, and total body trauma. Sometimes injuries were received from our own people caught in crossfires. When all hell breaks loose at night in the jungle, a nineteen-year-old boy under ambush will fire at anything that moves.

How do you insulate yourself against all this? We relaxed when we could, and we put a lot of stock in friendships (the corpsmen were like our kid brothers). We played pranks and sometimes took the launch ashore to Da Nang. Occasionally we were invited to a party ashore and a helicopter came out for the nurses. The men wanted American women at their parties.

There were some people who had the idea that the only reason women were in the service was to be prostitutes or to get a man. Coming back from Vietnam, I was seated next to a male officer on the plane who said to me, "Boy, I bet you had a great time in Vietnam." I had my seat changed. When I got home and was still in uniform I was once mistaken for a police officer.

On the *Sanctuary,* we had Vietnamese patients too. But our guys were distrustful of them, especially children who had been observed planting mines (probably in exchange for a handful of rice). The Vietnamese were often placed under armed guard. I have friends who were nurses in country who harbor a real hatred for the Vietnamese.

I heard a story of a Vietnamese child running up to a chopper that was evacuating casualties and tossing a grenade into it. Everyone on board was killed in a split second; both crew and casualties, because they paused to help a child they thought needed them. A soldier I knew said, "If they're in the fire zone, they get killed." War really takes you to the lowest level of human dignity. It makes you barbaric.

After Vietnam, I was stationed at the Naval Academy in Annapolis to finish out my duty. There I dealt basically with college students—measles and sports injuries. It was a hard adjustment to make.

In Vietnam, nurses had a great deal of autonomy, and we often had to do things nurses normally aren't allowed to do. You couldn't do those things stateside. Doctors saw it as an encroachment on their areas of practice. I'd been a year under extreme surgical conditions in Vietnam, and then in Annapolis someone would ask me, "Are you sure you know how to start an IV?"[36] It was hard to tame yourself down. Also, in the civilian setting, mediocrity was tolerated. I heard people say, "That's not my job." Nobody would have said that in Vietnam. There, the rules were put aside and everybody did what they could. When we got back to the states, there was no one to wind us down, deprogram us, tell us that Vietnam was an abnormal situation. . . . It was as if no one cared, we were just expected to cope and go on with our lives. . . .

I guess the hardest thing about nursing in Vietnam was the different priori-

36. An "IV" is an intravenous mechanism.

ties. Back home, if we got multiple-trauma cases from, say, an automobile accident, we always treated the most seriously injured first. In Vietnam, it was often the reverse. I remember working on one soldier who was not badly wounded, and he kept screaming for us to help his buddy, who was seriously wounded. I couldn't tell him that his buddy didn't have a good chance to survive, and so we were passing him by. That was difficult for a lot of us, went against all we'd been trained to do. It's difficult to support someone in the act of dying when you're trained to do all you can to save a life. Even today, I have trouble with patients who need amputations or who have facial injuries.

It is most important to realize that there is a great cost to waging war. Many men are living out their lives in veterans' hospitals as paraplegics or quadriplegics, who in World War II or Korea would not have survived. Most Americans will never see these people—they are hidden away from us. But they are alive.

Maybe the worst part of the war for many of these boys was coming home. The seriously wounded were sent to a military hospital closest to their own homes. Our orthopedic ward at Great Lakes Naval Hospital had forty beds, and it was like taking care of forty kid brothers. They joked around and were supportive of each other. But quite a few of them got "Dear John"[37] letters while they were there. Young wives and girlfriends sometimes couldn't deal with these injuries, and parents sometimes had trouble coping too. All these people were "casualties of war," but I believe that these men especially need our caring and concern today, just as much as they did twenty years ago.

[*On her discharge from the United States Navy in August 1969, Helen returned to nursing. She married in 1972. She and her husband, an engineering physicist, have two children. Helen returned to school and received her B.S. degree in nursing. She is now a coordinator of cardiac surgery and often speaks and writes of her Vietnam experience. She also actively participates in a local veterans' organization. When her daughter was in high school and offered her mother's services to speak on Vietnam to a history class, she was rebuffed by the teacher, who said, "Who wants to hear about that? We lost that war!" Both Helen and her daughter (who is proud of what her mother did in Vietnam) were offended.*]

37. A "Dear John" letter is one that breaks off a relationship.

9. Photograph of Nick *(right)* with Some Buddies in Vietnam.

Nick

[*Nick was born in 1946 in a midsize southern city. Both his parents were skilled factory workers. Nick graduated from high school in 1964 and wanted to work for the fire department, but he was too young for the civil service. He got a job at the local utility company and married in 1966. Nick was drafted in 1967. He served in the United States Army with the First Cavalry Division.*]

I suppose I could have gotten a deferment, but I didn't know they were available. My wife was pretty scared when I got drafted, but neither of us ever imagined that I would shirk my duty.

I did my boot camp at Fort Benning [Georgia]. About 80 percent of the people in boot camp with me were draftees. A number of the draftees were black. I had worked with blacks before the Army, had many black friends, and never saw any racial problems. We were then sent to Fort Polk, Louisiana, for advanced infantry training. They had built simulated Vietnamese villages that were very similar to what we later encountered in Vietnam. Overall, we were trained pretty well, but we were still pretty scared.

I arrived in Vietnam on December 12, 1967, and was assigned to go out on "search and destroy" missions. Even though I was prepared mentally, I was still very frightened. I was wounded once when we got ambushed while we were setting up an ambush of our own. Another time I got hit with some shrapnel from a 60 mm mortar. That was at 3:00 A.M. and the medics didn't arrive until 7:30.

I'm not proud of everything I did in Vietnam, but I won't run away from it either. You got so hard at seeing friends killed and things like that. We desecrated their dead, just as they did ours. We used to put our unit's shoulder patches on the VC dead (we nailed 'em on) to get credit for it.

I didn't like the Vietnamese themselves. Most of the civilians were VC sympathizers, and the South Vietnamese army just wouldn't fight. I was in some kind of culture shock. Here we were, trying to help these people, and some of them were living in grass huts. Once I asked myself, "What am I doing here?"

The highest rank I made was sergeant, but I was demoted when I caught a guy in my unit asleep on guard duty and busted him with a shotgun. I was demoted for damaging the shotgun, government property.

I got back to the States in December 1968. There were some protesters at the Seattle airport, but they just marched with signs and didn't harass us at all. Over time, I lost my hostility to the antiwar protesters, although at the time I despised them. Except for Jane Fonda[38] (who went too far), I have no bad feelings for them at all. I have a friend who threatened to run his daughter off because she had a Jane Fonda workout tape.

I'm no hero and didn't do anything special. But college students today need to know that the people who fought in that war are no less important than people who fought in World War I, World War II, or Korea.

[*Nick returned to his position with the utility company. He and his wife have two sons, born in 1969 and 1972. He never talked about Vietnam and wanted to throw his medals out, but his wife made him keep them. When his sons started asking questions, he told them about Vietnam. They convinced him to bring his medals out and display them. Since returning from Vietnam, he has never voted "and never will. . . . I have no use for politicians at all." He is now enjoying retirement.*]

---

38. Movie star and antiwar activist Jane Fonda organized shipments of food and medical supplies to North Vietnam and traveled to Vietnam during the war.

10. Photograph of Robyn as a College Student.

Robyn

[*Robyn was born in 1955 and raised in a Wisconsin farming town of around fifteen hundred people. Her father owned a small construction business and, like many other men in town, had proudly served in World War II. Her mother was a high school teacher. Robyn has three sisters and three brothers, none of whom served in Vietnam.*]

I remember starting to watch the war on television when I was about ten. I asked my mother, "How come they're killing each other?" She said that America was the land of freedom and that we were in Vietnam to help make the people free. As a teacher, though, she always encouraged us to think for ourselves and find our own answers.

The guys in town started going away [to Vietnam], and in a town that size, everybody knows. When my ninth-grade algebra teacher suddenly disappeared, no adults would talk about it. Later, we found out that he had received CO status. In my town, that wasn't much different from being a Communist. The peer pressure was tremendous.

I have always believed the United States is the greatest country in the world, but it's not perfect. The more I heard about the war, the more I realized something was wrong. Although only in high school, I felt obligated to let the government know that I thought it was in the wrong. And yet at no time while I was protesting the war was I *ever* against the guys fighting it. My quarrel was with how the government was running the war.

I recall one of my first "protests." I was in the high school band and we were playing "The Star-Spangled Banner" at a basketball game. Although I stood and played with the rest of the band, I turned my back to the flag. When I came home that night, my father hit me for being disrespectful. So much for the right to free speech we were fighting to protect.

When I left for college in 1973, one brother had just gotten a medical deferral, and another would soon be registering for the draft. The war was becoming more and more personal. I skipped classes to attend rallies and antiwar events, and I wrote lots of letters to politicians. When the POW-MIA bracelets[39] came out, I helped sell them. There were quite a few heated discussions with some protesters who thought that wearing a bracelet (my guy is still MIA) was contrary to the cause. In those days, I tended to "discuss" things in decibels.

My second year of college ended with me skipping classes to watch the televised returns of our POWs. I would have loved to hug each one, so this was my way of saying "Welcome home" and to bear witness. I cried the whole time—for them, for their families, and for all the agony we'd all gone through during the war. Then I dropped out of school and just "vegetated" for a year. My idealistic perceptions of humanity had been severely challenged, and I was drained.

After Vietnam, I got involved in some projects that were targeted to help Vietnam vets. One of my best and proudest experiences will always be my work at the Vietnam Veterans Memorial in Washington, D.C. I worked at the wall as a volunteer every week for almost ten years. Unlike past memorials, this one doesn't honor the war. It's the Vietnam *Veterans* Memorial, not War Memorial, and it honors those who fought it.

I have seen firsthand its healing effects on vets and their families. And on me. At the wall, the former protester and the Vietnam veteran share something in common—our great sadness for those who were lost and those who haven't yet returned. Vietnam vets also don't seem to have the glorified view of war that older vets do.

The government's lack of support for Vietnam vets (during and after the war) might be part of the reason. If more people were aware of the other side

---

39. Bracelets bearing the names of American POWs (prisoners of war) and MIAs (soldiers missing in action) were worn to remember those soldiers left behind in Vietnam and to urge the United States government to act on securing their return home.

of war, the side the vets saw, they'd have a lot more incentive to work things out. Instead of seeing war as an alternative solution, people would finally realize that war is simply the result of our failure to find a solution.

[*Robyn returned to college and eventually graduated from law school. She worked in Washington, D.C., for a nonprofit education organization and as a government relations consultant. Robyn now works at a public and government relations firm. She continues to work with Vietnam veterans and, in particular, on the POW-MIA issue.*]

✦

Questions to Consider

The interviews in this chapter were conducted between 1985 and 1992. As you read through the seven interviews, try to get a sense of the tone and general meaning of each one. Then try to establish the respective frames of reference for the interviewees by comparing and contrasting their backgrounds. From which socioeconomic class does each person come? From what region of the country? What do you know about the interviewee's parents and friends? What did the person think was expected of him or her? Why?

After high school, the interviewees' experiences diverged greatly. Eventually, Mike, M.M., Eugene, and Helen enlisted in the armed services. What reason did each of them give (if any) for enlisting? How different were their reasons? For his part, Nick was drafted. What was his reaction to being drafted?

Both John and Robyn became involved in antiwar protests, but for very different reasons. Why did each become involved? Would John and Robyn have agreed on why the war should have been opposed?

Return to the five veterans. What were their feelings about the Vietnamese people? What did they believe were the reasons for American involvement in the war? What were their reactions to events of the time—the draft, antiwar protests, Kent State, and race relations in the armed services? What were their feelings about their respective roles in Vietnam? What did they think about the situation of returning veterans? Some of the interviewees seem to have made the adjustment to civilian life better than others. Can you think of why that might have been so? Finally, what do you think each of the seven veterans or civilians learned from his or her personal experiences during the Vietnam War era?

Now look at the photographs closely. Are they posed or unposed? For whom might they have been intended? What image of each person is projected? How does each person help create that image?

Now consider carefully the interview that you conducted. You have done some important historical work by creating this piece of oral evidence. Now you must analyze it. What does your interview mean? In other words, how does it fit into or modify what you know about the Vietnam era? Begin by comparing and contrasting your interview with those in this chapter. Do the same with the interviews conducted by other students in your class. What major similarities and differences can you identify in the responses to the Vietnam War among members of this birth cohort? Do you see any patterns based on race, geographic region, socioeconomic class, or other factors? If so, describe and explain these patterns.

The majority of the people we interviewed had never met one another. Do you think they could meet and talk today about the Vietnam era? What might such a conversation be like?

Epilogue

In the spring of 1971, fifteen thousand antiwar demonstrators disrupted daily activities in the nation's capital by blocking the streets with trash, automobiles, and their own bodies. Twelve thousand were arrested, but the protest movement across the country continued. In June, the Pentagon Papers, a secret 1967 government study of the Vietnam War, was published in installments by the *New York Times*. The Pentagon Papers revealed that government spokespersons had lied to the American public about several important events, particularly about the Gulf of Tonkin incident.

As part of his reelection campaign in 1972, President Nixon traveled first to China and then to the Soviet Union and accelerated the removal of American troops from Vietnam. "Peace," his adviser Henry Kissinger announced, "is at hand." Withdrawal was slow and painful and created a new group of refugees—those Vietnamese who had supported the Americans in South Vietnam. Nixon became mired in the Watergate scandal and resigned from office in 1974 under the threat of impeachment. The North Vietnamese entered Saigon in the spring of 1975 and began a "pacification" campaign of their own in neighboring Cambodia. Nixon's successors, Gerald Ford and Jimmy Carter, offered amnesty plans that a relatively small number of draft violators used. Many who were reported missing in action (MIA) in Vietnam were never found, either dead or alive. The draft was replaced by a new concept, the all-volunteer army.

The Vietnam veterans, who had no homecoming parades upon their return and who had been alternately ignored and maligned, finally got their memorial. A stark, simple, shiny black granite wall engraved with the names of 58,000 war dead, the monument is located on the mall near the Lincoln Memorial in Washington, D.C. The idea came from Jan Scruggs (the son of a milkman), a Vietnam veteran who was wounded and decorated for bravery when he was nineteen years old. The winning design was submitted by twenty-year-old Maya Lin, an undergraduate architecture student at Yale University. A representational statue designed by thirty-eight-year-old Frederick Hart, a former antiwar protester, stands near the wall of names, along with a statue dedicated to the nurses who served in Vietnam. All one hundred U.S. senators cosponsored the gift of public land, and the money to build the memorial was raised entirely through 650,000 individual public contributions. Not everyone was pleased by the memorial, and some old emotional wounds were reopened. Yet more than 150,000 people attended the dedication ceremonies on Veterans Day 1982, and the Vietnam veterans paraded down Constitution Avenue. Millions of Americans have viewed the monument, now one of Washington's most visited memorials.

As for the baby boomers, many have children old enough to have served in Operation Desert Storm, Somalia, Bosnia, Afghanistan, and the invasion and occupation of Iraq. A good number have put their Vietnam-era experiences behind them as they pursue careers, look forward to retirement, and await or play with grandchildren—a new birth cohort.

By the first decade of the twenty-first century, it became obvious that for the United States the Vietnam War was not a military aberration. Rather, it appeared to have been a *harbinger* of wars the nation would be forced to fight in the future: guerrilla-style conflicts in which the enemy, not unlike the Viet Cong, would strike suddenly and then melt away into the countryside or into the civilian population. In such military engagements, modern technology cannot be brought to bear so easily against what Americans increasingly refer to as "terrorists." Still unanswered is the question of whether the American military or civilians possess the tactics or the patience to triumph in such a "new" kind of warfare.[40]

Thus, for many reasons, Vietnam is a chapter in American history that has not yet been closed. Does that era contain lessons that Americans—and historians—still need to learn?

40. In fact, Americans are hardly strangers to guerrilla warfare. Perhaps the most dramatic instance was the crushing of the Philippine insurrection after the United States acquired the Philippines from Spain in 1899—a particularly bloody affair.

11

A Nation of Immigrants: The California Experience

♦

The Problem

In the late nineteenth century, the French contributed a quarter of a million dollars toward the construction of a monument intended to commemorate Franco-American friendship and shared democratic ideals. The rest of the money, nearly a half million dollars, was raised in the United States. The site was on an island in New York Harbor, where sculptor Frederic Auguste Bartholdi created an enormous statue of a woman holding a burning torch in a raised hand. Measuring 305 feet from her pedestal to the top of her head, the Statue of Liberty was dedicated in the fall of 1886 to great public acclaim.

The inscription on the statue's pedestal was taken from a poem written by Emma Lazarus for a literary auction, one of the many fundraising events held to aid the construction of the statue. Lazarus was one of thirteen children born to a prosperous Jewish family, descendants of seventeenth-century Portuguese immigrants. Shy, quiet, and sheltered, she published her first book of poetry at age eighteen. She later wrote and published more poetry, novels, plays, and magazine articles,

as well as important English translations of Hebrew literature. In spite of her prolific literary output, however, Lazarus is best remembered for the few lines of her poetry that many generations of school children had to memorize:

> . . . Give me your tired, your poor,
> Your huddled masses yearning to
>   breathe free,
> The wretched refuse of your teeming
>   shore.
> Send these, the homeless, tempest-tost
>   to me.
> I lift my lamp beside the golden door![1]

The Statue of Liberty immediately became a symbol of hope and of economic, political, and social opportunity for the millions of southern and eastern European immigrants who poured into the United States from the late nineteenth century until the outbreak of World War I. Ironically, however, by the 1920s, the United States had drastically curtailed immigration, a policy that basically continued until the

1. Emma Lazarus, "The New Colossus," *Poems of Emma Lazarus* (Boston: Houghton Mifflin, 1889), Volume I, p. 203.

1960s. As immigration restrictions were eased in the 1960s, it became obvious that the origins of the immigrants had shifted. Of course, some Europeans continued to emigrate, but the so-called fourth wave of immigrants came primarily from Latin America, Asia, and the Pacific Islands.

In this chapter, you will look at some of these fourth-wave immigrants in California. Why did they come to the United States? What were their lives like once they arrived here? Does the United States still offer the "golden door" of opportunity promised by the verse on the Statue of Liberty's pedestal?

◆

Background

The United States has been described as a "nation of immigrants" or a "nation of nations"—and for good reason. The first wave of immigrants included the great voluntary migrations of English and northwestern Europeans as well as the involuntary emigration of enslaved Africans during the seventeenth century. In the second wave, the Protestant Scotch-Irish who came to North America in the early nineteenth century were joined by nearly two million Roman Catholic Irish trying to escape poverty and the potato famine in the 1840s and 1850s. Also included in this second wave of immigration were the Germans, many of whom were fleeing the political revolutions of the 1840s. Somewhat better off financially than the Irish, German immigrants often established small businesses or became independent farmers. Nevertheless, the Irish and Germans of the second wave of immigration tended to cluster in visible communities and display definite ethnic identities and cultural activities. The Irish were further set apart by their extreme poverty and Catholicism. Early nativist movements, such as the Know Nothing Party, were a reaction against the second-wave immigrants.

The rapid industrialization of the post–Civil War era created a nearly insatiable demand for workers at all levels of skills. Many of these jobs were filled by the "new" third wave of immigrants from southern and eastern Europe, many of whom were either Orthodox, Catholic, or Jewish. Arriving between 1870 and 1890, with little but the willingness to work hard, more than 7.5 million immigrants moved permanently to the United States. In 1892, Ellis Island was opened to filter out people with contagious diseases, criminals, and other "undesirables," but only about 1 percent of the immigrants were turned back. Most of these new-wave immigrants lived in urban areas, crowded into tenements and slums, and often depended on the work of women and children to supplement the family income. They had a major impact on city politics, which were usually run by urban machines, and were the target of various Progressive reformers, such as social settlement workers, visiting nurses, American-ization advocates, and vice commis-sions.

In the West, Chinese immigrants who had worked in the mines during the gold rush of the 1850s were joined by newcomers who labored on the con-struction of the railroads and in small businesses and agriculture.

Different from the dominant Anglo pattern in culture, religion, and some-times race, these third-wave immi-grants from southern and eastern Eu-rope and Asia encountered prejudice and often violence in the United States. Anti-Catholic and anti-Semitic organi-zations were formed in the East and Midwest; by the 1920s, the new Ku Klux Klan was active throughout the country. In the Far West, restrictive laws against the Chinese (and, later, the Japanese) culminated in the Chi-nese Exclusion Act of 1882. Only the personal intervention of President Theodore Roosevelt in the 1906 Gen-tlemen's Agreement averted a crisis with Japan over a California school board's segregation of Japanese chil-dren.

When the massive third-wave immi-gration resumed after World War I in spite of a new literacy test require-ment, public pressure forced Congress to limit the total annual immigration. The National Origins Quota Act of 1924 not only greatly reduced Euro-pean immigration (from 850,000 in 1921 to 150,000 in 1924), but also ex-cluded Asian immigrants totally and gave preference to people from north-eastern European countries. Mexicans, who were not included in this legisla-tion, continued to migrate to the west-ern states during the 1920s. This re-strictive immigration policy remained basically unchanged for the next forty years, with the exceptions of the occa-sional admission of a small number of refugees and a quota increase in the 1950s.

In 1965, without much debate, a new Immigration Act removed the quotas for various European countries and al-lowed family members of U.S. citizens to emigrate without being counted in the annual total. But by the 1980s, im-migration was again becoming a hot political issue. About 600,000 legal immigrants, mostly Hispanics and Asians, were coming to the United States each year, while illegal (or un-documented) immigrants were esti-mated at another 500,000 annually. As had happened before, these fourth-wave immigrants had a visible pres-ence, were often quite poor, and dif-fered culturally and racially from the dominant Anglo pattern. They also had a noticeable impact on local and state politics, and opinion polls reflected the American public's concerns with such issues as crime, education, health care, and other social services.

Today, California is the most popu-lous state in the United States, and it serves as a kind of "mirror" for what is happening in America. As contempo-rary observer and author Haynes John-son has noted, California has always been "the pacesetter, the place where national cultural and political trends started."[2] The most ethnically and ra-cially diverse state in the nation, Cali-fornia provides the ideal location for

2. Haynes Johnson, *Divided We Fall* (New York: Norton, 1994), p. 98.

studying recent immigrants and their experiences.

California's early prosperity was tied to its natural resources, which included gold, lumber, fish, salt, borax, and range land. In the latter half of the nineteenth century, California became a magnet whose population doubled every twenty years until the mid-1920s, with one-third of the increase due to the birthrate and the remainder from immigration and in-migration from other states. Ethnic tensions and violence against minority groups were common.

The early twentieth century also witnessed the growth of new sectors of California's economy, such as the birth of the Hollywood film industry, the development of the oil industry, the establishment of wineries, and the rise of the agribusinesses of the Central Valley. At the same time, Progressive reformers moved to restrain the political influence of railroads and big business and began efforts to conserve some of the natural beauty of the state, such as that of the Yosemite area. Ethnic tensions were still evident, however, as Chinese residents were confined to Chinatowns and Japanese residents were denied access to property ownership and education. During the depression of the 1930s, Mexican Americans along with Mexican citizens were forcibly returned to Mexico. Even the displaced "Okies" and other Americans fleeing the Dust Bowl of the Great Plains states were often barred from California's towns and cities.

The two worst outbreaks of prejudiced behavior in California occurred during World War II. The forced relocation and internment of over 100,000 Japanese, two-thirds of whom were U.S. citizens, caused them enormous psychological and financial hardship. Although most returned to California after the war, only about 10 percent of their assets remained; the majority had to start all over again. The other instance, called the "zoot-suit riots" because of the gangster-style clothes worn by some young Mexican Americans, took place in 1943, when about two hundred United States Navy sailors went on a rampage in East Los Angeles, attacking members of the neighborhood Hispanic gangs. The Los Angeles Police Department stood by and watched, maintaining that it was the job of the shore patrol and the military police to control the rioters. Only after a formal protest by the Mexican government did the riots finally end.

The cold war and the increase of defense-related industries such as aircraft and electronics benefited California economically. But the 1960s, a decade that seemed in some ways to hold out the promise of a better life for all, had a darker side, even in California. Militant Native Americans occupied Alcatraz Island in San Francisco Bay as a symbolic gesture of cultural and economic protest. Cesar Chavez, leader of the United Farm Workers, exposed the terrible living conditions and exploitation of the migrant agricultural workers whom he was trying to organize. The *bracero* (day laborer) program that had permitted "temporary" work by immigrant Mexicans ended in 1964, but illegal workers continued to pour across the border. At the same time, more public concern focused on the young people in the barrios who were deeply involved in gangs.

Preceded by smaller riots in eastern cities and followed by riots in other major cities, the Watts riot of 1965 in Los Angeles shocked many Americans with its violence and revealed poverty and despair in the midst of what had appeared to be prosperity and optimism. After an incident involving a drunk-driving arrest, African American rioters looted and burned buildings in that inner-city ghetto, where the population was ten times greater in 1965 than it had been in 1940. During the six days that the Watts riot lasted, it spread to adjoining areas, and the National Guard was called out to help contain it. Thirty-four people were killed, more than a thousand were injured, and $40 million worth of property was damaged or destroyed. In 1970, and again in 1992, more riots broke out in Los Angeles.

During the 1970s, 1980s, and 1990s, California experienced major changes in its economy, population patterns, and politics. The economy, particularly the large sector dependent on federal defense spending, plunged into a recession as cold war tensions decreased and U.S. foreign policy changed. Blue-collar jobs contracted, low-paying jobs in the service sector expanded only slightly, and, as technical and communications skills became more important for job seekers, access to good education became crucial.

During the 1990s, many young people moved to California to take part in the rapid growth of businesses connected with the use of personal computers and the Internet. The dot-com boom, as it was called, created a large group of newly wealthy people whose demand for housing drove up the cost of renting and purchasing homes to astronomical heights. Even after the failure of many of the new, technology-driven businesses in 2001 and 2002, housing prices remained so high that they were out of reach for most working-class and middle-class families.

Continuing economic instability has contributed to the wide gap between the rich and the poor. Moreover, the uneven recovery experienced by some economic sectors and geographical regions has not spread to other sectors and regions that remain depressed.

Equally striking were changes in the population. After 1965, when the United States began to loosen immigration restrictions, the country experienced another "new" wave of immigration: from Latin America, especially Mexico, and from Asia and the Pacific Islands. For example, between 1970 and 1983, over one million Hispanics, Asians, and other foreign-born people moved to the county of Los Angeles. Because of this wave of immigration, California's population grew so rapidly that Hispanics and Asians often crowded into poorer inner-city areas such as Watts, where African Americans were already living. Conflicts increased between the African Americans and some of the newer immigrants, such as Korean store owners, and even at times between earlier immigrants such as the Chinese and the newer arrivals. Beginning in the late 1960s, politics reflected the new ethnic and racial identities and awareness.

The United States Census taken in 2000 showed that Hispanics numbered 35.3 million, or almost 13 percent of the population; non-Hispanic blacks and African Americans (35.4 million) were also nearly 13 percent. The Asian population was 11.6 million, or approximately 4 percent. In comparison, the Hispanic population was 32.4 percent of the population in California; the non-Hispanic black and African American population was 6.7 percent. Asians accounted for approximately 11.2 percent of California's population. People who identified themselves as Caucasian (white) constituted 75.1 percent of the U.S. population and 59.5 percent of California's population.[3]

These figures make it clear that California has received a disproportionately large number of fourth-wave immigrants. Why do these newcomers continue to settle there? What are their lives like after they arrive? To what degree does California still serve as a land of opportunity for immigrants?

◆

The Method

Most of the evidence in this chapter is in the form of interviews, memoirs, or autobiographies. This kind of evidence is especially useful in giving a historical "voice" to people whose stories or viewpoints are not usually represented. Like all autobiographical material, however, these stories may not always be completely accurate. For example, they may contain exaggerations or create situations that are intended to convey a particular message to the reader or listener. Writer and poet Carlos Bulosan, a Filipino migrant farm worker in the 1930s, described riding a freight train into a little southern California town: "We were told . . . that local whites were hunting Filipinos at night with shotguns."[4] Without corroborating evidence, the historian cannot evaluate the factual accuracy of this statement, but the message—and the perception—of the author are clear.

In using the evidence in this chapter, try to identify first *why* the immigrants came and *what* their experiences were (including the obstacles they encountered). What were their goals? their accomplishments? The central question then asks you to evaluate the degree to which the opportunity to succeed in achieving their goals still exists for people who are part of this newest wave of immigrants.

3. Hispanics may be of any race. For U.S. Census figures, see http://www.census.gov/index.html. For state figures, choose Quick Facts and select California.
4. Carlos Bulosan, *America Is in the Heart: A Personal History* (Seattle: University of Washington Press, 1973 [originally published 1943]), p. 144.

♦

The Evidence

ASIAN IMMIGRANTS

Source 1 from Nathan Caplan et al., *Children of the Boat People* (Ann Arbor: University of Michigan, 1991), p. 5.

1. Two Vietnamese Proverbs.

An uneducated person is like unpolished jade.

A knife gets sharp through honing; a man gets smart through study.

Source 2 from Al Santoli, *New Americans* (New York: Viking, 1988), pp. 209, 232–233.

2. Celia Van Noup, a Cambodian Refugee and Owner of the House of Donuts in Southern California.

I started this business from almost nothing at all. I named it House of Donuts, my own franchise. I spend most of my time in this shop, seven days a week. . . .

I get to the shop at 5:00 in the morning to open for breakfast, and I usually leave around 7:00 P.M. I work behind the counter, serving customers, and do the cleaning and sweeping. I work by myself most of the time. My youngest daughter, Parika, just began college, but she comes with me at 5:00 A.M. to help. At 10:00 A.M., she goes home to study, before she attends afternoon and evening classes. . . .

Another reason that I work and try to save money is to be able to sponsor my cousin and her family from Cambodia. She is just like my sister. . . .

That's one of the main reasons I want to have this donut shop and try to keep it open. There're three reasons: for my children, for my cousin's family, and for the little house that I dream of.

Whenever I can, I drive around and look at "For Sale" signs on houses. When I see a beautiful house on sale, almost new, I write down the phone number. I call up and say, "How much do you want?" They say, "It costs this much. Is this your first house? How much money do you have?" Of course, it's always too much. I don't have the money now. But the dream is always there.

I want the house not only for myself—for everybody to live in. My daughters, my relatives from Phnom Penh—they could live in the garage if we fix it up nice. We wouldn't have to pay rent and be bothered all the time. It's my American dream to have that little house.

Sources 3 and 4 from Joan Morrison and Charlotte F. Zabusky, *American Mosaic* (New York: E. P. Dutton, 1980), pp. 306, 333–334.

3. Betty Chu, a Chinese American Homemaker from San Francisco.

My son is in high school now. With him it was one big adjustment right after the other. He had to learn the different dialect in Hong Kong, and then he had to learn American here. I don't know how the guy went through it, but he never stopped behind in his class. I don't know how he did it. I just don't know how he did it. He's always been a quiet boy. He just doesn't have that many friends. It does still worry me. [*Sighs.*]

One of my son's biggest disappointments is that my daughter doesn't speak Chinese. Well, she was a year and a half when she came over, and she thought she was American all along. Now she wants to grow up to be an Italian.

Last year, December, we became citizens. The doctor at the hospital where I work invited us over for a party. He surprised us by standing up and announcing it. He said, "Something very wonderful happened last week," and told everybody that we were citizens now. He gave us an American flag as a present, and everybody drank to us. It was very heartwarming.

4. Su Chu Hadley, a Chinese American from Taiwan Living in Northern Rural California.

[*At this point in the interview, Su-Chu's two daughters come into the room to say good-bye before going to the beach. They wear bikinis and carry a picnic basket and a transistor radio. After they leave, Su-Chu looks out the window for a moment. Then she speaks softly—*]

You can't know how it makes me feel to see them go off like this. They are ten and twelve, and when I was ten and twelve I was working in the fields all day. . . . Sometimes in the evening I cry, thinking of everything that has happened, and my children say, "Daddy, how come mommy cry?"

"She's remembering bad things from long ago," he tells them.

And then I look at him and at them and at my house here, and I say, "Well, at least I have a happy ending."

Source 5 from Bong-youn Choy, *Koreans in America* (Chicago: Nelson Hall, 1979), p. 333.

5. Bong-youn Choy, a Korean Restaurant Owner from Berkeley.

. . . We soon found that the restaurant business was one of the hardest businesses, but a rewarding one. My wife was the master chef and I was the manager, doing everything from marketing to janitorial work. My two sons, David and Francis, who were still in public school, helped us as dishwashers and waiters. Both of them were very good workers and became valuable assets to the business. My daughter, Cora, also helped whenever she visited us. The restaurant was open six days a week, and every Tuesday night my wife conducted cooking classes.

We worked from fourteen to sixteen hours a day. During the first six months, we lost a little money because we did not know how to run the restaurant and lacked customers.

Source 6 from Mary Paik Lee, *Quiet Odyssey* (Seattle: University of Washington Press, 1990), pp. 4, 129. Courtesy of Washington Press.

6. Photographs of Mary Paik Lee, a Korean American Store Owner, with Her Family in 1905 (Korea) and 1987 (Santa Cruz).

[*In this portrait of the Paik family taken in Korea in 1905, Mary (center) is the youngest child in the picture.*]

[*Here, Mary (center) is shown with her sons, Tony and Allan, and two of her grand-daughters, Sarah and Katie, in Santa Cruz in 1987.*]

[*Mary Paik, her parents, and her ten siblings emigrated to California in the early twentieth century. All eleven children rose to middle-class status through hard work. Most of the next generation, their children, and almost all of the third generation, their grandchildren, attended college and entered the professions.*]

Source 7 from Paul Ong, Edna Bonacich, and Lucie Chen, *The New Asian Immigration in Los Angeles and Global Restructuring* (Philadelphia: Temple University Press, 1994), p. 104.

7. Ethnic Composition of the Asian American Population, Los Angeles County, 1970–1990.

Ethnic Group	1970	1980	1990	1980–1990	Increase, 1980–1990 (%)
Chinese	40,798	94,521	245,033	150,512	159.2
Filipino	33,459	100,894	219,653	118,759	117.7
Korean	8,650	60,339	145,431	85,092	141.0
Japanese	104,078	117,190	129,736	12,546	10.7
Vietnamese		27,252	62,594	35,342	129.7
Asian Indian		18,770	43,829	25,059	133.5
Thai		9,449[a]	19,016	9,567	101.2
Other Southeast Asian[b]			31,920		
Other Asian	3,300[c]		28,349		

[a]Based on the number of immigrants born in Thailand.
[b]Approximately 28,000 Cambodians, 3,700 Laotians, and 300 Hmong.
[c]Estimated from Public Use Micro Dataset.
Sources: U.S. Bureau of the Census, *Census of Population and Housing, 1970, 1980, 1990* (Washington, D.C.: Government Printing Office, 1973, 1983, 1993); and *Census of Population and Housing, 1970, 1980, 1990 Public Use Sample: 5% County Level Sample* [computer file] (Washington, D.C.: U.S. Bureau of the Census [producer]).

Source 8 from Ivan Light and Edna Bonacich, *Immigrant Entrepreneurs: Koreans in Los Angeles, 1965–1982* (Berkeley: University of California Press, 1988), p. 274.

8. The Brief Life Story of Young Korean Gas Station Owners from Los Angeles.

Dad worked in the gas station 6 am through 12 pm at night. I worked 3 pm to 7 am. Although it was hard and tiring, we thought since we had an opportunity, we ought to work hard. . . . So finally we got the gas station on our own account. We started our own business for the first time. That night my husband and I couldn't sleep. We cried for a long time and promised each other that we would work harder. We didn't even have a bed so we were sleeping on the floor. (Life History)

Source 9 from Victor G. and Brett DeBary Nee, *Longtime Californ'* (Boston: Pantheon, 1973), pp. 165–166.

9. Lisa Mah, a Chinese American Employee of the Chinatown Neighborhood Arts Program in Berkeley.

When my parents would talk about the outside being a bad place, they would refer sort of generally to "the whites out there," they always called them *sai yen*. To me, of course, that meant the whites right around us. It meant the bar downstairs where there was an Irish tavern, Cavanaugh's, that we could hear coming up through the floor every night. We'd hear this crashing, singing, people being thrown around down there, they would have brawls and they would pee on our doorstep. Every other day we would go down there with a bucket to wash it off. But at the same time my parents kept reminding us that "the whites out there," the same people who would vomit and pee on our doorstep, were the people who had the power to take our home away from us. We had to do a little placating of them. Every Easter, every Christmas, every American holiday, I would be sent on a little tour of all the local businesses. I would go to the bakery across the street, the barbershop down the street, the realty company, and the bar. I would deliver a little cake to each one. We wanted to be known as that nice Chinese family upstairs or down the street, you know, whom you wouldn't ever want to hurt in any way.

HISPANIC IMMIGRANTS

Source 10 from June Namia, *First Generation* (Boston: Beacon Press, 1978), p. 179.

10. Graciela Mendoza Pena Valencia, a Mexican Agricultural Worker from Salinas.

The contractor said, "You have never picked strawberries?"

"No."

"Oh! That's easy. Have big trees. You just pick the fruit off the trees."

I come here and I see those strawberries on the floor, oh! It's more hard. I came with my friend. When I come here the first day, I saw the big rooms. I feel like I'm going in jail. Only the little beds, no chair, no nothing, only the bed. For a bedspread you got a gray color. I was in a room with twelve people. . . .

I don't work now. Last year I work at celery, in the shed packing. Now, there's more good places to work. If you come here alone first, it's more complicated. When I know the place and everything, I bring my brothers and my mother and my sister. She marry a good man, they got a big house. My brother's got a new car. I was the first one to do farm work in this country. Second, my sisters; next, my brothers. Because if you here first you don't know nothing. When they come here, my husband have a good job and he help my brothers. It's more good to come like that than alone.

I like it here. I am happy with my kids, my husband, the house.

Source 11 from Ernesto Galarza, *Barrio Boy* (Notre Dame: University of Notre Dame Press, 1971), pp. 203–204.

11. Excerpt from the Autobiography of Ernesto Galarza, a Mexican American Economist and Author.

We cut out the ends of tin cans to make collars and plates for the pipes and floor moldings where the rats had gnawed holes. Stoops and porches that sagged we propped with bricks and fat stones. To plug the drafts around the windows in winter, we cut strips of corrugated cardboard and wedged them into the frames. With squares of cheesecloth neatly cut and sewed to screen doors holes were covered and rents in the wire mesh mended. Such repairs, which landlords never paid any attention to, were made *por mientras,* for the time being or temporarily. It would have been a word equally suitable for the house itself, or for the *barrio*. We lived in run-down places furnished with seconds in a hand-me-down neighborhood all of which were *por mientras.*

Source 12 from Joan Moore, *Going Down to the Barrio* (Philadelphia: Temple University Press, 1991), pp. 76–77.

12. What Gang Membership Meant to Mexican American Teens in East Los Angeles.

[Teenaged boys]

To me it was my life, my one and only way. [What do you mean, "your life"?] My only mission . . . [You were all for your barrio? Could you please tell me how you felt?] Well, I felt that was the only thing going for me. It was my neighborhood. They were like my brothers and sisters. I mean, at that time, that's the only thing I had. It was them and my grandparents.

It was the most important thing in my life at that time. There was nothing that came even close to it except maybe my own personal family. But even then at the time there was no problems at the home, so my gang life was my one love.

[Teenaged girls]

The year that I was there it was like, umm, they were like family, because we would all take care of each other. . . . I think they were like my own family. I think I was more with them than my own family, because I left them for a while.

It was very important. Because that's all I had to look forward to, was my neighborhood, you know. That's all. It was my people—my neighborhood, my homies, my homeboys, my homegirls—that was everything to me. That was everything, you know. It wasn't all about my *familia;* it was all about my homeboys and homegirls.

Sources 13 and 14 from Armando Morales, *Ando Sangrando* (La Puente, Calif.: Perspectiva Publications, 1972), pp. 71, 100ff. Courtesy of Perspectiva Publications.

13. Mrs. Barba, a Mexican American: Testimony Given Before the U.S. Civil Rights Commission.

Saturday, November 9th, at about 1:30 a.m. an officer from Hollenbeck Police Station called me to go pick up my son who had been arrested for burglary. I asked him, "What time did you pick him up?" He said about 10:20. I said,

"Why are you letting me know so late?" He said, "Because your son fell down." I started crying. He told me, "Don't worry, it's a small cut." I believed him. The next day I knew he had lied to me. I took my son to the White Memorial Hospital. My son had 40 stitches in his head and two fractures in the vertebrae. Also, the 13th of November, he had surgery for a hernia. I have very much faith in God. I know very well Officer Beckman is lying very much about my son. But I have faith in all the people that are helping me. This, I will never forget. And I hope we can accomplish justice. This *cannot* happen to *any* other boy.

14. Photographs of a Police Recruiting Billboard (top) and Child Demonstrators, East Los Angeles.

Questions to Consider

California has always been a magnet for Hispanic immigrants, the majority of whom work in the enormously productive and labor-intensive agricultural system of the Central, Imperial, and Salinas Valleys. Other Hispanics, Mexicans and Chicanos, along with Asian immigrants, live and work in cities such as Los Angeles. Although Source 10 provides some insight into the life of a Mexican agricultural worker, most of the sources in this chapter focus on the experiences of the fourth-wave urban immigrants.

First, quickly skim through all of the evidence to get a sense of the diversity among the immigrants and the variety of their experiences. Source 7 further clarifies who is included in the category of Asian immigrants. Use a piece of paper folded in half lengthwise to help organize your notes. Write one question at the top of each side of the paper: Why did they come? What were their experiences? (Be sure to include the ob-

stacles they encountered under the latter heading).

Now go back through the evidence more slowly. What reasons do the immigrants give for their immigration in the stories told by Sources 2 through 4 and 8? What work experiences are described by Sources 2, 4, 5, 10, and 8? What do the proverbs in Source 1 indirectly advise Vietnamese immigrants to do? According to Source 12, why do Mexican American teens join gangs?

Notice the difficulties encountered by the immigrants in Sources 3, 5, and 8 through 14. Are there any patterns here? How did the immigrants respond to these problems? Consider also the information revealed in the photographs of Mary Paik Lee and her family (Source 6). Finally, after reviewing your notes about the fourth-wave immigrants' experiences, to what degree would you say that opportunity still exists for newcomers to this country?

Epilogue

Throughout the late 1980s and 1990s, the national debate about the impact of the fourth wave of immigration continued. Were the new immigrants a drain on our educational institutions and social services, especially our already troubled health care system? Or did the immigrants, as several studies showed, generate more through their productivity and the taxes they paid than they

consumed in the form of government services? On a different, much more racist note, some groups began to complain publicly about the "browning" of the United States.

Focusing on some of the problems connected with illegal immigration, Congress has passed four major pieces of legislation in the last fifteen years. The 1986 Immigration Reform and

Control Act offered amnesty and legalization to some three million seasonal agricultural and other workers. Special provisions in the Immigration Act of 1990 facilitated entrance for highly skilled immigrants, while the Illegal Immigration Reform and Immigrant Responsibility Act of 1996 set aside new money for border patrols and made it easier to deport illegal aliens. In 2000, yet another effort was made to encourage illegal aliens to obtain visas or be sponsored for citizenship applications through the Legal Immigration and Family Equity (LIFE) Act.

As certain parts of the California economy weakened during the 1980s and 1990s, and as the racial and ethnic composition of the state's population continued to change, the backlash against the newest immigrants intensified. In 1992, Los Angeles again experienced devastating riots that began in response to the acquittal of white police officers who had beaten a black motorist. The riots expanded, however, into the looting and burning of stores owned by Asians, especially Koreans, in neighborhoods occupied by African, Asian, and Hispanic Americans. Two years later, California voters approved Proposition 187, intended to exclude illegal aliens from public schools and nonemergency medical care. Although a court challenge prevented the proposition from becoming state law, many

of its provisions were later put into effect by California's governor. In 1998, Californians voted by a two-to-one margin to replace bilingual teaching with English immersion classes for immigrant children.

In the twenty-first century, Hispanics have led the way in the effort to rebuild Los Angeles after the riots and subsequent Anglo flight to the suburbs. In many ways, working-class Latino families have begun to restabilize Los Angeles and other smaller California cities. As urban historian Mike Davis points out, these cities are now characterized by a dynamic, vibrant Hispanic culture.[5] Both Hispanics and African Americans continue to exercise considerable political influence on the local and state levels, although they are increasingly faced with serious problems in the areas of public education and social services.[6]

Since the 9/11 attacks, much of the concern about potential threats to U.S. security has focused on illegal immigrants and the borders with Canada and Mexico. The state of California, deeply in debt, has continued to question the benefits and costs of newly arriving immigrants. Nevertheless, fourth-wave immigrants continue to come to California, and they will continue to influence the economic, political, social, and cultural life of the state and the nation.

5. Mike Davis, *Magical Urbanism: Latinos Reinvent the Big City* (New York and London: Verso, 2000).
6. Peter Schrag, *Paradise Lost: California's Experience, America's Future* (Berkeley: University of California Press, 2004).